P9-DNG-263
A LITTLE BIT
SIDEWAYS

A LITTLE BIT SIDEWAYS

SCOTT HULER

MBI Publishing Company

First published in 1999 by MBI Publishing Company,
729 Prospect Avenue, PO Box 1, Osceola, WI 54020-0001 USA

MBI Publishing Company books are also available at discounts in bulk quantity for industrial or sales-promotional use. For details write to Special Sales Manager at Motorbooks International Wholesalers & Distributors, 729 Prospect Avenue, Osceola, WI 54020-0001 USA.

Library of Congress Cataloging-in-Publication Data
Huler, Scott.
A little bit sideways: one week inside a NASCAR Winston Cup race team.
p. cm.
ISBN 0-7603-0455-6 (pbk.)
1. Stock car racing—United States. 2. Filmar Racing (Team) I. Title.
GV1029.9.S74 H85 1999
796.72'0973—dc21 98-46892

On the front cover: The Square D team's number 81 car. *Don Hunter*

Printed in the United States of America

❖

*This book is for David, Michael, and Joe,
and to the memory of Gerald Martin*

Contents

INTRODUCTION

THE FAITHFUL GATHER

Thursday Night, September 25

The first fans show up at Charlotte Motor Speedway almost two weeks before the UAW-GM Quality 500.

Stop in front of the huge sign announcing the Winston Cup race on October 5, but instead of turning right into the speedway, turn left into one of the broad, green fields across Highway 29. Do this in the evening, on September 25—11 days before the race. Find the motor home closest to the driveway into the field; it's a nice, 1994 Southwind, in perfect condition. Park your truck and knock on the door. Thurman Lawson, a big man of about 55 or 60, barrel-chested and hefty but in a friendly sort of way, will answer. It's dark out and he's not expecting anyone, so the way he'll look at you is a little scary.

But he's racing, he's good people, so he'll let you explain why you dropped by. And once you tell him you're just trying to understand this whole racing thing—trying to understand why he's already here to enjoy a race that doesn't start until *next month*—Thurman will swing open the screen door, invite you in, set you down on the couch. He'll sit back down on his blue plush captain's chair, turn down the baseball game on the TV, and tell you anything you want to know.

"I used to come down here several times in the 1960s," he says. "I was here when Fireball Roberts got hurt. I started going to Darlington in the 1950s. We've been coming here regular since 1973. We used to come Friday night, and camp right by the, um, facilities." That's a public rest room that used to be on this land.

"But now you have to come eight or ten days before if you want to get a good spot." That's Helen, Thurman's wife, sitting at the motor home's tiny dinette table. She explains how they've been following racing for a couple of decades together. "My husband likes Earnhardt—she shoots him a little glance, the way people who have been married for years and years will shoot each other little glances—"But we like Jeff Gordon. And we support all of 'em."

All the racers. They support all of them.

They're here this early because they're with the Cabarrus County Baptist Association. The association will put up a tent, which they'll use for worship, for cooking, for lost and found, for all the things close to 200,000 race fans might need and might like to do for one another. "They'll put up the church tent first of the week," Helen says. "They'll serve a full breakfast, the Baptist men will. Sunday morning, 5:00. Troopers first, then everybody else is welcome."

The other motor homes and campers will start trickling in over this weekend, and by Monday or Tuesday the fields surrounding the speedway will have the unmistakable look of a NASCAR Winston Cup race week. A traveling circus of some 150,000 or 200,000 people in varying combinations, showing up anywhere from Atlanta to California, from New Hampshire right back here to its home in Charlotte, 32 race weeks a year plus extras like two races in Japan, the Winston all-star race here at Charlotte, and the madness of Speed Weeks in Daytona in February.

Fifty or so race teams run the schedule, dragging 18-wheel haulers filled with race cars and equipment around the continent, setting up shop for three days at every track. Millions watch the races each week on ESPN, CBS, ABC, TBS, or TNN.

But TV just can't touch what Winston Cup racing really is. People tailgate before Green Bay Packers games, but people do not show up in motor homes 10 days before the game, set up makeshift houses of worship, and feed the masses the way people do during a Winston Cup race week. People buy souvenirs from temporary stands outside Oriole Park at Camden Yards, but two or three dozen 18-wheel retail emporiums and countless smaller trailers do not park outside the stadium, filling acres with key chains, hats, shirts, stickers, models, and electronic equipment bearing the names of their heroes the way they do during a Winston Cup race week.

And people attend sporting events of every kind, but they do not live in the very stadium itself for four days, drinking, eating, and howling at the moon, becoming one with the event, with the athletes, and with each other the way people do in the infield during race week at the Charlotte Motor Speedway.

People make trips to see a bunch—or even all—of the major league baseball or football stadiums. But people do not retire, buy motor homes, and follow an entire circuit the way Winston Cup people do.

Thirty years ago, people began climbing into Volkswagen buses and Dodge vans to follow around an unusual band called the Grateful Dead. Selling food and gewgaws to keep body and soul together, the fans and their festivals became as much a part of the experience as the music. The band's concerts became more than concerts; they became events, where an entire culture got together, embraced itself, and let loose. Outsiders couldn't understand, but insiders couldn't get enough. It changed their lives. It became their tribe.

About the same time, an entirely different group of people started getting in Winnebagos and Southwinds and going to races farther and farther away, staying longer and longer, going to more races each year. Food and souvenir vendors—

often the fans themselves—followed. Now the festival of the fans in their campers, the souvenir trailers, the fans on the infield, with their coolers and their viewing platforms and their decline-of-Western-civilization three-day Bacchanalia have become almost as much a part of the experience as the race itself.

And the race itself. Fans howl during the kickoff of a football game, they cheer the first or last pitch of a baseball game, they roar when the lights go down and music comes up and the Chicago Bulls come out into the spotlight.

But let that pace car peel off into the pits after the pace laps that have let 43 eight-cylinder, 3,500-pound, 750-horsepower cars warm up and approach 200 miles per hour. Let that green flag drop, and let those cars explode into Turn 1 like the coming of the apocalypse, and then let's talk about screaming, let's talk about release, let's talk about a by-God experience.

Fifty or so race teams are at the core of this. A couple of thousand folks, mostly guys, spending $4 or $5 million a year per team—at least—trying to find a way to go fast. Hundreds of sponsors standing in line to put up all that money, just so race fans will see their name, their colors, their products, going fast. Fifty drivers, who make their livings going fast—driving at 200 miles per hour—and standing still, signing autographs. Forty or 50 owners, flying around in private planes and wondering what made them think this would be fun. Anywhere from 15 to 50 crew members per team, pushing stuff around and taking stuff apart, welding at the shop and changing four tires in 20 seconds at the track, working 10 hours a day 7 days a week for 11 months a year, and thanking God for the opportunity.

Race parts shops. Tire manufacturers. Automobile designers. Manufacturer's reps from the companies that make racing wheel rims, racing uniforms, race car seats, space-age heat insulation to keep exhaust gases from blistering race car drivers' feet to the bone. Guys who supply Gatorade to race teams. Guys who supply Gatorade stickers to race teams. Guys who walk around the garages, checking to see whether the Gatorade stickers have made it onto the race cars.

Computer guys who design programs that can tell crew members which cylinder isn't hitting during a test lap and make a graph to show it. Pretty girls whose job is to carry cigarettes around to team members, girls married to race drivers, girls standing around available because they'd like to do something, goddamnit, only they don't know how. And even, as things start to change, the occasional pretty girl who turns out to be an engine metallurgy chemist.

Thousands of fans who go to dozens of races a year. Millions of fans who go to at least one. Tens of millions of fans who watch on television, religiously—and amazingly—buying everything NASCAR says to buy. They show up at the mall at 4 A.M. when Jeff Gordon is going to be there for an hour at 11, and they bring not just cards and posters and notepads for him to sign but race tires and car doors.

And once a week, everybody gets together. The teams park inside the track, most of the fans park outside, but that's about the only difference. The teams spend two days practicing, flinging engines and tires around like they're Legos. The fans watch everything they do. The teams run qualifying laps and get set, spending their evenings comatose in motel rooms, or if they're awake, looking for that last missing detail, that last thousandth of a second that can mean the difference in the race. The fans spend the evenings chatting, or playing cribbage, or drinking and screaming and playing Lynyrd Skynyrd as loud as they can until they pass out.

And then, Sunday afternoon, that green flag drops and everybody knows why they came.

It's a religion. It's a culture.

It's a love fest, in a way. "I guess it's your friends you meet racing," Helen Lawson says. "You keep in touch with them over the years," Thurman adds.

"It's a pretty close-knit family," Helen says, using the most common metaphor for the huge Winston Cup scene. The drivers, the teams, the sponsors, the racing journalists, the PR people, the fans all say it. We've chosen this life. We're carnies. We're separate from everyone else, but we're together. We're family.

Helen Lawson has been around racing so long she's been invited to join the Winston Cup Racing Wives' Auxiliary. "I enjoy that. I go to the meetings when I can." The group engages in charity work, mostly. It raises money. It puts on events. It helps.

Thurman chimes in, "The fans are the same way. They'll help." They will. They take care of each other. They're a big family, a group, a subculture.

A tribe.

Concert promoter Bill Graham once famously said about the Grateful Dead, "They're not the best at what they do—they're the only ones who do what they do."

Just so here. Winston Cup racing isn't the best sporting event, or entertainment event, or shopping experience, or weekend festival. It's more that there's nothing quite like it.

And so you have to understand it.

You have to come to Charlotte for the race, but to get the whole picture, you have to see the whole week. You have to experience race week. You have to see what it looks like, to the fans, to the sponsors, to the drivers, to the teams.

The Charlotte race is 11 days away, but Charlotte race week, of course, has already started. It started when the Lawsons got here. Or it started weeks ago when workers started setting up hospitality tents outside the speedway on its own grounds. Or it started in May, when the spring Charlotte race ended, the staff took a day off, and started in on the October race.

Race week? Race week goes from Sunday to Sunday. The Charlotte race is 11 days away. This week's race is in Martinsville, Virginia—100 miles north. The race teams' haulers, each carrying a race car and a backup, extra engines, tools, carts, and everything else the team will need for a weekend, are at this moment already on their way there. Tomorrow morning at 6, before the sun is up, they'll be pulling into the infield and setting up their weekend shops. Race week for Charlotte starts on Sunday, with the running of the Martinsville race.

On your way out the door of their trailer, the Lawsons press into your hands a magazine called *Sports Spectrum*. It's about 90 percent racing and 10 percent earnest evangelical Christianity. It's well produced, and like everything connected with racing, it promises—and delivers—treasure unimagined. "Joe Gibbs gave us cases of these magazines about the drivers," Helen says. "I'd like you to have one." You thank the Lawsons genuinely and get in your truck. The lights of Charlotte Motor Speedway shine on the big white sign tower and on the glittering seven-story glass-and-steel tower that functions as the track's offices and houses its Speedway Club and some of the suites and the best seats. Inside, though, the track is dark, the seats are empty. A few other motor homes dot the surrounding fields—early arrivals like the Lawsons. But for a last few moments Charlotte is still empty, waiting, ready.

So you head for Martinsville. Race week starts on Sunday, and you don't want to miss anything.

CHAPTER 1

WAITING FOR A WINDOW

Sunday, September 28

Rain. Sunday morning, race day—and rain. Gray clouds, low in the sky, hanging like a thick blanket over Martinsville Speedway. A half-mile of damp concrete track, two long straightaways connected by two maddeningly tight, almost hairpin, turns. Think of the outline of a giant paper clip. Or, as some racing people like to say, of two drag strips connected by two bootleg turns. Seventy thousand seats on concrete-and-aluminum benches, all covered with puddles. Uncounted acres of slanting grass and red clay parking areas in the hills of the south central Virginia piedmont, all turning into swamp, beneath the pickup and camper tires of 70,000 fans showing up despite the rain.

Martinsville Speedway is NASCAR Winston Cup racing's oldest track. Neatly trimmed azaleas and boxwood shrubs line the concrete walls inside those tight turns. It's NASCAR's most beloved bandbox, sort of the Wrigley Field of big-time racing. Martinsville Speedway shows up well in a lot of situations.

Rain isn't one of them.

Race cars cluster in Turns 1 and 2 of the speedway, under soggy car covers that ape the cars' garish paint jobs with broad strokes—a few orange and yellow arcs for the Tide car, number 10; a big red 28 on a black cover for the number 28 Texaco Havoline car. And a yellow stripe canted on a blue background on the number 81, the Filmar Racing Ford Thunderbird sponsored by Square D Electrical Distribution systems. Forty other cars in two long rows, huddled under their covers, look as sodden and dispirited as scouts who went to bed after a bonfire on a weekend camping trip and awoke to see that it came up rain.

Dressed in coveralls and brightly colored team shirts, crowding under the shelter of the narrow wooden eaves of the single infield food counter, dozens of race team members light cigarettes, sip watery coffee, and warm their hands around small, white Styrofoam cups. Huddled around the counter in their Pennzoil yellows, their John Deere greens, their Square D blues, they look like a mixed flock of tropical birds waiting out a rain forest downpour. Some, in rain suits or ponchos or carrying team-color umbrellas that fail to brighten the dreary day, venture out along the damp asphalt infield on some errand among the 50-some tractor-trailer haulers in which the race teams make their offices.

They squint into the sky, shake their heads. They look at each other and laugh. It doesn't look much like they'll race today. "You never know," says Eddie D'Hondt, wearing a blue button-down shirt covered front and back by a huge, yellow embroidered D in a square, itself surrounded by a dozen other embroidered sponsor names. Eddie is the team manager for Filmar Racing, the team that runs the number 81 car driven by Kenny Wallace. Eddie has narrow eyes that miss nothing, slicked-back dark hair and a constant five-o'clock shadow—and a thick New York accent that makes him sound streetwise.

"They call it the NASCAR window," he says of the seemingly miraculous meteorological cooperation NASCAR seems to get for its Sunday afternoon races, finding a three-hour, race-sized gap of clear skies when radar shows clouds for miles around. He tries to muster a chuckle, but it doesn't really work. He's just joined the Filmar Racing team—this is his first race with them—and rain is exactly what they didn't want. Wallace drove the car to a sixth-best qualifying position—"sixth quick" in racing parlance—and was fastest in yesterday afternoon's last practice, called Happy Hour. The team's been having a tough year, and this looks like it might be their best chance for a top-five finish or even, if the team dares to imagine it, Wallace's first Winston Cup victory.

And then rain.

Rain is the worst possible news on race day. Unlike other racing series, NASCAR simply doesn't run in the rain. Without treads, race tires can't grip the banked speedway track when it's wet. Without windshield wipers, race car drivers can't see through the thinnest mist, so nothing brings out the red flag during a stock car race as fast as even the briefest, lightest rain. Two hundred miles an hour, almost 2 tons of race car, less than 2 inches between the cars, and rain?

Nope.

So on the morning of September 28, 1997, everybody involved in the Hanes 500, the 27th of 32 races on the Winston Cup circuit, faces a lot of grim realities.

At best, the rain will result in a long day of waiting culminating in a race run under conditions completely different than those for which the race cars were prepared, or set up, on Friday and Saturday. The cars were set up—tire pressures adjusted, shock stiffness set, springs chosen, track and sway bars positioned—for a hot track, covered with tire rubber built up during a weekend of practice. Now the rain will have washed the track clear, and a weekend's worth of choices and adjustments are worthless. The first laps of the race, under cloudy skies and on a clean track, will be a guessing game.

That's at best. At worst, the rain will force a complete postponement of the race to another day or even another weekend, possibly taking away the only free weekend race team members were likely to have until late October. This has already happened once this season. The second Talladega race was postponed for a week, because there happened to be a free weekend following it. Teams left cars and trailers at Talladega and returned to their shops near Charlotte, North Carolina, to work, returning the next weekend and missing a rare weekend with their families. They still grumble about it.

A postponement in racing is not the same as a postponement in, say, baseball. In baseball, a game's rained out, you play two the next day, or the next time you're in town. Maybe, if it's late in the year, you have to play on an off day, or even reschedule a flight and play an afternoon game. Players and coaches kill the rain delay playing cards. The fans take home a rain check good for another game whenever they feel like coming. The local TV station throws on *Godzilla Versus Megalon*; it's not a big deal.

In racing, it's a big deal. Baseball schedules 2,430 games a year. The NASCAR Winston Cup Series, the top stock car racing series in the world, has 32 races scheduled for 1997. So in the little red brick office outside of Martinsville speedway, behind the locked doors of the office in the Winston Cup trailer, in the ESPN trailers parked out in the marshy grass around the speedway, and in the halls of every brightly colored race team hauler angled along the Martinsville infield, it's a big deal. And people are talking.

Those Martinsville Speedway seats hold more than 70,000 fans; even in rain, no seats will go empty. The doors opened today at 7:30, and fans have been filling the rows of seats ever since. Fans in ponchos, fans in rainwear, fans wearing garbage bags, to be sure, but fans in the seats just the same. Another several million people will watch the race on ESPN; millions more will listen on Motor Racing Network, which feeds hundreds of mostly country radio stations nationwide.

This happens 32 weeks a year, in a season stretching from mid-February to mid-November, just as it has for a half century. NASCAR—the National Association for Stock Car Auto Racing—was founded in 1947 in Daytona, when after a three-day meeting in the Streamline, a beachfront hotel, with racing promoters from throughout the South, promoter Bill France took his Daytona beach races, stitched them together with moonshine races in the Carolinas and Alabama and short track shows up and down the East Coast, and called them a league. With a large-scale sanctioning body, he reasoned, races could have safety standards. They could have insurance. Purses could be guaranteed, and amenities could be improved—and he and his fellow promoters could draw more fans and make more money. Racing could move a little closer in from its Saturday-night outlaw status to a Sunday-afternoon family entertainment.

With the Daytona Beach race that France promoted as one of its mainstays, NASCAR prospered. New tracks were added, and before long some tracks were paved. California drag bums and New England grease monkeys filtered down over the next decades, as did sponsorship money from major car manufacturers and tobacco and alcohol producers. In the early 1970s tobacco money, looking for someplace to go when TV ads for cigarettes were outlawed, showed interest in the circuit. R. J. Reynolds looked closely at racing, with its huge base of fans, especially in the South, tobacco country. The Grand National Championship became the Winston Cup, and the Winston Cup it has remained ever since.

What R. J. Reynolds learned first, everyone else has continued to learn. Race cars sell stuff, because race fans buy it.

In the mid-1970s, Gatorade sponsored a car—and sold Gatorade. The capitalists discovered that a 200-mile-per-hour billboard moved product, and the race was on. There has been a Country Time Lemonade car. There is now a Tide car. There has been a Hayes Modem car. There is now a Cartoon Network car. All of those companies lay down the $3 or $4 million (at least; it's up to twice that for the top teams) it takes to keep a Winston Cup team running for a season. For that, they get to put their names on its hood and on its rear quarter panel. A company can get its name on a fender for less—maybe $250,000. Companies stand in line to put their names on race car fenders.

And for good reason. People involved with NASCAR racing estimate that if you walked into the great American workplace on any Monday morning and asked, "Hey, whadja think of that race yesterday?" some 20 million people would be able to give you an intelligent answer.

So 20 million people are now wondering whether this race is going to run. Only a few of them can do anything about it.

In the ESPN trailer, producer Neil Goldberg is dispatching camerapeople and planning his race coverage—while trying to keep in touch with his offices in Bristol, Connecticut, to determine how long to stay on if the race is delayed and what to do if the race is postponed. Companies have paid hundreds of thousands of dollars for commercials during the race on ESPN, but they paid for commercials in front of millions of viewers on Sunday afternoon, not about a third as many some other time.

In the Winston Cup trailer, Gary Nelson, Winston Cup Series director, checks his computer weather monitor, keeps in touch with the officials coming in and out of the trailer as the morning gets started. He's concerned about safety, about running a responsible race. But he's also concerned about ESPN, about the Hanes company that sponsored this race, and about the Martinsville Speedway, which put up a lot of prize money and has a whole raft of other problems to solve if the rain postpones the race.

In the press box above Turns 1 and 2, with a view of the entire track, track owner Clay Earles, track president Clay Campbell, and public relations executives watch the drizzle. They've sold 71,000 tickets, and their only obligation is to provide a race. If not today, then hopefully tomorrow. And if it rains tomorrow, well, NASCAR rules specify the race will be run "the next raceable day."

That's a problem. Their parking areas are staffed by people working extra jobs. Their souvenir stands and refreshment stands are staffed by people working extra jobs. If the race is run tomorrow, how many of them will give up a Monday of work to pick up that extra cash? There are security guards and ticket takers; there are the extra police organized to keep the miles of backed-up traffic moving along U.S. Highway 220, just south of tiny Martinsville, Virginia, and a couple of miles north of the North Carolina border. There are emergency medical service teams and wreckers, ambulances, and a Medevac helicopter. Where do they all stand if the race is postponed to "the next raceable day"?

Ah, the next raceable day. Might be the weekend of October 19, the next free weekend in the schedule, and the only weekend some team members are expecting to have off since June. Then again, could be tomorrow—Monday—which would drastically cut into the preparation time teams have for the next week's race, at Charlotte, on October 5.

In the 40-plus haulers painted in bright team colors, jammed in to avoid the rain or sitting out front in lawn chairs in the shelter of the lift gates that stick out like drawbridges, team members grumble about a postponement. The blue-and-yellow hauler of the number 81 Filmar Racing Square D Ford is no different.

"It'll be our one weekend off, and now that'll be gone too," says engine man Frank Good, a tall, thin man of around 30 with a shock of straight brown hair and a perpetually wry look on his long face. "Two other weekends we had off this entire year. One of them we had to go back to Talladega. The other we went to St. Louis with Kenny [to run a Busch Grand National Series race]. And we didn't even make that race." He shakes his head, taking a rattly drag on a cigarette that's a little spotted from the rain.

"Sucks."

Gas man Don Stiteler just laughs. "Typical fall race at Martinsville," he says. "It has to rain at least one day." A postponement won't mean that much to Don; he's a weekend warrior. That means he doesn't work at the team shop near Charlotte, so he's not worrying about what he's not getting done. He's a kind of fellow traveler to Filmar Racing. For a per diem of about $25, free air fare, and a room he shares with someone else on the crew, he flies to the race every weekend from his job in Pennsylvania, at a heating and air conditioning business. He doesn't have to do anything at the shop to prepare to upend a 11-gallon gas can into a race car on race day. So when he shows up, he helps out, doing whatever is necessary. And if the race is postponed and he has to stay an extra day? "I own the business." He too lights a cigarette, his weathered face breaking into a grin.

A postponement will complicate lives, no doubt. But for the number 81 car, more than anything else, a postponement will complicate the preparations for next week's race. Next week's race is at Charlotte, and Charlotte is not just another race.

❖

Charlotte is NASCAR racing's Mecca, its hometown. A good 90 percent of the 50 or so Winston Cup race teams are based in Charlotte. Bruton Smith's Speedway Motorsports, which owns Charlotte Motor Speedway, owns four other Winston Cup tracks and parts of others (NASCAR owner Bill France's International Speedway Corporation owns only four), and it's from Charlotte that Smith runs a racing empire whose decisions will affect the future of Winston Cup racing.

Most of the support services that racing engenders—companies that make uniforms; companies that make wheels; companies that sell equipment and seats and supplies—are based in Charlotte. Local community colleges offer courses in motorsports management. Clemson University, not far off in Clemson, South Carolina, has a motorsports engineering major in its mechanical engineering department. Local radio shows feature drivers every week.

For stock car racing, Charlotte is Ground Zero.

Which wouldn't mean much in itself, just a race weekend where team members get to sleep at home.

But it's much more. A race at Charlotte is something like a convention. Every sales rep for every shock and spring will be working the garage; every team member looking for a change will be having murmured conversations with crew chiefs and team owners.

And more important than anything else, every sponsor will be at Charlotte. Race teams that work free from on-site interference most of the season, with little more than a Monday-morning phone call to remind them where the money comes from, will suddenly have people looking over their shoulders. Not merely because Charlotte is one of the season's big races; along with the race at Indianapolis and two races each at Daytona, Talladega, and Darlington, races at Charlotte are the season's high points. But Daytona, Talladega, and Darlington races are races some people attend, races a lot of people attend. The races at Charlotte are races people who spend millions of dollars to sponsor teams simply don't miss.

"That's headquarters," says Eddie D'Hondt. "The people we deal with will be in Charlotte. You're under the boss's eye."

And the team running the number 81 car doesn't particularly want to be under the boss's eye just now. By every measure, 1997 has been a hard year for Kenny Wallace and for Filmar Racing.

And, especially, for crew chief Newt Moore.

About 5 feet, 9 inches tall, Newt might weigh a wiry 150. But if his bantam frame looks a little tense in his blue-and-yellow Square D uniform, if his ice-blue eyes look a little fierce as he tries to stare through the rain, tries through force of will to burn the clouds away, don't feel alarmed. Newt Moore isn't trying to frighten you.

But as he will be the first to tell you, Newt Moore has a lot on his shoulders. He says that a lot, actually pointing to his shoulders when he says it, a plaintive look surfacing in his eyes for an unguarded second. The pressures he feels are real.

At 35, Newt started this season as the shop foreman for Filmar Racing, the team, sponsored by Square D, that runs the number 81 Ford Thunderbird driven by Kenny Wallace. As shop foreman, Newt was a hard-driven but wisecracking guy. In charge of fabricating the race cars at the team's shop in suburban Charlotte, he was also the spotter during each week's race, which meant from a position atop the racetrack he'd talk to Wallace by radio, keeping him aware of who was around him, where any trouble lay on the track, which car he was racing for position and should engage, and which cars were laps ahead or behind and should be avoided.

As shop foreman, Newt would stop almost anything he was doing to talk racing. Once a driver himself, he was two-time track Mini-Modified Stock Car champion at Nashville Speedway, a 5/8-mile NASCAR-affiliated track considered one of the best in the South. Newt has lived racing for as long as he can recall. When he recognized that he was never going to be a top-level driver himself, he moved into the shop and worked his way toward the top from the inside. Filbert Martocci, a Nashville owner of lighting stores and a financial services company, bought into a race team with his friend Gil Martin as crew chief in 1988; Newt was on board by 1990. The team started out in NASCAR's second-level series, the Busch Grand National series, which runs slightly smaller cars but many of the same tracks as the Winston Cup.

The team, like all new teams, shuffled some, going through a driver or so and turning over people in every element of the team'mechanics, fabricators, engine guys, as well as the guys who work in the pit crew and at the track race weekend. Kenny Wallace, younger brother of 1989 Winston Cup champion Rusty Wallace and a guy with Busch Series wins and some Winston Cup experience, joined up in 1994, and the team started winning races at the Busch level and running some Winston Cup races. They moved to Charlotte—the suburb of Concord, actually, where the speedway also sits—in 1995. Newt moved his wife away from her family, but there wasn't any question.

In 1996, the team fielded a Winston Cup car for every race on the schedule, qualifying for all but one race and finishing 28th in points. The team was poised for improvement in 1997.

But 1997 hasn't gone according to plan—not at all.

After an okay-to-start-the-year 22nd-place finish at the season-opening Daytona 500, the Square D Thunderbirds that Kenny was driving blew engines in the next two races. Following that, Kenny got into a wreck in Atlanta and had finished only one of the first four races. Despite poor qualifying runs he finished strong in the next two—in the top 15 both times—and then blew another engine at Bristol after qualifying fourth.

Feeling snakebit, the team came to Martinsville for the spring race in April and had its best weekend. Kenny qualified fastest, winning the pole and the $5,000 that goes with it. He ran a great race, battling his brother Rusty in a duel that was constantly shown through the in-car camera he happened to be equipped with for the race. He finished sixth. The team had a moment of cautious optimism.

But that was about as good as things got for the Filmar Racing team in 1997.

After further disappointments, owner Filbert Martocci, with regret and under circumstances he still doesn't like to discuss, let go longtime friend and crew chief Gil Martin.

Suddenly Newt Moore, one-time Nashville Speedway race champion, experienced mechanic, and a guy who could talk about racing full-time, was in charge of a Winston Cup race team.

Some members of the team say they haven't seen him smile since. As crew chief he's the chassis man, making decisions on springs and shocks, as well as running the entire program. He's suddenly in charge of every element of running the team, from ordering uniforms to making sure new cars get built. It's an awesome amount of work, and though he wanted it badly—as soon as Gil was gone, he met with Filbert to sell himself for the job—everyone on the team can see it's overwhelming.

Not that they have trouble with Newt—far from it. The members of the Filmar Racing team would go through a wall for Newt. He's conscientious to an extreme, and members of the team worked alongside him before they worked for him, and they don't think he's changed.

The five races immediately after Newt took over in Dover in June combined weak qualifying, weak races, and two wrecks, and things looked bad. At Michigan, in June, Kenny qualified poorly—33rd—but it didn't make a difference. His engine blew on the first lap. The next week, at the inaugural race at the new California Speedway in Fontana, Kenny did not qualify, his only DNQ of the season. Newt's shoulders started hurting worse.

The second half of the season hasn't gone much better. Kenny has been finishing in the 20s and 30s. No engines have blown, but there hasn't been a top-10 finish, either. Kenny did win another pole—at Bristol—and the team still appreciates that Newt took his share of the $5,000 prize and distributed part of it to every member of the team.

But even before that Bristol race began, Kenny, live on ESPN, assured viewers that though his car might be starting up front, it wouldn't stay there. He knew the team hadn't found the right setup for the car during the practices after qualifying. And in truth, when the green flag dropped, he fell to the back of the pack in a hurry and finished 39th. He didn't lead a lap. He hasn't, in fact, all season.

The failure of the team to finish better is wearing on Newt. Nobody was happier than Newt when Kenny qualified so well for this week's race. Briefly it even looked like he might win another pole. The team needs a good finish. Kenny needs a good finish. And with Charlotte coming up, Newt needs a good finish. Martinsville and Charlotte—this week—is crunch time for this team.

And now rain. "I know I'm not that great a chassis man yet," Newt says. "I don't say I am. I know I need help. But I'll do whatever I can. I'll do whatever I have to." He stares out into the rain, hands in the pockets of his Square D blue pants, his face set. He walks off into the drizzle, heading toward the tent still set up above the empty Square D pit area.

Eddie D'Hondt, watching Newt, shakes his head. "Nobody knows how much pressure is on that guy. It's his first year as crew chief. That's incredible. Plus with a team that hasn't been going good, like these guys, you know what I'm saying? Plus next week is Charlotte, where this team historically doesn't do so good." No, it doesn't—drivers, like athletes in any sport, have places they perform well and places they don't. Kenny does well at shorter tracks like Richmond and Martinsville; at Charlotte he's never had much luck. In fact, when the team tested at Charlotte a week ago, they weren't merely bad, they were terrible, almost a full second in lap times behind the other teams testing Fords around the 1.5-mile track.

One final pressure spot: points. The team stands in 34th place in the Winston Cup points total. Of the teams that have entered every race, they're running dead last. As harsh as that is, it has a significant and looming financial result. According to the Winston Cup distribution of sponsorship money put up by R. J. Reynolds, teams in 30th place or higher at the end of the season assure themselves of a $7,000-per-race bonus in the next year's season. In 1996, their first year running the full circuit of Winston Cup races, the Filmar Racing team finished 28th, and the $224,000 this year has made a difference. Considering getting by without that money next year—or, really, going to sponsor Square D, after a terrible season, and asking for more money—can cause Newt's eyes to take on the long stare that has become so familiar to his teammates.

Newt says every chance he gets, "We need to get up after those guys running in front of us." He means the green number 90 car, driven by Dick Trickle; the bright red number 8, driven by Hut Stricklin; the pale rainbow 42 that Joe Nemechek drives; and the 75 driven by Rick Mast. Kenny Wallace, with 1,932 points, is 240 points behind Mast, who's in 30th place. That's a lot of ground to make up in the six remaining races. On the other hand, Dale Jarrett, in third place, is a little less than 200 points behind Jeff Gordon for the points lead and less than 100 behind Mark Martin for second, and people are saying it's a great championship race. Only the 8 car is starting ahead of the 81 at Martinsville; Stricklin qualified fourth. Nemechek is eighth, but Trickle and Mast are back in 31st and 38th. If the team is going to make up 240 points, Martinsville looks like an opportunity. Nothing is impossible. And Newt Moore would like to do the impossible.

So with all that on his shoulders, a good run with a well set up car would have been perfect. It would have been a step. Instead, rain.

❖

Newt isn't the only member of the Square D Filmar Racing team under pressure. For one thing, Filmar Racing is a completely independent team. It runs the number 81 car and only the number 81 car. Independent teams win fewer and fewer races. For example, between them, in 1997, the multicar teams owned by Jack Roush and Rick Hendrick had won 16 of the 26 races so far, and each planned to grow in 1998. So the Filmar team may be trying to do something that just can't be done anymore. When the 1997 season ended, in fact, independent teams had won only 5 of the 32 races.

So the Square D team is fighting from the back of the pack before the hauler ever pulls into the infield on race weekend.

In the back room of the Square D hauler, Filbert Martocci sits quietly, thinking.

Thinking about how to get Newt the kind of support he needs to get the team on the right track; thinking about what Filbert might need to do himself; thinking about his businesses back in Nashville that will need long-distance attention if he needs to stay at Martinsville another day.

Thinking about what it's going to cost if the race has to be rescheduled.

"Figure it costs $85,000 to $90,000 each race for a medium-budget team, more like $145,000 to $150,000 for high-budget teams," he says. "But that's just taking our expenses for the year and dividing it by the number of races."

But if the race is postponed until another weekend and the teams have to come up on a Sunday to run? "A one-day show? No motels? That would probably cost us . . . $25,000." He tosses the figures out not because he is a man comfortable tossing around $25,000 but because he is involved in racing, and in racing the figures are large. He will only say that he's invested "significant sums of my own money" into his race team, but driver Kenny Wallace says he's certain that Filbert drops a million dollars a year into Filmar Racing to add to the $3.5 million or so Square D ponies up.

That's some dough. Does he hope the race is run tomorrow, then? "No," he says, sighing. "Because then I'll lose my pit crew. They have full-time jobs. Most of my pit crew doesn't work for the race team. Anyway, it's hard to say what I'd prefer, because they won't ask me."

On that, he's right. Even the Roushes, the Yateses, the Hendricks—owners of the multicar teams whose drivers are currently fighting it out for the Winston Cup points championship—don't have much of a say in NASCAR decisions. In fact, owners can feel like they don't have much of a say in anything. Their crew chiefs make virtually all the decisions on the cars; the driver does the driving and the high-profile pitching of the sponsor's product. Aside from signing checks and fretting, owners can seem left out of the loop.

But Filbert knows better. He's a businessman, and he sets the tone for his organization like the owner of any business. A short man in his 50s, he has a deep tan and the pressed jeans, cowboy boots, and Filmar Racing shirt that identify him as a team owner as surely as the credential that hangs from his collar: "Filbert Martocci, owner, number 81."

Filbert has spent a lot of money trying to make his race team competitive. He's worked hard to get a driver he's comfortable with and a sponsor he can depend on; both are now under contract through 2000.

"But it's like an orchestra," he says. "You can have the best driver and the best crew chief and the best car and still not win. You have to keep changing positions until you find what wins. It's chemistry." He's willing to make changes, and he's willing to spend what it takes to win.

On race days, Filbert now works as spotter—and in fact, his proudest moment in racing came when Jeff Burton was driving for his team in the Busch Grand National series, and Filbert, from the spotter's position, coached Burton from 3/4 mile back into winning the race. Filbert believes deeply in leadership and coaching, and he's looking hard for someone to take that role for Newt, to take the weight off Newt's shoulders and help him along. "Newt's like a sponge; he absorbs everything," Filbert says. That's great when he's learning about racing, but not so great when he's just absorbing the stress caused by inexperience and uncertainty.

But Filbert believes Newt is his guy. He just doesn't know when the next race is going to run.

Like everybody else, he'll wait.

❖

All morning, in the drizzle, as race fans file along the rows of the bleachers, carrying wet coolers and trying to get excited over an upcoming race that might not run, the race teams work equally hard, and with just as little success, to make their race day routines feel authentic.

But as the rain turns to mist and then to drizzle and then back to rain again, as occasional moments of sun again give way to clouds and wet, the spirit of the race struggles, wavers, and finally appears to die. On the infield, the racetrack has the feeling of going to the prom with the girl you didn't really want to date. There is an event, but it's clear something is missing. During the early morning, teams have gone through elaborate, pages-long prerace checklists taped to the sides of the cars—tightening bolts, adjusting air pressures, checking fluids, leaning over engines and filling the air with the throaty rumble as an engine man gooses the throttle from under the hood. In the garage area of a Winston Cup race, the most common sight—the *sine qua non* of NASCAR racing—is a gang of identically clad guys pushing a race car. Pushing it to get gas, pushing it to be inspected by NASCAR officials, pushing it to or from the garage or hauler. Everywhere you see groups of guys in blue-and-red jumpsuits, or in bright orange shirts and baseball hats, or in any of the vibrating team colors, shepherding silent race cars around like movers trying to place a piano for an indecisive homeowner. "That's our job," a yellow-clad member of the Pennzoil team said to me once. "Pushing stuff around."

Car after car completes its inspection, is filled with gas, and takes its place, covered, in the soggy line in the first turn. The teams connect each car to a little rolling generator, which runs a heating system that warms the oil pan and the oil tank so that the car is ready to start. But these gestures feel symbolic. It's going to be a long time before any gentlemen start their engines.

The pits themselves are stocked. Hoses to air wrenches are neatly coiled, wrenches tried out, then covered with tarps. The huge cart that each crew sets up in its pit is called a war wagon. It has seats on top for the crew chief and a couple of other team members; it has a satellite television hookup so the team can watch a telecast of the race as it's going on, and a computer hooked up to the feed for NASCAR's official scoring program. The cart has special drawers for the jacks used during the pit stops, the sign the crew holds out to show the driver where to stop, drawers for tools and fluids, rags, and the omnipresent duct tape. The electrical cords connecting the war wagon to the nearest outlet are duct-taped to the ground, and then even the ground is covered with another tarp as the rain refuses to let up.

Each team had set up a little tent over its pit to keep the car dry while they performed their prerace checks. Now, with the cars bunched in the turns, the tents look empty and kind of sad. Team members hang out underneath them, trying to kill time. Every now and then somebody tilts an electric fan under the tarp covering the pit area, rippling the tarp as hot air blows to make a weak attempt at drying the asphalt beneath. But it's desultory and tired, and they eventually give up. Dry, today, is not an option.

❖

At about noon, the infield public address system crackles briefly to life: "Come on, boys, let's get it over with."

On a little flatbed stage at the start-finish line, where if the day had been nicer previous champions and NASCAR legends like Ned Jarrett, Richard Petty, and Junior Johnson would have been introduced, stands a narrator and a Miss Winston—a pretty girl in a Winston Cup uniform of white pants and a white shirt with the Winston logo on it. She holds an umbrella, and as the announcer calls out the names of the drivers in reverse qualifying order, they walk quickly across the damp flatbed, hunch under the umbrella for a quick handshake, and hustle down the stairs. An arc of yellow balloons, part of what once was the number 50 made of balloons before the rain made them superfluous, lends an air of strained gaiety to the proceedings.

The fans try to work up the energy to cheer for the drivers as they're introduced, but it's a long way to go. Most of the drivers aren't even wearing their fire suits. They're in baseball hats and golf shirts, wearing jackets supplied by their sponsors, collars turned up against the rain.

Jeff Burton, who qualified 10th, and brother Ward Burton, who's on the pole, get the largest cheers. They're from nearby South Boston, Virginia. Points leader Jeff Gordon is roundly booed.

Kenny Wallace, who qualified sixth, gets a smattering of applause and then comes down the stairs and hustles back to the Square D hauler.

Waiting for him there is Winston Kelly, one of the voices of Motor Racing Network, which broadcasts most races to nearly 500 stations nationwide. Like their counterparts on ESPN, the MRN guys have long since given up on meaningful race talk and are now just looking to fill up time.

Kenny, with his Herman Munster–style bellow of a laugh and his willingness to say or do almost anything, is a good catch, and Kelly grabs him.

"How were y'all in practice?" Kelly asks, and Kenny, laughing, lets loose such a stream of race cliches—"Oh, we really feel dialed in, but it's racing, you never know, Winston, in this short-track racing anything can happen" that Kelly says, "You know what, Kenny, you ought to interview me."—Kenny lets out a burst of that laugh—"HUH-huh-huh-huh-huh"—and says he will. He dons a headset from a nearby scanner, leans over Kelly's microphone, and waits for the lead-in Kelly has told him will come. Kelly will hear, "Well, Winston, what do you hear from Kenny Wallace and the Square D race team?" and Kenny will just come directly onto the radio. Team members and his public relations representative, Danielle Randall, push together around him, ready for the joke.

But the lead in is slightly different than anyone expects, and Kelly expertly responds, asking Kenny about his hopes for the race.

Kenny is a pro. "Well, last time here we started first and finished sixth. This time we start sixth, so . . . ? You never know. We did good in what I call monitor racing—we had a good car in Happy Hour. I feel good about the car, and the team. We keep digging every week. Our goal now is to gear up for next year."

All in all, not too different from the cliches he originally spouted, but good enough for genuine thanks from Kelly, who goes off in search of more filler.

Kenny loves the term "monitor racing," which is what he calls the unofficial race for bragging rights to see whose car ran fastest in Happy Hour, the final Saturday afternoon practice before the race. As soon as possible after the Saturday race is finished—at Martinsville it was a Craftsman Series Truck race, at Charlotte it will be a Busch Grand National Series race—the Winston Cup cars line up at the gate out of the garage, racing onto the track for a precious last hour making final adjustments to set up the car just right. During those practice laps the NASCAR scoring computer is turned on, so lap times are compiled, and cars are ranked on monitors according to their fastest lap. When Kenny turned in the fastest lap during practice on Saturday, he excitedly told Filbert about it. Filbert was less enthusiastic. "So where's our trophy?" he asked dryly.

Kenny genuinely loves talking to the reporters. He genuinely loves talking to the team members, to the fans, to anyone. Kenny just loves people, and it's made him a popular driver. The sponsors love him because he utterly charms the crowds in their race-morning hospitality tents and at personal appearances. The press loves him because of his self-deprecating humor, honesty, and willingness to laugh.

And he keeps the team loose by refusing to get down. Not a man plagued by self-doubt, Kenny wears a gold watch given to drivers as part of the inaugural festivities at the California 500, the race for which he failed to qualify. And though the Martinsville drivers' motor home paddock is small and supposedly limited to top-25 drivers (Kenny, recall, is currently 34th), when the nice lady and man who watch the gate to the paddock tell him, out of sheer favoritism, he'll never be excluded as long as they're around, he has his motor home inside without a hint of abashedness. He knows he belongs. He's a race car driver. And if the greater part of that job involves entertaining sponsors, signing autographs, and being fun to be around, well then, hell—he's perfectly well suited for that too.

After Kelly's gone, Danielle comes up and puts an arm around Kenny. She's got him scheduled to be one of the drivers present at the unveiling of a new NASCAR video game on Tuesday night. She's got a copy of the game, and he'll be racing Jeff Gordon in front of TV cameras at a Charlotte restaurant.

"I didn't give a copy to Jeff," Danielle says. "Aren't I awful?"

Kenny takes the copy of the game back to his motor home. And that's how he spends the rest of his afternoon. "I even went to K Mart and got a steering wheel," he says later. "I love that game."

❖

The day drags on another hour or so, and time seems almost to stop. Team members looking to jump teams have surreptitiously approached every crew chief they can productively approach; guys with products to represent or ideas to push have done what they can. Even the crowds around the weather monitor at the Winston Cup trailer have dwindled: There's only so much cloud-cover green you can look at. The snack bar's pink hot dogs, mealy hamburgers, cigarettes, and tepid coffee have long since lost any charm. Under the sodden tents on pit road and sitting on the counters in the haulers, team members are reduced to the age-old time-killer of men everywhere with nothing to do.

They're telling stories.

Under the Square D blue tent, Don tells a story about a crew member who stuck a long-handled brush over the wall to scrub tire fragments off the car's grille during a pit stop—standard practice. But he didn't pay attention to where the other guys were, and in the frenzy he clotheslined the front tire-changer. Don repeats the story, acting out the part of the changer, doing a sort of limbo to show how his legs flipped out from under him, a finger under his Adam's apple to represent the offending brush. A train goes by on a track along the backstretch, and he's reminded of a tight race during which a passing train stopped long enough for the engineer and workers to lean out their windows and watch the end.

Steve Baker, a hulking weekend warrior whose job is to hand the gas cans over the wall to Don during pit stops, shares a tale about the pressurized water tanks each team wheels to the pits for race day—the water is used in case a radiator dumps or is changed. "One time, right before a race, when the pit was packed, a guy from the team next to us loosened the top of his tank without checking the pressure." The tank was still pressurized. "Boom!" Baker says, indicating with his hand the top of the tank flying up, hesitating, and plummeting down. "We didn't even have time to yell. It came down and sank about 6 inches into the asphalt." Steve has the long hair, droopy mustache, and comfortable bulk of a biker, and he rides his bike to the races most weekends, wherever the team is. He's divorced and works construction, living out of a suitcase wherever he happens to be working.

"My home? I guess this is," he laughs. This turns out to be true. At one point, lost for anything else to do, Steve cleans out his little locker in the hauler. Besides the expected papers, food items, and forgotten uniform parts ("Man, I was wondering where that was"), came a single work boot.

The group's attention next turns to Jim "Two-Can" Murray, general mechanic and the guy in charge of the car's gears. They plead with him, as someone always does when there's a new face around, to tell the story of his nickname. He's in his 50s and has been racing for decades. He's been on championship teams and has done it all. He smiles, lights a cigarette, and walks off. "Another time," he says. "I'm busy right now." He seats himself on a lawn chair under the hauler's lift gate, opens a copy of *Speedway Scene*, and falls asleep.

❖

It seems like this will never stop. But as the afternoon drags drearily onward, there's a sudden quickening of the pace. At a little before 3 P.M., NASCAR spokesman Kevin Triplett stands on the bottom stair of the Winston Cup trailer. "Tomorrow," he tells everybody checking in. "Tomorrow, 11A.M." The day is finally looking like it might clear, but by the time the track is dried, it's unlikely there will be time to run the full 500 laps of the race before it's too dark to continue. Martinsville has no lights. NASCAR likes to give its fans a full race; so does the speedway. So it's come back tomorrow, and the scramble is on. A sheet of NASCAR stationery is posted on the trailer: "All cars will remain as parked in Turns 1 and 2 and covered for the evening. Tomorrow at 7:30 A.M. each team must wait to be escorted by two NASCAR officials before working on the cars." Then the air filter can be changed, the oil warmed, plugs changed, and tire air pressure changed. Everything else must be left as it is.

For the first time all day, movement means something. Teams, finally given work to do, scramble like fighter pilots given an alarm. Toolboxes roll toward haulers; crash carts, filled with supplies needed if the car is in a wreck, are covered with tarps. War wagons, already covered with tarps, get covered more carefully, their tarps fastened with duct tape or held down by bungee cords, tires, wheel rims, or floor jacks.

Back at the Square D hauler, Eddie is on the phone in the back office, trying to rebook their rooms at the hotel. He's largely successful. Word spreads among team members that the garage opens back up at 7 and the race starts at 11.

Newt already couldn't look like he's under any more stress, so his demeanor doesn't change. Eddie has made a few quick decisions and sent home his weekend warriors. Don stays, but the other weekenders head home. What that means for the crew he'll figure out tomorrow. If he's short a tire changer or another pit crew member, he'll just have to scavenge one. Steve Baker, with his construction job to return to, shakes a lot of hands and heads off to his hog. Everybody else, just pleased that the race was postponed for a day and not into their free weekend, finishes closing down the hauler. Two-Can grabs a couple of beers from a cooler by the door, puts one in each pocket, grins, and with the rest of the crew, joins the stream heading for the exit.

The team goes back to their hotel, orders pizza, and spends the remainder of the day watching football on television.

❖

The fans don't go anywhere.

That is, the fans can't go anywhere. The grandstand empties with an eerie quiet. Nothing about racing is supposed to be quiet, and many fans who showed up today haven't heard so much as a single race car engine growl. Fans stream out behind the metal grandstands. The simple metal latticework from underneath looks like nothing more than a large set of stands at a high school football stadium. Another train passes the track along the backstretch, hooting into the finally clearing sky.

Inside the speedway, the still-standing tents, red, purple, yellow, black, green, along pit road look dreary among the puddles from the day's persistent drizzle. Piles of tires, some covered with tarps hastily, others neatly, look almost but not quite ready for . . . something. For tomorrow, then.

The rolling lawns surrounding the speedway have been long trampled into a slippery, red muck. The famous clay of the Piedmont covers boots, shoes, tires.

The track is at the dead end of a narrow residential street off Route 220. Houses line one side of the street, and a grassy lawn slopes precipitously downward on the other side. A dirt road leads down into what is almost a ravine, and cars have parked in every corner of the lot. Some of those cars have left, but the dirt path is now a thick red soup, and cars without front-wheel drive aren't moving very well. The sound of revving engines and spinning tires fills the air, though it's probably not quite what fans had in mind when they showed up in the morning. At the east end of the parking area is a little lake, usually quite pretty but now an almost shocking shade of pinkish orange, viscous with clay silt.

Though the race haulers are staying in the speedway, other cars that have been parked inside are crawling out, joining a sluggish flow of vehicles leaving the parking lot across from the houses and other parking areas adjacent to the speedway. The asphalt road is striped with heavy orange mud picked up by car and truck tires.

There's much less camping at Martinsville than at larger tracks, where fans can camp on the track infield and in acres of campgrounds adjacent to the speedway. At Martinsville, with no infield and only 70,000 seats, a much larger percentage of the fans come for the day. Since the movement of traffic leaving the speedway is almost indiscernible, many of them line the little street, hoping to see a driver or crew member exit. Kids in Mark Martin hats and Jeff Gordon shirts watch wide-eyed, hoping against hope. Groups of three and four people, a little rain-dampened, a little bedraggled, stand in knots and discuss what to do about dinner, whose spouses or bosses have to be called. Where they're going to stay'if they're going to stay.

Rod, a 35-year-old maintenance worker from Republic, Ohio, is wearing a raincoat and a number 24 cap as he watches the procession with his wife and a couple of friends. This is the first race they've ever been to, and they don't mind that they're going to have to stay another day to see the Winston Cup race. "Oh, I've done stupider things," he laughs. After seeing races on ESPN, he and his wife thought they'd give Winston Cup racing a shot. And yesterday, during the Craftsman Truck Series race that ran under a cloudless sky, they knew they'd made a good decision. "My wife leaned over to me and said she could really get to like this," Rod says, obviously pleased.

His wife at that moment runs off, squealing. He doesn't pay much mind. Thinking for a minute about watching a race, he mentions the advertising slogan NFL football is using, "Feel the Power." He says that anybody who's ever been to a motor race looks at that slogan and laughs. "Couple years ago we went to

Norwalk, to the drag races," he says. "I tell you, my body organs was vibrating." Now that's power.

His wife comes back, breathless. A van creeping along the street held members of Jeff Gordon's pit crew, and with crew chief Ray Evernham's autograph on her DuPont Paints cap, she's in heaven. Another car crawls by drawing a crowd. Its driver, Geoff Bodine, is keeping his window open and signing autographs or just chatting with the fans. "Yeah, thanks," he says, or "I know." It's all comments about what a great driver he is or the weather. Good fan relations consists of about 90 percent listening.

Jimmy, a 37-year-old firefighter from Roanoke, Virginia, says he'll stay for tomorrow's race, "if I can get it off." He's wearing an Earnhardt hat and has been going to a few races a year for a good dozen years, he says. "But I still haven't seen him win!" He laughs. Earnhardt has won seven Winston Cup championships and 70 races. Managing to see more than a dozen races without an Earnhardt win is something of an accomplishment. Jimmy laughs—maybe tomorrow will be the day. "If not, I'm not out but $30."

But the fans lining the street are racing's apple-polishers, well-behaved fans, with kids or still kids themselves, hoping for a glimpse of a hero.

Down in the grassy parking ravine, the scene is a little more varied. Pickups with camper shells and 4x4s have their tailgates down, tarps draped everywhere. Fans in damp black Earnhardt T-shirts laze in lawn chairs; Weber grills send tendrils of smoke into the clearing sky. Everywhere, guys with bellies and boots stand, holding cans of beer, thoughtfully staring. Every now and then the line of cars gives a lurch and a small cheer goes up, but mostly the people with the cars and trucks remaining have decided to wait it out, and in the sloppy, muddy mess of the sloping parking lot, it's postrace time, even if there wasn't a race. A line of trees along the back of the meadow makes an excellent rest room, and these folks are at peace.

Gary, a 29-year-old vinyl siding worker from Wilmington, North Carolina, wears a Mark Martin hat and enjoys a beer. He says he goes to about five races a year—here, Charlotte, Richmond, Darlington, and Rockingham, probably seeing both the spring and the fall races at one of those tracks. And he's not worried about having to head back to work tomorrow. "No, my boss is here," he snickers. "I ain't dumb." In fact, Gary doesn't have to worry about much. "When we got up this morning and it was raining, we booked our rooms for another night." So he blithely drank his way through today's rainy waiting, and tomorrow is race day all over again. Sometimes it's a great world.

In fact, that's how it feels around the parking area—something like a folk festival where the weather isn't quite as planned but the music is still going on. Race fans usually don't mind drinking, talking, racing, and hanging around racetracks with other race fans, and that's what they've done all day today. For them, the postponement isn't a problem—it just extends the party.

A friend of Gary's emerges from a little makeshift tent of blue tarps. He's wearing a long white Rod Stewart wig and a Mark Martin T-shirt, and he has the Mean Drunken Stare that says the party's been going on for him for quite some time.

"Mark Martin's the king!" he shouts. "Jeff Gordon's queer, Earnhardt sucks, and Mark Martin's the king!" He lights a cigarette and goes back to the Stare. Gary offers a chicken wing, but it may be about time to leave the parking area—traffic has started to move smoothly.

Glancing back over the little hollow, it looks a bit like a Civil War encampment. Hutches and tents of plastic and canvas have sprung up, with more fires going as people cook food they couldn't eat in the morning's steady rain. Everywhere, people stand and lie about in attitudes of repose. Some sing, some shout, some drink. The overcast clears further, and a little purple and high blue peek out of the sky. There's no moon, but a couple of stars are visible, growing stronger as the light fades and the clouds break apart.

It's like a camp of soldiers who prepared for battle but met no foe for the day. They've been given a reprieve, and if they're glad to last another day they're still somehow unsatisfied because they didn't face the excitement they expected.

But tomorrow's race day again.

❖

Those who aren't camping or driving home are in trouble if they didn't follow Gary's example and book motel rooms for the night.

All over south central Virginia, bedraggled race fans form noisy, cranky crowds in motels, filling tiny lobbies with Bill Elliott T-shirts and rainbow-striped wind jackets. Cars and pickups with Rusty Wallace decals or the number 3 of Earnhardt pull into parking lots. Someone peers into the lobby or jumps out and makes a foray. He comes back shaking his head, and the car moves on a little farther down the road, to the next motel, and the next, and the next.

Motels during race weekend are filled as far away as Danville, Virginia, and Eden, North Carolina—20 miles and more away. So fans who checked out of their motel rooms Sunday morning are combing the countryside like locusts, scavenging any room they can find. Motels and restaurants that put extra help on Friday and Saturday night are overwhelmed by the unexpected bounty on Sunday, further clogging the works. Drive-through lanes at McDonald's and Hardee's stretch into nearby streets, and parking lots overflow into used car lots and vacant lots.

Somewhere along North Carolina Route 87, east of Eden on the way toward Ruffin and Yanceyville, a motel so dingy that it doesn't even have a name other than Motel has rooms. The Asian man behind the counter, astonished to be called away from his meal on a Sunday night, can't figure out how to work the credit card machine, so if you can't pay cash, you're out of luck at Motel. You'd better have your own food, too—across the street is a boarded-up supermarket, but that's about it for the neighborhood. A few nearby lights illuminate the patchy clouds from below, and the sky shines with stars.

Unloading the trunk of their weather-worn green Grand LeMans four-door, two men in "Caution: Speed Zone" and Joe Nemechek T-shirts wearily carry luggage into their room. No different, perhaps, than weary fans all over the region at that moment, but for one thing: Abdul and Amir are black.

They laugh. "No, not too many brothers at the race," Abdul says. "But we have a unique perspective. We're hustlers."

Abdul is 32, with a comb sticking into his bushy beard and wearing a kufi; Amir is 45, and he's drinking ginger ale from a two-liter bottle. They avoid alcohol because both are practicing Muslims. They're from Philadelphia, and ticket hustling is their living. No less than the crew members or the fans with their campers, Abdul and Amir are part of racing. "We've been doing racing for ten years," Amir says. "Following the circuit, hustling tickets." They learned the same thing that R. J. Reynolds and Tide and Gatorade learned: That's where the money is.

You won't see many black faces at a race. There are one or two black crew members, and the very occasional black fan. Once in a while a black journalist will cover a race, and sponsors sometimes bring black fans around to the races. But overall, racing is as white as white. Recent efforts by famous athletes to start black-owned race teams have garnered a lot of press, but racing people generally agree that until there's a black driver black people won't embrace racing. Nonetheless, anyone paying attention can see that NASCAR would love to have black fans—black fans buy products; black fans buy tickets.

But at the moment, unarguably, it doesn't have black fans.

So even as hustlers, Abdul and Amir stand out.

"We've had good and bad experiences," Amir says. "I've been called Leroy, I've been called boy, you know." Says Abdul, "The race crowd is a real Dixie crowd. Here in Martinsville, the crowd is pretty good. But in Georgia, in Tennessee, the fans get a few beers in 'em, the Dixie comes out." Amir says, "And we have learned not to stay where all those campers are. When it gets dark, we don't go down there."

But then, like almost everyone in racing, Abdul and Amir are tired of that topic. Racing is an almost exclusively white sport. It'll change at its own pace. Abdul and Amir are much more interested in the troubles they face as ticket hustlers. "The law enforcement," Amir says. "They know we're not going to the race when they see us. So unless it's legal, they automatically come after us."

Martinsville isn't a bad track for police, they say. Different tracks get bad at different times, depending on who's trying to get elected to what or whether the track owner had a complaint from a friend or notable recently. But mostly they're left alone to do their job—an important one, they say.

"Fans who need tickets to a sold-out race, we have 'em," Amir says. "Ticket brokers come to us to fill their orders. And we're not buying them up from the track and scalping them. We're buying them off the fans." He kicks off his shoes and leans back on one of the room's two beds, clicking an NFL game on with the remote.

Getting hassled by police is part of their job, and they just factor the occasional bail or confiscation of their stock into their overhead.

In many ways they're like every other person working in racing. They travel together, leaving families they wish they could spend the weekends with. They can make up to a few thousand dollars on a good day, "but on a bad day you can get stuck," Abdul says. "Like today. Tickets were moving good yesterday, and even this morning until the rain got heavy."

Amir says, "It was raining when we got up, and we started thinking of strategy then." We said, "Let's just sell what we got, and if we buy, we gotta buy real low."

Like race teams, they have to have different plans for different tracks, different circumstances, different weather. A track where demand was high in the spring can add 5,000 seats before the fall race, briefly destroying a market. A market can be good all morning and suddenly crash, leaving them with seats they sell for less than they bought them for. It's like the stock market, and they're speculators. "Each track is different," Abdul says. "Some places, 30 minutes before the race starts everyone is in their seat. Other places, an hour after the race started, people are still dwindling in." Charlotte, they say, is the worst town for selling in. Police are aggressive and inflexible, especially near the track.

"It depends on how we do tomorrow," Abdul says. If they do well enough, they'll drive back home. If they haven't made enough money, they'll go to Charlotte; but they'd rather skip it.

They'd rather not have to worry about it, because they'd rather not have been rained out today. If they have to go to Charlotte, it's going to be a tough race week for them too.

But like everyone else on the circuit, they can't control the weather. They've done what they can today, and they'd better get some rest. Tomorrow they'll have to get up early.

Because it's race day.

CHAPTER 2

OVER THE WALL

Monday, September 29

PART 1: PRERACE

Race day dawns fine and clear, perfectly clear, breathtakingly clear—a high blue sky unmarked by clouds. Abdul and Amir are nowhere to be seen, not even in the parking lot by the abandoned seafood restaurant where they said they'd be. It's probably just as well. With yesterday's rain and the number of people who had to go back to work today, it's clearly a buyer's market for tickets to the Hanes 500. Still, the usual crowds press the souvenir trailers around the track and line the road to the crossover gate in Turn 4, where team members enter the infield. The bright red mud lining the street is drying at the edges, already starting to turn brown and crumble. By the time the teams roll down that street at 7 A.M., a truck is already circling the track, heating it with a jet-powered gas heater. Wreckers drag around tractor tires, helping to not only heat and dry the track but to replace a smidgen of the rubber that had washed off the track in the rain.

Fans begin filing into the speedway bleachers almost as soon as the teams arrive, but this morning there are no yellow and red ponchos, no plastic rain jackets and garbage bags. Today it's Mark Martin T-shirts and the rainbow stripe of Jeff Gordon's number 24 car, uncovered and bright in the thin, early-fall sun.

The infield, seething with activity, still carries a strange energy—somewhere between the intense, focused hustle of race day and the lassitude of a practice session, the teams carry themselves as if this Monday race is real, but not quite. It feels like going to school the day of a test, but there's a substitute teacher. The test goes on, but things just feel different. The teams fold the EZ-Up tents they had set up over the pits and lean them against haulers to dry in the sun; car covers, drenched, flop over the infield fence, again making the scene look like the day after a soaked Boy Scout Jamboree, with tents and tarps drying on every available surface and everybody rushing around pursuing merit badges that seem somehow just a jot less important for the delay.

Each team sends a single crew member dragging a little gas-powered generator on a cart to Turns 1 and 2, where NASCAR Winston Cup officials in white-and-red uniforms (Winston colors, of course) guide them to their cars.

The team members start the generators, plug the cords into little sockets on the rear bumpers or quarter panels of their cars, and head back to their teams. The generators power heating elements inside and surrounding the oil tank, heating the oil to prepare it for the race.

Along pit road, members of the Square D team try to ready their little corner of the track for the race. Much was done yesterday. The blue-and-yellow war wagon, with its jacks, air wrenches, and other race-time equipment, is already in place, under a tarp. The tarp is peeled back, the shiny blue seats on top wiped down with dusty red gas-station rags. The nine sets of tires purchased for the race are liberated from their own tarp, wrapped tight with duct tape. The pit itself, where the car will stop for tires and gas during the race, is itself under a tarp. Many teams weight the tarps down and tilt hot-air blowers underneath, hoping to more quickly dry the asphalt. Jack-man Stephen "Duze" Dluzniewski, a swarthy Bostonian of about 30, pushes a squeegee, herding pooled water through a hole in the pit wall toward an infield drain. He's assisted by a member of the number 33 car's team, whose pit is just to the rear of the Square D team's.

This kind of desultory cooperation is second nature in the garage and pits—a slow-going car being pushed by too-few teammates toward garage, inspection, hauler, or gas pump will likely get a push from a stray crew member of another car. When a team is hurriedly changing front springs in the garage during practice, a quick method of changing both at once is to jack the car up on both sides and, using the two jacks as fulcrum, have a few crew members lean on the back of the car, tilting the front end into the air for quick adjustment. Three guys leaning on the rear deck can comfortably raise the front, and if there are only two, a nearby member of another team will, almost unconsciously, drift over, lean, exchange a smile, a nod, or a smoke, and then leave after a minute and a half, when the springs are changed.

But cooperative or not, there's just not much for crew members to do in the pits this morning. Lines to the air wrenches are carefully coiled, but they were ready yesterday. The camera, tools, antennae, and coolers need to be arranged in the pit area, but that was mostly done yesterday, too. In the Square D pit, Two-Can and Don putter around with gas cans and tire pedestals, but they're basically just filling time.

The pages of prerace checks were all completed yesterday, and the limited changes to tire pressure and spark plugs that can be made according to the special rules this morning have been made. By 9 A.M. teams are pushing their cars, one by one, into Turn 4, where their windshields glint in the sun. Their brilliant blues, yellows, and greens almost glow, seemingly restless with the energy of being penned in yesterday.

Frank Good, his eyes still looking a little sleepy, leans on a drying stack of tires and smokes a cigarette. He describes his morning.

"I went to the car and plugged it in. Then I waited for the clusterfuck to stop so we could push it to pit road. We warmed the oil up, warmed the engine up. We jacked up the rear and spun the wheels to warm the gear up." He took off the oil pump top and used a drill to pump hot oil into the engine. They could have changed plugs, but he didn't. A NASCAR official looked over his shoulder as he worked to make sure he didn't make any unauthorized adjustments.

Could he have if left alone?

A smile. "Oh, yeah, I'm sneaky enough. Like I could have changed the timing." Timing, which determines when the spark enters the cylinder to cause the gas to explode, driving the piston and turning the drive shaft, affects how the car runs and where in its rpm ladder the engine delivers the most horsepower. "Advance it too much and it detonates," Frank says. "Retard it too much and it runs like a dog." On a damp day like yesterday the timing was advanced slightly—to give the fuel a tiny fraction of a second more to mix with damper air and combust. "Now this is the kind of day you wanna be retarded a little bit," he says. Too bad; changing is against the rules.

Don is someone who can actually take advantage of the few extra minutes. He's in charge of gas during pit stops. He's the gas man, hoisting an 11-gallon can of gas on his shoulder, dumping it into the car, handing the empty to the guy standing next to him, taking another can and dumping it too, while the other crew members are changing the tires. Gas weighs about 8.9 pounds a gallon, so that's about 100 pounds he's horsing around on one shoulder.

But while the car is running—and all weekend long during practice—Don keeps track of gas, by weight. Using an electronic scale connected to the war wagon, he weighs the empty gas can, then drags it in a little cart, gets it filled, and weighs it full. Throughout practice, the team counts laps the race car does and figures out how much fuel it's using per lap, and how that fuel mileage varies according to weather, track conditions, and changes in the setup of the car. With a sense of how long the race car can drive without running out of gas, Newt Moore can plan pit stops and tire changes accordingly.

After each pit stop during the race, Don will weigh the gas remaining in the second can and subtract that from the 22 gallons he knows fill the tank to determine how much gas the car used since the last pit stop. Dividing that by the number of laps the car has run gives him a number. He adds it to the lap on which the stop took place and scrawls it on a little card and hands it up to Newt, standing on top of the war wagon. The gas figures—and information he's getting from Eddie, who's working on tires—help Newt decide when the car needs to stop next.

So do events on the track, like wrecks, other cautions, or information he's getting from the driver about how the car's handling.

Don's weighing the empty can just to get his settings straight. Like every aspect of the car's performance, gas has its own white binder, with reports from every race at every track since Filmar Racing started running a Winston Cup car. "At superspeedways [like Talladega or Daytona] we'll get like 6.8, 6.5 miles per gallon," Don says. "A regular track, like Dover, it's around 4.27, 4.3. Martinsville averages 4.1, 4.2, something like that." The constant acceleration and braking on the short straightaways and tiny turns keep the engine running harder and getting less motion out of its run, so Martinsville is one of the poorest-mileage tracks. "We'll probably get about 150, 160 laps here," or less than 80 miles out of the 22 gallons in the tank, Don says.

"But it don't matter," Don grins his crooked grin. "The tires won't go that long. After 100 laps, these guys'll be screaming like dogs."

That's true. The sound of drivers complaining over the radio about their tires going away late in a long green-flag run is one of the truly pitiable sounds in racing, comparable to the wails heard in prisoner-of-war camps or day care centers. Late in a run tires have been worn almost completely away, making them slippery. The car, with poor traction, starts to get wobbly in the corners. If the back wheels give up traction first, drivers say the car gets loose. Loose means the driver feels the rear of the car sliding around to the right as he tries to wrestle it through the turn. The car gets a little sideways, and the driver has to gather it back in by getting out of the throttle for a moment. That reduces, or "scrubs off," speed, which is the last thing you want to do on a race track. If the front tires go first and the front of the car wants to climb up the track, refusing to turn (think of how your car feels when it's hydroplaning in a rainstorm), they say it's tight, or pushing.

So when the tires start to go, you can bet the drivers wail about it to their crew chiefs over their two-way radios.

Eddie D'Hondt is spending his extra time this morning trying to avoid just that—he's checking and rechecking the air pressure in every one of the tires in the sets Filmar Racing purchased for the race. He measures each tire with a tape measure he's never without. Each tire is made differently. The right side tires are made of a stiffer compound to reflect the different forces on the tire (the right side bears much more force through the turns, as the car is pushed toward the outside of the track), and the right-side tires are slightly larger, too, to help keep the car turning left. Fronts and rears are the same, except the seam where the tire is joined is different. Eddie gets his sets of tires from the Goodyear trailer each race and then separates them into their four positions on the car. Then he patiently assembles sets of tires to be used in different situations: sets with slightly greater stagger—the measurement of how much bigger the right side tires are than the left side—sets with slightly less, sets that are fairly even. Sets whose right-side tires are to be used if the team chooses to make a right-side-only pit stop; a set whose lefts are to be used in the opposite circumstances.

He tapes to the side of the war wagon a list of the different sets. Each tire in each set is identified by codes on the side of the tire, by air pressure, and by other numbers Eddie himself has scrawled on the tire with a marker. Eddie marked the tires and made the sets yesterday, but he moves from tire to tire adjusting air pressure, using a little black tank the size of a doctor bag to fill each tire. Then he sits on each tire and uses a wire brush to buff the five lug holes in each wheel, then applies a thin line of yellow weather stripping. That holds on the lug nuts, tightly enough so they don't fall off, but loosely enough that the strip stretches when the wheel is slammed onto the car during a pit stop. One of the most common sights before a race is somebody in every pit area first cleaning the lug nuts, then buffing the holes, then stripping the nuts onto the wheels, 36 or so wheels per team—180 individual gluing jobs per team. Metal disks sit on top of the nuts once they're glued on to keep them in place.

Every team glued on its lug nuts yesterday—and every team has someone chipping off the dried weather stripping today, cleaning the nuts, and reapplying so that the goo has the proper amount of stretch in it.

Along the entire pit road, each team engages in similar last-minute preparations. Fans blow onto asphalt; rags wipe war wagons. Tarps are folded, jacks assembled. There's even, occasionally, the whiz of someone checking the trigger of an air wrench. Maybe it's starting to feel a little like race day after all.

❖

Watching the activity from the press box above Turns 1 and 2 are Dick Thompson, director of public relations for Martinsville Speedway since about 1966, and Bob Latford, who has been involved in racing since, as a 12-year-old boy, he hung around the famous 1947 Daytona Beach meeting that NASCAR founder Bill France Sr. organized at the Streamline Motel. Latford and his pals ran out to pick up lunch on their bicycles for the promoters as they invented NASCAR and hammered out the race series that is now the Winston Cup. Latford, in fact, later invented the points structure by which the series determines its champion: 175 points for first, 170 points for second, and on down, first by fives and then by fours and threes, to 31 points for 43rd—last—place.

With the morning stretching on and the race nearing, Thompson, a florid, comfortable man of about 60 sitting at a little built-in desk in the corner of the hundred-seat press box in front of a 1996 oil portrait of himself, chuckles as he admits that the celebrations he had planned for before the race yesterday are never going to take place. He had luminaries like Richard Petty, Cale Yarborough, Ned Jarrett, and Buddy Baker lined up to parade around the track, celebrating its 50th anniversary. Yellow balloons, in the shape of a 50, were going to arc over the drivers as they walked across the flatbed truck parked on the front stretch that served as a stage for driver introductions. Today, he says, they'll just introduce the drivers and get started. Some things just don't postpone.

In a way, though, that's fine. Martinsville does things in a low-key way, a lot more like your local Saturday-night racing than most other NASCAR Winston Cup tracks. "This is a kind of back-to-the-roots track," he says, leaning back in his chair. "What we sell people, actually, is a memory. The racing surface, the contour of the track, is no different than it was in 1947, except it's paved."

Martinsville, in fact, is older than NASCAR itself. "Bill France helped Clay Earles run his first race here," Thompson says, selling programs and parking cars, just learning what he could from Earles. Thompson points out to the track, where trucks drive around, still drying it. He motions to the crossover gate in Turn 4, the only spot where cars and trucks can enter or leave the infield. Closed during races, of course, it's closed now too. "That's where Clay and Bill France sat down, and Bill told him he thought stock cars were the thing of the future." Earles had been planning to run what were then called AAA cars—Indy cars. France convinced him that Americans would prefer to watch cars that looked like the cars they drove. Earles bought it, and he scheduled a stock car race for his track.

And oh, that first, pre-NASCAR, Martinsville race. Most NASCAR fans—and probably every child growing up in Martinsville—can recite that story. As stock car racing grew in popularity after the war, Earles determined that a racetrack at Martinsville would make him some money if he could bring the outlaw sport of racing to the Sunday-go-to-church crowd. At the same time, Bill France, down in Daytona, was thinking about expanding the audience for his beach races. Like Earles, he recognized that the cars running Friday-night challenge races among bootleggers and shade-tree mechanics could entertain families if they were just cleaned up a little.

So Earles did that. Instead of a bullring of a quarter of a mile or less bulldozed out of somebody's tobacco field, he built a track of more than a half-mile—it's 0.526 now—with slightly banked turns and a good 5,000 seats. Best of all, he figured that the packed red clay of his track would get rid of the awful cloud of dust that characterized the rough outlaw racing that most people associated with stock cars.

It turned out that only 750 of those seats had actually been installed when September 7, 1947, rolled around, but Earles went ahead and ran his first race anyway.

"We estimate we had 10,000 people," Thompson says, still in awe 50 years later. "We had 6,013 that paid," and an estimated 4,000 or so more who didn't but stood and watched the race anyway. Those early fans took Earles at his word when he said racing could be a clean, upstanding sport worthy of decent folk. Many came right from church, and fancy dress was much in evidence.

Which was a pity, because though the five decades since have proven that Earles had it right on the money about racing's appeal as a wholesome, family sport, he had it dead wrong about the dust. People describing Martinsville always say that, about 15 minutes after that race started, it looked like an atomic bomb had detonated at the speedway. The column of red clay dust that rose from and hovered over the speedway was unlike anything Earles—or anybody else—had ever seen.

"I still run into people who were at that race, and they tell me about all that dust," Thompson says. Well, yeah. Finding someone in racing who *wasn't* at that race would be the trick. Like a no-hitter, like Woodstock, like the Beatles at the Cavern, like every epochal event since, probably, the dawn of time, that first Martinsville race in September, 1947, now appears to have entertained a good hundred times the original estimate of 10,000 people. Talk to anyone in racing who's over 50. If you don't get a story about bathing three or four times to get the dust off, about wearing Sunday-best clothes to a race and coming home looking like a chicken leg rolled in flour, about a red-silt bathtub ring that took two bleachings to clean, then you just aren't trying.

But you know what? An awful lot of those stories may be true. One of the miracles of NASCAR racing as it explodes into its newfound mainstream popularity is that it comes to the culture at-large close enough to its golden age to have its heroes still around. At a time when major league baseball is so divorced from its vaunted history that it runs commercials with fake interviews with people pretending to be Ty Cobb, you can't pace the infield of a Winston Cup race without stumbling over a genuine racing legend, and chances are he'll talk to you if you stop him. Junior Johnson, the bootlegger and driver lionized in Tom Wolfe's famous *The Last American Hero*, owned and ran a race team until a couple of years ago. He is racing's Babe Ruth, and until recently he was still walking around the infield, with a gray buzz cut, a stopwatch, and a scowl. Richard Petty, the sport's Mickey Mantle, still runs a race team—a team getting more competitive every year—and, instantly recognizable in his feathered cowboy hat and shades, he signs a card, hat, or T-shirt for anybody who stops him, in the garage or in the crowd. Ned Jarrett, surely the Lou Gehrig figure of the circuit, dragging the sport into respectability on his own by taking a Dale Carnegie course and committing himself to developing relationships with fans and sponsors, is now a television and radio commentator and even more beloved as an announcer than he was as a two-time circuit champion.

Petty. Johnson. Jarrett. Benny Parsons. Buddy Baker. The Wood brothers. They were giants before the flood, but they are still here, still involved in racing.

Thompson, sitting in the rec-room interior of the Martinsville press box, is such a relic—or in any case he's a long-termer. He started doing public relations for Martinsville only in 1966, so at 30 years he's a relative newcomer compared to Latford, who paces the back of the empty press box near the soda machine and the omnipresent packs of free cigarettes, taking long, strong drags on his own smokes and wryly adding the snap to Thompson's stories. These guys have been working together for 30 years, and they've done this routine before. Latford has slicked-back salt-and-pepper hair, a waxed handlebar moustache, and the creases in his face of a man who spends a lot of time in the sun and a lot of time smiling. Latford currently publishes *The Inside Line*, a newsletter whose history and behind-the-scenes facts save the jobs of racing journalists every week. But he seems to take more seriously his responsibility of being racing's occasionally forgotten sense of humor.

Say Thompson tosses out the story of how Martinsville gives winning drivers a grandfather clock, instead of just handing out another hunk of tin to clutter up a driver's rec room. "It came about because we knew the drivers had a lot of trophies," he says. "After a while when you get so many they're really just dust collectors. We thought, why not give 'em something useable? To hand down through the generations." Latford lets Thompson have his say, and then offers another thought: "So you can say this is the only track where they race against time and for time." Then a throaty smoker's laugh.

Thompson picks up the thread again. In a box by his feet, loosely wrapped in crumpled newspaper, is a trophy, a loving cup, on a plaque, a slab of wood carved in the shape of the state of Virginia, with various wheel-shaped gewgaws attached. It says, "Hanes 500 Champion." But what about those famous grandfather clocks? What's with the trophy?

"It's a fake," he says, to hand to the winner after the race. "Gives him something to hold onto for the pictures. He can't hold a clock above his head." Then, from Latford, the twist, concerning Jeff Gordon's first Martinsville win: "When he got home, he called up and wanted to get a trophy made like that one." He won a race, he wanted a goddamn trophy; maybe he had a little extra dust he didn't know what to do with.

Richard Petty won 15 races at Martinsville. "They say Randleman [North Carolina, where Petty lives] chimes on the half hour now," Latford says, and Thompson smiles. It's an old routine, but they love it.

Latford has done everything from run public relations for tracks (he started departments at various times at Charlotte, Atlanta, Daytona, and Darlington) to working for CBS in its broadcast of the 1979 Daytona 500, another race about which everyone has a story. It's generally considered the beginning of the modern era for stock car racing broadcasting. It was the first 500-mile race ever broadcast flag to flag.

"Before that, it was a few minutes of racing in between wrist wrestling and cliff diving," Latford says of the old Wide World of Sports–style race coverage. But in 1979 CBS decided to broadcast the entire Daytona 500. Coincidentally, a blizzard socked in almost the entire eastern seaboard, and millions of people were housebound with nothing to do but watch the Daytona 500.

The race was a barn-burner, with Cale Yarborough and Donnie Allison door handle-to-door handle on the last lap. The lapped car of Donnie's brother Bobby came on the scene, the two leaders wrecked, and Richard Petty came from almost half a mile down and won. Yarborough and the Allisons, meanwhile, got out of their cars and into a nationally televised brawl in the infield.

And all over the country, Latford figures, people were leaning forward on their couches saying, "Good Lord, what the hell is this? *And why didn't I know about it before*?"

"I worked that show for CBS as chief statistician," Latford says, "and we saw the ratings. They kept going up every 15 minutes." Nobody turned off that race—and nobody's turned off since, it appears. "Stock car racing is kind of unique," Latford smiles. "It's like country music: Nobody likes it except the public."

He starts flicking off numbers: Two-time series champ Ned Jarrett won $289,000 during his career; his son Dale has made more than $2 million so far this season. And as the money has increased, so has the competition. "This is the closest of fields," he says of the cars now evenly lined up, glinting in the sun along the front stretch, each connected to its little generator whose putting can be heard even here, behind glass in the booth. "Gary Bradberry was .32 seconds off the pole," Latford says. "And he went home." That is, the fastest qualifier was Ward Burton in the number 22, who completed his qualifying lap in 20.272 seconds. He gets to start first. Bradberry's number 78 car was loaded into its hauler on Saturday after he failed to qualify for the race, and his team will be watching today's race on ESPN.

When the difference between go first and go home is .32 seconds, that's competition, a kind of parity stick-and-ball sports only dream of. "Only four guys starting today," Latford says, nodding and taking another drag, "have not led a race this year."

❖

Uh-oh. One of the four cars that hasn't led a lap this year is Kenny Wallace's number 81 Filmar Racing Ford Thunderbird sponsored by Square D.

"Two poles and we haven't led a single lap," says Frank Good by the bright blue-and-yellow Square D hauler. "You can't like that."

But the moment for liking or not liking has passed, at least for today. In fact, the time for doing anything but racing has passed. It's around 10 A.M., and the car sits in its starting position on the outside of the third row, basking in the bright sunlight with 42 other cars on the speedway front stretch, each car with its putting little generator and a heavy insulating quilt, in team colors, over the windshield to keep the inside of the car from warming up too much. The pit area is set up. Every hose is neatly coiled, the two air wrenches have been tested, and a backup is hooked up. The handles have been wrapped in sandpaper, to make gripping easier for the tire changers. The tires are laid out according to Eddie's directions, in sets of four, making a grid nine tires deep and four wide. Every lug nut is glued in place. The war wagon is set up, its satellite dish pulling in ESPN for the race. The gas scale computer is hooked up, and a computer is connected to the racetrack's online scoring system. Everything is ready.

So it's lunchtime. Around the hauler, crew members hang around, drinking sodas and bottled water from the round orange Gatorade coolers lined up as a sort of fence between the Square D yard and the yards of the haulers on either side. Hauler driver Dave Ensign grills burgers and hot dogs, which he doesn't particularly like to do. Some teams pride themselves on the quality of their racetrack cookery; while teams work in the garage, some hauler drivers spend their days marinating ribs and chicken, preparing vegetable dishes; others simply send out, and big disposable aluminum catering pans of corn or baked beans can often be found in the piles of trash left behind after a race.

Dave is kind of in the middle. "I can do soup," he says of his cooking approach. As to the hot dogs he's grilling, he actually prefers boiling: "When they blow up, they're done." The Square D team, he figures, has other things to worry about than food quality.

At the moment, they certainly do. Bustling around the tiny hallway leading between the hauler's two rows of storage compartments, the crew members change clothes, pulling on pressed deep blue shirts and trousers, all with the Square D logo embroidered on the front and back and other sponsors in smaller letters around the shoulders. Guys going over the wall to change or carry tires pull on jumpsuits, equally embroidered. Meanwhile, Don leans on an aluminum counter just inside the door, poring over a piece of paper that has been taped up on one wall all weekend: the list of race time responsibilities.

A pit stop is planned to a degree that makes an orchestra concert look like a spontaneous decision to go to the movies: Everything from who carries the gas can to who puts the tires on the wall to who scrubs the car's grille with a brush on the end of a long pole is listed so everybody knows what they're supposed to do. But today a lot of lines on the photocopied sheet are scribbled out. Losing weekend warriors like big Steve Baker has complicated the team's plans for the race. None of the guys actually going over the wall have left, but ancillary jobs—running empty gas cans to get refilled, holding the metal sign that shows Kenny where the pit is as he races down pit road—are open. Plans are great, but this is reality. Small team, extra day, no helpers: big trouble.

Doubling up on tasks and pulling in efforts by friends and acquaintances gets most of the key jobs taken care of, and Don and Newt huddle by the back door of the hauler. Don points toward the guys in the hauler, where I am standing, and I look to see who he might be pointing at. He points again. Newt sighs, then nods, and my heart sinks.

❖

You have to understand that actually working the race with the crew for the number 81 Square D Filmar Racing Ford was something I fervently did not want to do, and with good reason. As a journalist I appreciated the team's willingness to answer questions as I followed them around the previous weeks; I appreciated their allowing me to be underfoot during a very busy—an especially busy—race week. But none of this Plimpton stuff for me.

The reason is, I tried it once, and it went rather poorly.

I became fascinated with everything about Winston Cup racing during a newspaper story I once did for which I spent a weekend among the fans on the infield at Charlotte Motor Speedway. That led to a story about what a pit crew did during an average race weekend, for which I spent a weekend with the crew of the bright yellow number 30 car, then sponsored by Pennzoil (which currently sponsors the number 1) and driven by Michael Waltrip (now driving the 21). For my greatest understanding, the team's public relations guy demanded that I perform the service of passing a water bottle to the driver during pit stops. I was supposed to hand him the bottle by means of a long pole not unlike a pool skimmer.

I didn't really want to do that. I had enjoyed learning what the crew did, but I by no means considered myself a crew member in training, and I just wanted to stay out of the way. Nonetheless, I ended up standing in the pit, as Waltrip roared in during the first pit stop I had ever witnessed from up close.

The beginning of a pit stop is the kind of explosion of activity that you almost don't believe even as it's happening. A bunch of guys are standing around, watching the race from the pit; they're checking in on the ESPN broadcast on the TV in their war wagon; they're peering close at the computer monitor that shows the position, lap time, and seconds behind the leader of each car. They're chugging Gatorade from the powder mixed with water in the orange coolers Gatorade also provides, for the privilege of also distributing to each team a big green paddle that says "Gatorade" and sticks up from their war wagon. They're drinking bottled water, they're talking to the amazing number of people—fans, family members, friends, corporate types—hanging around the pits. Then there's a caution, and everybody puts out their cigarettes, zips up their jumpsuits, adjusts gloves and knee pads. Those who wear goggles put them on. The gas man hoists his first 100-pound can of gas, and his helper readies the second. Then the crew chief squawks over the radio "Here he comes!" and in a roar of engine noise and a swirl of grit and dust, the car screeches in. Suddenly the 14 or so people in the pit are a madness of energy, flinging tires and cans of fuel through the air, splattering lug nuts onto the pavement, running at full-tilt, and then the jack man drops the car, the crew chief is screaming "Go! Go! Go! Go! Go!," the back end of the car is briefly visible fishtailing onto the outside lane of pit road in another whirl of sand and dirt, and then everything slows down to normal speed again. It's like being hit by a tornado, and the noise is just about the same.

Back when I tried to help the Pennzoil team by giving Michael Waltrip his water, Bill Elliot, then driving the number 11 car sponsored by Budweiser, had the pit just behind Waltrip, and he pulled in just before Waltrip did. That limited Waltrip's access to his own pit, so Waltrip pulled in slightly at an angle. It was a hot day at Martinsville, and he gestured frantically to me for the water. Rather panicked by my first glimpse of the sudden explosion of activity, I did what I could to lean over and get him the bottle. But because of the angle he was a little farther away than I expected, and I couldn't reach him. So I did something that seemed natural at the time: I took a step closer. I put one leg over the pit wall.

I then thought my head had exploded, but what really happened was Doug Hewitt, the crew chief of that car, started screaming over the headset at me. He then picked me up and flung me bodily back over the wall. I did manage to get the bottle of water to Waltrip, though.

The mistake I had made, of course, is that NASCAR rules say only seven guys can be over the wall during a pit stop. In my panic at the sudden noise and melee, I just sort of lost it. My stepping over could have caused Waltrip to be penalized. Fortunately, either I was never the eighth guy over or no official saw me, so no penalty. In any case, the crew—and the driver, over the radio—were laughing about it five minutes later.

I believe I was able to laugh at it within a year or two, but I still consider it a highly traumatic event. The fact that it occurred at this very track makes me remember it, and makes me even more crestfallen when Don crooks his finger at me.

"You're our sign guy today," he says. "Rich will show you what to do."

That's Rich Vargo, a mechanic in the shop who carries the front tires over the wall during pit stops. He explains what I'll have to do and where I'll stand.

"There'll be two of us on your left, going over," he says—him and Ricky Turner, the front tire changer. My job is to hold the long pole with a big metal Square D sign on the end of it so that when Kenny's coming down pit road he knows where his stop is. (Kenny has a big container of water mounted in the car, which he sips at through a straw during the race; thankfully, he won't need me to hand him any water.) Rich walks me over to the pit to show me how to hold the surprisingly awkward sign, how to wave it so Kenny can see it, and how to lower it onto a line marked with duct tape on the ground so the car stops in exactly the right spot, where the guys can get to all four tires, where the jack man won't be fighting the wall on the inside, where the car will be equally positioned between the cars behind and in front of it, and where it can be seen well from the camera mounted on a long pole arcing over the pit. The pit stops are videotaped so that during the week the crew can study them and improve. They've spelled "Mart II" in duct tape in the middle of the pit so there won't be any confusion when they're viewing.

Once the car stops, my job is to pull the sign out of the way without knocking anybody over and pick up a bristle brush on the end of another long pole to scrub tire goo out of the radiator grille, being careful not to either trip or clothesline Rich and Ricky or jack-man Steve Dluzniewski as they come sprinting back around the front of the car to change the left-side tires. Don helps matters by repeating his stories from the day before about guys getting choked and flipped during pit stops by errant hoses and signs wielded by people who didn't know what they were doing. A ha ha ha ha ha.

I put on a blue Square D race-day team shirt with great trepidation. But when that trepidation leads me to the men's room, I find what I should have expected—a line of guys in brightly colored race-day uniforms of every color, headsets on, staring at the floor waiting in line. Plenty of guys, it seems, still get a little nervous right before the race.

Back at the hauler, Gloria Ray, the team secretary who functions as the team scorer during the race, stands up from the white plastic garden chair she's sitting in and leaves the infield in a small if widespread exodus of certain women from the other 42 teams. "Well, I gotta go sit down with my girls," she says, slips on her Filmar Racing leather jacket, grabs her purse, and walks off to the scoring tower. Each team sends a scorer for every race; it's part of the rules. ("You have to provide a scorer," Gloria says. "The driver can get out and change his own tires if he has to, but the entry form says 'scorer.' ")

Then Filbert steps out of the hauler, surveys the infield for a moment from the top step, picks up his briefcase, his headset, and hand-held mic control, and walks across the track to climb the stairs. On top of the press box, he'll join a row of 42 other guys, spotting for their drivers, telling them when a wreck happens, who's on the track ahead of and behind them, and anything else that might help them get or protect track position. He's been spotting again only for the last couple of weeks, but he clearly likes it. Just throwing money at the team isn't going to satisfy Filbert. He likes to be part of his enterprise.

Finally Newt leans out the door and lightly jerks his head inside. Everyone on the team follows him in, walking all the way to the back of the hauler into the team's private office. With a little table, a desk, a television set and stereo, and leather padded seats along the wall, it can fit six or seven for a meeting with any comfort. About 14 guys cram in.

Newt doesn't waste a lot of breath. "We've been through a lot this year, with engines and wrecks and personnel changes and all that deal. But today we need to focus on one thing: This is a race we can win." When he says "focus," he curves his fingers like he's holding binoculars, moving them back and forward in front of his eyes. "We've won a pole here and we can run here. Driver loves this track. We can win here, so we just gotta stay focused and do what we need to do. Pit guys, we got a good tire program set up here, Eddie's set us up real good with that deal. Guys in the number 90 crew said they had us clocked to be on the pole if we hadn't broke loose in Turn 4 in qualifying, so we got a car as fast as any out there. This could be our best finish of the year, and this would be a good time for it."

He talks a little more about focus, about everyone doing their own job. He could be a corporate vice president talking about how to make a business work: teamwork, fundamentals, focus, efficiency.

Then he says, "All right, let's go."

And they go.

❖

PART 2: LET'S GO RACING

The pageantry at the beginning of the race is mostly over. Brief driver introductions started around 10:30, and the drivers are in their cars. Newt and Frank stand at the car with Kenny, helping him inside, helping latch the driver's window net, and saying a few words before the race starts. In the pit, Vic Kangas and Eddie Jarvis take seats atop the war wagon. They'll be keeping lap times and keeping an eye on the scoring computer. The third seat is for Newt. Andy Thurman does knee bends and stretches; other crew members smoke cigarettes or watch the ESPN prerace show on the TV set in the war wagon. "This track is part pavement, part concrete, and all wall," Dr. Jerry Punch says into the camera. Kenny, sitting in his car, looks up into the grandstand. "Looks like a lot of people got off work today," he says. The stands look at least 90 percent full.

The national anthem plays. Each team lines up along the front of its pit, hats off, at attention, during the song. In the Square D pit, that means about a dozen of us, wearing blue shirts with that big yellow D in a square logo. There's an invocation by a preacher, and then, at last, the command from the flag stand: "Gentlemen, start your engines!"

"Engine's on," Kenny says over the headset, thumbing a button on his steering wheel to talk.

"Ten-four, Herman," Newt says. Kenny is nicknamed Herman by some, a name he was given in school after the rambunctious cartoon character Herman the German. Newt and Frank unplug the generator, bang the car once in salute, and head back toward the pit. Forty-two other teams do exactly the same.

The pace car gets ready to pull the field around the track a couple of times, giving the cars a chance to heat up their engines and their tires. "We're rolling," Kenny says. The pace car pulls the field past the pits so the drivers can set their pit road speed. With no speedometers, the drivers just find their rpms in a certain gear when the pace car is driving them at the required pit road speed. Kenny says, "4,600, second gear," over the headset. Newt says, "Ten-four," and writes the number down on a piece of paper. Every time Kenny comes in for a stop, he'll remind him of the pit road speed to keep him from speeding and getting penalized by NASCAR. At Martinsville, that translates to 35 miles per hour. Newt paces nervously during the pace laps; the rest of the team lines the pit wall, waving to Kenny on his first time by, or just holding up an arm in salute. I do as I have been trained, rocking my sign up and down as he paces by so he can see where the pit is on pit road. "Where are you guys?" he asks, going by—then, "OK, got it." Newt pulls me aside briefly to remind me that in certain race situations he'll tell me to stop Kenny short, a few feet in front of his mark.

"It makes it easier for him to get in the pit that way?" I ask.

"It makes it easier for him to get *out*," Newt says, and climbs atop the war wagon for the start of the race.

For all the madness of the start of a Winston Cup race in the grandstand and on TV, down in the pits the start feels almost subdued. Instead of the building excitement and increasing roar, what you hear in the pits, with your two-way radio headset on, is just the crew chief talking to the driver. With 43 cars lined up a few feet apart, if somebody gets out of line at the start, or starts too slowly or too quickly, the ensuing wreck could gather up dozens of cars. So each driver, instead of watching for the green flag himself, keeps his eye on the car in front of him and listens to his crew chief. Everyone else in every crew keeps quiet and watches the front stretch in front of them, the only part of the track they can see clearly.

"OK, pace car's in, buddy," Newt says. "Here we go. OK, wait . . . wait . . . wait . . . green-green-green!" The moment the man in the flag stand above the start-finish line drops that green flag, 43 crew chiefs tell 43 drivers to mash that accelerator. Forty-three pedals go down, and the race has begun.

In the pits, crew members see only the flash of the cars as they zip by on the front stretch. Very little of the rest of the track is visible from where they do their jobs. So they cluster around the TV sets on every war wagon (look down the row of war wagons along pit road and you see a neat line of little dish antennas mounted on each one, pointing the same direction like a row of sunflowers), or they keep an eye on the computer monitor showing the NASCAR scoring program, which collates the work done by the scorers in the scoring tower and picks up signals generated by transponders in each car as they go over a wire loop in the track. The system, a simple grid that looks pretty much like an Excel spreadsheet, shows each car, how many seconds it is behind the leader, and what lap it's on. It can take the program a moment to unscramble the order during pit stops or after a wreck, but it does the trick.

The cars circle the track a few times, working quickly up to their top speed: 120 miles per hour or so on the straightaways, down to 75 or 80 in the turns. The engines, tuned for this track to provide maximum acceleration and deceleration rather than power over a sustained run, grind up and down with each straightaway and turn, an alternating buzz and whine that sounds almost more like motorbikes than cars. Key at Martinsville are brakes; slowing from 120 miles per hour into a turn twice in a lap is more than 1,000 brake applications, as Two-Can told Kenny. "You gonna set those brakes for me today?" he asked, reminding Kenny to feather the brakes during the pace laps to heat them up and get the pads seated.

"Ten-four," Kenny replied. Kenny grew up around short-track racing. His father was a track champion at St. Louis-area racetracks, and Kenny, like his brother Rusty, has always done his best driving on short tracks.

The beginning of the race passes fairly smoothly. Ward Burton, in the number 22 car, starts on the pole and holds the lead for the first few laps, loses it to Mark Martin in the number 6, then regains it. Through the first 50 laps the cars remain bunched up, an almost stately procession around the track, as drivers feel out the track surface and find out how their cars, set up for a track covered with rubber from days of practice, handle on a track that's "green," cleared of rubber buildup by the rain. Kenny holds his spot in sixth, fighting off Rusty, who started seventh. Rusty gets by him, and he's beginning to have trouble with Jeff Gordon, who's crept up from eleventh.

Then there's trouble in Turn 3. Car 97, seemingly untouched, breaks loose and spins.

Almost simultaneously, every hand in the pits goes up above a head and makes a spinning motion. In the grandstand, the crowd looks like the people at the beginning of a Superman show: "Look! Over there!" Everyone stands, every finger pointed the same way.

The crews of every car respond in exactly the same way. First they crane their necks to see if they can see the spot on the track—they can't. Then they scramble. The cars will be in for pit stops as soon as the 97 car is cleared from the entrance to pit road. A NASCAR official stands with a red flag at the entrance to pit road while the cars slowly circle the track another couple of times, and then he clears out of the way.

The crew has made the pit ready for the stop: Don has hoisted one of the full cans of gas and balanced it on his shoulder. Right-side tires are balanced on the wall; left-side tires are waiting next, with guys prepared to put them on the wall when the others are gone. Danielle and any friends or corporate types have backed away, watching from behind the extra wheels. It's time for action, and they don't want to be in the way.

Filbert, from his spotter's position on the racetrack roof, tells Kenny there's no wreckage on the track to watch for, then tells him when pit road is open. Newt says, "Next time in."

Then Kenny pulls onto pit road—"4,600, Herman," Filbert reminds him. Newt says, "Here he comes guys, here he comes—five . . . four . . . three . . . two. . . . Here he is."

And the pit explodes into action.

❖

Say it once and get it over with: The over-the-wall gang.

The guys going over the wall to do pit stops in Winston Cup racing have to do more in less time than just about any athletes in any sport. Sprinters running 100 meters only have to run; hockey players skate full tilt for 45 seconds or so, but they're not carrying 50-pound tires, and avoiding a body check isn't the same thing as keeping an eye over your shoulder so you're not run over by the 3,500-pound race car behind you. Plus, even the hardest hitter on the ice, field, or court isn't liable to explode into a ball of flame if you mistime your play.

Think, for comparison, of the field goal unit on an NFL team—only say they have to start from the sideline, run to the middle of the field, set up and execute a successful field goal, and get back to the sidelines. All in 20 seconds, and there's no such thing as a time out.

The guys jumping over the wall to gas up and change the tires of the Square D number 81 Filmar Racing Ford are not what you'd call a team of craggy veterans. Frank Good has been with the team for two years, and he's about the veteran of the gang. In an arena where a tenth of a second can mean the difference between winning a race and coming in fifth, where teamwork and cooperation and practice mean thousands of dollars per tenth of a second—this team has been assembled from rookies and free agents. Still, that's who they are. That's having a small sponsor in a big-sponsor sport. That's being a single-car team in a multiple-car world. They're willing to take their chances.

Frank is the rear tire carrier: He carries the rear tires over the wall and hands them to Andy Thurman, who uses an air wrench to remove five lug nuts in just over a second, making the second most familiar sound in racing: that staccato Vrr!-Vrr!-Vrr!-Vrr!-Vrr! that is just the definition of "sounds fast." He'll let the nuts scatter. Fresh lugs, cleaned and buffed that morning, have been lightly weather-stripped on the new tire. He throws the air drill onto the ground, but not before slamming the switch on the top of it to reverse the rotation, so when he picks it back up it will be ready to tighten the new lugs. He yanks the tire off, flings it aside to his left—the jack man, after all, is to his right and won't do his job well if he has to dodge the wheels—and grabs the wheel Frank has carried over with him. The same procedure is going on with the front tire, where Rich Vargo hands a tire to Ricky Turner. Ricky, by the way, just joined the team today. He takes the place of a personal friend of Newt Moore's, who stepped in last week when two crew members quit unexpectedly.

If everything's going as planned, the jack man—in this case Duze—has done his job. He's vaulted the wall a half-second before Kenny came to a stop, carrying the jack and cutting to his right around the front of the car as it smoked to a stop. The jack weighs about 35 pounds, and many people say that the jack man leaping the wall with the jack looks like a running back cutting through a hole in the line. But Duze looks much more like a soldier rescuing a baby from sniper fire, cradling that thing, his back hunched over it almost protectively, ducking around the car and sliding the jack under a post identified by the paint scheme of the car and an extra arrow made of duct tape and magic marker. He's lifted the handle and jumped down on it, and he's lifted it again and gone another half pump with it, and the right side of the car's in the air. In the car, Kenny's got the clutch compressed and his foot on the brake, so the wheels don't spin while Andy is ripping the tire off and replacing it.

Frank has taken the second-and-a-half while he was standing around with nothing to do and lined up the holes in the tire with the lugs—the lugs were highlighted on the hub by magic marker, to make that easier. So the tire he hands to Andy is ready to be slammed onto the hub, lug nuts waiting on the wheel.

If one of the nuts flies off the lug as Andy's jamming the wheel on, Andy just reaches to his left and grabs one from a stiff wire loop clipped to Frank's belt—three nuts hang there as extras, ready to slip off the loop. Andy spins all five nuts onto the tire and leaps up, flinging the drill's air hose wide as he does so; if it gets caught on anything—the corner of the car, a tire, another crew member—the pit stop could be disastrously slowed, and if the hose ends up under Kenny's wheels and he drives over it on his way out of the pit, he'll be assessed a penalty.

As soon as the front and rear right side wheels are on the hubs and a couple of nuts are tightened, Duze twists the handle of the jack, drops the car, and races around to the left side of the car, finding space between the car and the pit wall to pump the jack a couple of times, while Andy and Ricky, having whacked their drills to reverse the rotation once again, have removed the lugs on the left side. Frank and Rich, after first rolling the discarded right-side tires toward the pit wall to keep them off pit road, have taken the new left-side tires off the pit wall, where they were placed as soon as the pit stop started, and handed them to the changers. Frank and Rich fit them onto the hubs with Andy and Ricky, who then spin on the five nuts.

Behind the rear wheel changers, meanwhile, Don has been filling the car with gas. He stepped over the wall with that 100-pound tank of gas balanced on his shoulder the second the car pulled in, and he jammed the nozzle into the car's gas tank, which has a spring-loaded receptacle. Stan Blaylock, at the same time, has placed the catch can (it looks a little like a sprinkling can for your houseplants) into the overflow hose that vents air from the fuel cell. Like shotgunning a beer, the gas pours directly into the tank (like the tank, the gas can is vented at the top), forcing air out the rear through the vent hose.

When Don's first can of gas empties—after say, eight seconds or so—he hands it to Stan and turns to the wall, where someone else—usually big Steve Baker—

hands him the second can. As soon as that's done, Stan tosses the empty back over the wall and Steve catches it. Stan and Don both lean into the car as close as they can, to stay out of the way of the rear tire changers, who are running around them to the right side of the car and back.

As soon as the tank is full and gas, instead of air, starts splashing into the catch can, Stan begins waving his arm so that Duze can see him—his signal that the car is refueled, so as soon as the wheels are changed he can drop the car.

The moment the final lug nut is tightened on the left side of the car, Duze twists the jack handle to release the pressure and drops the car. Kenny's signal to move is the car dropping, and he spins his wheels and is gone.

It takes a thousand words to describe it—gas cans and tires flung through the air, lug nuts spraying the ground like machine-gun fire, the car screeching to a halt and then roaring off—and it all happens in less than 20 seconds. When it's right it's ballet, it's a peak experience, it's scoring a goal and hitting a home run and running a sweep all at once. It's winning.

It's almost impossible to describe what it feels like. Stan Blaylock, who holds the catch can during the pit stops and flies Filbert's plane the rest of the time, explains. A pit stop doesn't feel fast, he says. In fact, quite the opposite. "When it's a good stop, it feels like slow motion." Hyperaware, Stan sees the tire changers and jack man running around the car as slow and smooth as an NFL Films highlight, and he can move out of anybody's way at any time. The flow feels almost magical, smooth and silent instead of machinegun fast and jackhammer loud. "It's when things are going wrong that it feels fast." There are so many ways for it to suddenly feel fast, like so much is happening while that race car is sitting in one place. Lug nuts fall to the ground. Tires go flat. Jacks fail to rise, or drop too soon. Tires bounce away. Lug nuts are not put on correctly and wheels fall off. That happened to the Square D team once last year. It happened once to Dale Earnhardt and cost him a Winston Cup championship. At Martinsville, the cars are going 120 miles per hour on the straightaways. A car is about 200 inches long, so call it 16 feet. Driving 120 miles per hour means a car goes about 180 feet per second, about 11 car lengths. Brace it all out, and that means that under green flag conditions, every 10th of a second in the pits costs a racer one car's worth of position on the track. Come in in fifth place and have somebody drop a lug nut and take less then half a second extra to replace it and you could go out in tenth. So, Blaylock says, you definitely don't want to get that flickery, Keystone Kops feeling during a pit stop. It means things are going wrong, and the result can be dire.

But that's the worst case. "Otherwise it doesn't feel fast until the car's pulling away," Blaylock says. "When you back away from the car again, everything catches up to full speed."

❖

The first stop at Martinsville, on lap 57, goes without a hitch. I keep my cool, wave the sign, and lower it perfectly—it hits the ground right on the duct tape stripe and at that exact moment the nose of the race car bumps it. The tires, left and right side, go on without a hitch. The jack works. I use the brush on the grille without beheading Duze or the tire changers. The gas goes in, and the car goes out in a shade less than 19 seconds, 18.8, which is a strong stop even for a team that has worked together for months, much less a bunch assembled race morning.

"Great stop guys, great stop," Newt says from the roof of the war wagon. Crew members slap each other on the back, pull headsets off to shout "Great job!" into each other's ears over the roar of the engines.

But just for a moment. Then there's too much to do. Eddie stands the finished tires up and measures them with a pyrometer and a durometer, checking temperature and wear, which will give clues to the car's handling and help him prepare the next set for the driver. He scrawls temperatures in yellow directly on the tires: "200—220—215" across one tire, showing the range of temperatures the rubber has reached.

Other guys are getting the next set of tires prepared, leaning them against the wall. Newt is talking over the headset to Kenny about the car. "I need a little more bite in the right front," Kenny says, and Eddie gets to work, scrambling his sets of tires before Kenny's finished his statement.

"I'm OK right now," Kenny goes on, "but I could use a little more bite, right where I get from the asphalt to the concrete" at the end of the turns.

"Ten-four," Newt says. "Everybody's probably having the same trouble you are. But don't worry, we're gonna take care of you."

Don finishes his gas calculations and shows the book to Newt, showing him how many laps Kenny can go before he'll run out of gas. Newt nods. Filbert chimes in from the roof: "Newt, you need to ask about the 44 car. He came out after us." Newt says 10-4 and asks a NASCAR official, who straightens things out; passing under caution is not allowed, and cars commonly have to shift positions after coming out of the pits under caution, depending on the judgment of the officials watching them leave pit road.

Within minutes the pit area is cleaned up. The old tires are out of the way; the next set is on the wall and ready for the next stop. Don has prepared the extra gas cans and sent them off in a cart to be refilled. Finally each team sends someone over the wall to sweep the pit itself, keeping lug nuts and other junk from getting in the way of the next stop.

And then it's back to Gatorade, cigarettes, and waiting in the hot sun to the roar of the engines.

❖

Kenny stays in the top ten, floating around sixth and seventh position, for another hundred laps. Two cautions come and go, but the leaders don't pit, so Kenny doesn't. "Stay out there, Herman," Filbert says. "Just keep driving." He's holding tight, and at about lap 100 he pulls into fifth place for a while. The race is a fifth over, and Kenny is racing with the leaders. The mood doesn't so much tense in the Filmar Racing pit as deepen. This is what it's all about. This is why they're here. Eddie's working like crazy on his tire sets, fine-tuning to find any edge. It's possible, once a pit stop or two have gone by, to begin thinking of strategy—when to pit under the green flag if there isn't a caution. Try to gain track position by changing only two tires instead of four, saving five or six seconds? Then again, try that and after about 30 laps the cars with four new tires will be passing you, racers say, like you're tied to a stump.

All stuff to think about, and nobody's relaxing. Kenny goes hard toward the bottom of the track to fight off his brother Rusty on lap 131, and when he shows up next time around on the front stretch he's got a tire doughnut—a black circle where the tire rubbed against Kenny's car—from Rusty on his door. The team cheers him on.

Then, on lap 141, the number 7 car tries a little too hard to get around the 90. Both cars spin, collecting the 46, and it's time for another round of pit stops under the caution flag. Again Newt counts Kenny in, again the team attacks the car, again everything goes fine—until Duze drops the car for Kenny to take off. Which Kenny does, only to discover down pit road that he has a flat left rear tire.

"Coming back around!" Newt calls. "Cut left rear! Two tires! Two tires!"

The team, about to begin reorganizing the pit, is instantly scrambling again. Kenny roars in, they change the two tires on the left side, and he roars back out again. He's lost track position, dropping all the way back to 33rd place. But because the pit was under caution, he's remained on the lead lap.

The mood in the Filmar Racing pit is somber, but not dead. "Just our luck," Duze says, walking around the pit, shaking his head. "Just our motherfucking luck!" It was almost worse, Duze says. He was fixing the jack when Newt said Kenny was coming back in. "That fucker had air in it," he says. "I ran behind the pit box to fix the jack, and then he had a flat, so I grabbed that other jack I never use, so that was like a happy clusterfuck." Crew members cast back to the race two weeks before, at Richmond. Running OK but losing position, the team gambled on a strategy called short-stopping, in which instead of waiting for the leaders to pit, a car pits 20 or 30 laps early, losing track position and probably getting lapped in the short run but coming out with fresh tires that can help the car regain the lost position and more. Then, if it can hold out until the next round of pits, whether under caution or under green, the car can retain the 5 or 10 positions it gained by taking the chance. So Newt pulled Kenny in, costing valuable track position—and before he was even back on the track, a spin brought out the caution flag, putting Kenny not only on tires no fresher than his competitors' but a lap down at the back of the field as well.

And now this flat. They think back to the blown engines, the untimely wrecks, the missed race in California. It begins to seem like the bad luck they've been wrestling all year long won't let up.

They look down, but they don't quit. Today Kenny's car is still hooked up well. It's running as well as his car has run all season, and nobody's giving up on this race. Eddie especially focuses in on his tires. He starts separating sets of tires. He's got a plan.

At lap 185, a NASCAR official walks by and nods at Newt, making a little circular motion with his hand. This happens at about the middle of most Cup races. From now on, an eighth man will be allowed over the wall, but only to clean the driver's windshield, now getting covered with grit and tire goo. As the race wears on into the hypnotic middle laps, Kenny is still running well, picking off a driver or two every few laps. Still, the leader is running better, and Kenny's in danger of going a lap down, killing any chances for a strong finish. "That's the leader, half a straightaway behind you," Filbert tells Kenny on lap 199. During the middle of the race, a mesmerizing peace descends on pit road—the rhythmic, overwhelming roar of the engines douses any other sound; the sun pounds down, reflected with the sound into the infield from the track and the stands. The heat, light, and sound form a kind of sensory womb, and people in the pits enter an almost dreamlike state: there's only the race, only the noise. Everything else kind of disappears. It's not a powerful awareness, it's just the opposite—almost a sort of floating unconsciousness of everything beyond the race, and even of the race. It's just happening, and it's not so much that they're aware of the race as they just *are* the race. A few puffy clouds dot the sky, and when one covers the sun, for example, everyone in the pit instinctively flinches, glancing up. It's almost like they are awakened from a nap.

Eddie climbs up to the war wagon and Newt leans over, looking at tiny 3x5 cards on which Eddie has scrawled information. Newt nods. Something will have to give if Kenny is to fight off the leader and remain on the lead lap.

Then finally there's a spin on lap 204. "Two tires! Right side only!" Newt yells, and with precision Kenny comes in, gets his change, and goes out. The two-tire stop helps. Kenny is 13th after the stop. "God damn, it's about time!" Kenny yells into the radio. The team exchanges high fives, and Kenny starts complaining about the feel of this set of tires. Newt remains calm: "Give those right sides time to build up pressure." He's also watching the track: "That outside groove is the way to go now, Herman." Another spin on lap 237, but Newt shakes his head. "We're staying out," he says. "Track position is too important."

On lap 264 another spin brings Kenny in; coming out of that he's back to 20th position, but he's picking off cars one by one. He's lost position, but his car's running right. Newt and Filbert start coaching in earnest now. "Good job, buddy," Newt tells Kenny, urging him not to waste the tires rushing by lapped cars. "Save your stuff until you get ready to race 'em." Then, "Good lap, buddy, keep it up, Herman. Good and smooth. Way to roll through there. Looking good."

By the time another caution comes out on lap 321, the number 81 car has fought back to 15th place. Newt and Eddie call for another two-tire stop, and on his way out of the pit Kenny almost runs over a tire that has strayed from the pit of the number 10 car, one slot ahead of him. "Those sumbitches think we're rookies," Kenny says. "Tell 'em if they do that one more time. . . . We'll get 'em."

Newt is about to calm him down when Kenny starts giving him updates on the car: "It's loose—it's baaaad loose!" "Ten-four, buddy," Newt says. "We're working on it right now." Eddie scrambles to set up a set of four tires for the next pit stop, which comes under caution on lap 370. The car is in and out for a four-tire stop in 18.35.

"Great job, fellas, great job!" Newt shouts from the war wagon. And it's starting to feel like maybe something has shifted for the guys in blue and yellow. Kenny's 13th, with about 130 laps to go.

"OK buddy, good and smooth," Newt says. "Take care of your equipment"—code for either "don't waste a lot of effort racing with guys who are a lap down" or "we're working our asses off down here: Stay out of any wrecks and finish the damn race."

But taking care of equipment gets harder to do as the race nears its end. "Tell Ward to give me a break!" Kenny yells at one point, when he's having trouble passing Ward Burton's 22 car, which started on the pole. "Nudge him a little bit," Filbert suggests. Kenny moves up to 11th, and every car on the track has at least a couple of those tire doughnuts by the time the 400-lap mark comes and goes. Kenny's in 11th, racing the number 75 in tenth and the number 28 in ninth. When Kenny nears the 75, Newt yells, "The 75 car is for position." Kenny tries to get a nose underneath him in Turn 1, and he can't quite get there. Finally he opts for the outside, and he passes him a lap later. The crew, standing on the pit wall, cheers and applauds. "Good job! Good job!" Newt yells. Two-Can uses a stopwatch to take lap times, for his own benefit. Rich, his gloves off, sits on the pit wall, sweating.

But Kenny's tires have been on for 100 miles, and if he weren't concentrating so hard on racing, he'd be doing as Don said and screaming like a dog. Filbert, on the roof, sees other cars losing their handling as their tires give out: "Go after the number 10, he's backing up to you," he says. "And the 6, he's backing up to you." But Kenny's losing his tires as well, and he's running out of luck catching anybody. Something will have to give.

Finally, on lap 450, there's another wreck—the 21 cuts a tire and slams head-on into the wall, collecting the 31 when it bounces off. It's time for the final pit stop of the race; risking all, Eddie and Newt decide on another two-tire change. By the end of the remaining laps the unchanged left-side tires will be shot and Kenny will be running on much less car than the other top-10 cars. He'll have to work like hell to protect his spot, but that's the only way they can gain track position. The wreck that brought out the caution is in Turn 4, and by the time it's cleaned up and pit road is opened, it's lap 460.

"All right, boys, let's get ready," Eddie says, staticky over the headsets. "This is the race right here."

Newt looks down at me and nods toward the sign. "Stop him short," he says. The first five cars—the 2, 99, 24, 3, and 94—slide in, and their pits scramble. Four tires for everyone.

Then here comes Kenny. Newt counts him in. "OK, he's off the track . . . he's on pit road . . . here he comes . . . three, . . . two, . . . one, . . . OK, here!" He stops two feet before the mark, exactly where Newt wants him.

The car explodes in, and for the last time, with everything on the line, the scramble is on. Duze is across the pit before the car's even stopped—grit and tire fragments still fill the air like dust in a windstorm, and he squints and frowns as he rushes into the breach. Rich and Frank have the tires in place and ready to go by the time the jack lifts the car to its full height, and with lug nuts splattering the asphalt Ricky and Andy pull the tires off. Frank and Rich hand over the replacements.

No failures among the lugs, and Andy and Ricky step away from the car. Newt has wiped the window, Don has jammed in a single can of fuel, plenty for the final 40 laps. He's tossed the fuel canister back over the wall, and he and Stan, waving his hand to show he's done, back away too.

Then the jack drops, the wheels spin, and Kenny roars out of the pit, speeding out just ahead of the 33 car behind him and in plenty of time to establish a position on pit road before the 10 car ahead of him is even dropped. In fact, he pulls out so close to the 94, which pitted way back in Turn 4, that both cars grind by the 22, even though it has the lead pit and is on the ground by the time they come up on him.

Changing only two tires works. After the pack prowls around the track and picks up the cars that pitted on the backstretch, Kenny's number 81 car shakes out in seventh place. "Good job, guys, great job!" Newt squawks over the headset. "Great job!" He stalks around the pit, slapping hands and backs, exchanging a long nod with Eddie. Then he climbs back onto the war wagon.

"OK, K. W., you're in seventh position," he says to Kenny. "It looks like one more time around [before the green flag drops for the restart], so get ready to rock and roll. Concentrate like you've never concentrated before." There are 34 laps to go, and on the restart they're driving to win the race.

There's one last piece of drama in the pit, though. Ken Schrader, in the number 33 car, had the pit right behind Kenny's. When he raced out himself seconds after Kenny, he cut through the Square D pit. He ran over the hose of the rear air wrench, and the wrench caught in his wheel well, stretching and stretching the cord.

"Look out! Look out!" guys yelled in the pit as the hose stretched tighter, but nobody could hear. The guy in most danger, though, was already on the ground. The hose caught Stan Blaylock by the legs as Schrader took off, and flipped him onto his back. When the hose finally gave out and snapped back, the gun stayed stuck in Schrader's car for half a lap. Nobody was hit. Duze walks around shaking his head.

"An official wanted to know where the fucking gun was," he yells into the roar. "It got *misplaced*! Motherfucking Schrader tried *stealing* it. It's on the fucking backstretch!"

As they approach the green flag for the final laps of the race, Kenny clicks on for a second: "OK, " he says, "it's gonna be a barn burner." Kenny's brother Rusty, leading the race in the number 2 car, jumps the green flag on the restart, almost passing the pace car. NASCAR officials put out the black flag for him, requiring him to drive onto pit road for a stop-and-go penalty. He does; an official in his pit, hands out, guides him to a stop; as soon as the car ceases to move, he waves it on by like a bullfighter. Furious, Rusty roars back out and finishes 15th, the last car on the lead lap.

Up front there's a little more bumping and banging between Jeff Burton's 99 and Bobby Hamilton's 43, but Burton wins comfortably, with Hamilton fading to third behind Dale Earnhardt. Kenny closes up on the bumpers of Jeff Gordon and Bill Elliot, but he spends more time fighting Ward Burton off his own sixth position.

"Cover the bottom, Kenny, cover the bottom!" Eddie yells over the radio at one point as Burton gets the nose of his number 22 underneath Kenny's left rear quarter panel in Turn 1. Kenny covers the bottom, and he crosses the finish line in sixth place.

"Beautiful job, guys—you did a hell of a job!" he yells over the radio as he finishes, and Eddie and Newt do the same: "Way to go in the pits today, guys; Awesome job today. Awesome!"

Newt, walking from crew member to crew member, nodding his head, pointing, and slapping shoulders, seems not just excited by the strong finish but, for a moment, actually relieved. "I told you guys you could do it! Sixth-place finish; 500 laps, lead lap! Let's get this stuff loaded and get out of here." Dave Ensign walks over to lend a hand pulling the carts and equipment back to the hauler. "Hey, there's big D!" Newt says. "How you doing, buddy? How's everything?"

❖

The transition after the race occurs so quickly that it jars everyone but the crews themselves.

For more than three-and-a-half hours, the speedway has roared and boomed with noise so loud that as far away as the highest seats in the stands, to make yourself heard to the person right next to you, you have to pull aside some kind of ear covering and scream as loud as you can. The air has been filled with the climbing and descending of 43 engines humming up to 9,000 rpms and grinding back down again, twice a lap, for 500 laps; sand, tire fragments, and decomposing asphalt grit have filled the air like stinging hail. Then once the cars on the lead lap have finished, suddenly the noise abates. Car after car cuts its engine, quickly enough that the first sound you hear if you remove your headset to give your aching ears a rest is the crowd still cheering for the finish. But then that subsides too, as everywhere in the infield teams pull headsets off and start taking things apart and putting them away.

In Sunday's rain, groups of crew members huddling under the eaves of the infield concession stand looked like parrots weathering a rainforest storm. Now, hustling together in groups, responding to commands only they can hear, or doing jobs they don't need to be told to do, they look like tiny schools of tropical fish, changing direction all at once or suddenly swarming to a cart, to a toolbox, to a car.

In the Square D pit, talking almost stops. Jacks are taken apart and stored; air wrenches come off their hoses and gointo a drawer, the hoses are coiled into their spot in the war wagon. The TV is off, the dish slid into its panel. Computers are unplugged.

As every team scrambles to clean their area and head for home, the doors to the grandstand are opened, and fans pour into the infield, taking an already crowded garage area and pressing it further. The crew members barely notice; they push carts, stacks of tires, cans of nitrogen and gasoline where they need to go. The fans seem to get out of the way.

At the Square D hauler, the car rolls to a stop behind the lift gate. It's covered with tire fragments and doughnuts from Martinsville's tight turns. Kenny pulls himself out the window to congratulations and slaps on the back from Newt, Eddie, and the other crew members as they come back and forth from the pit. Eddie Jarvis, the driver of Kenny's motor home, is waiting for him with a cup of water with ice and a towel. Kenny, his face flushed, hair mussed from his helmet, drinks the water, smiling, leaning on the car. He talks about trying to run down Gordon, the series points leader and star, late in the race. "I had my nose right up under his ass," he says, but he never quite got by. "I was going to go outside like I done on the 75 car, but I never got time." Then, of course, his tires wore and his handling went away, and just holding off Burton was as much as he could do. It's pointed out to him that he finished higher than every one of the five cars that started in front of him, and he pops his head back, pleased. "Hey, let me think about that. Every car—I like that! That's good!" That he finished behind five cars that started behind him, including the 43 car, which started 22nd? That's just racing. The point is a top-10 finish. Newt pulls Kenny away, disappearing with him into the hauler office for a few minutes of debriefing.

For everyone else, it's endgame here. The lift gate of the truck, stuck out as a canopy all weekend, is lowered. The crew pushes the car onto the gate, throws aluminum chocks under the wheels, and then hits the button to lift it up to the top of the hauler. Leaning on the car as it goes up, they can feel that the hood, the tires, and the rims are all still hot. The car gets pushed into the space atop the hauler in seconds, and it's strapped in behind the backup car. Down comes the lift gate, and the load-out continues: the war wagon, the tool chest, the crash cart, the generators, the coolers, the chairs, the gas grill. Everything that has made the Martinsville infield a home to the crew for the last three days is loaded into the hauler, filling the tiny hallway with equipment.

Don comes up smiling with the gas cans, emptied at the collecting station. He saw a NASCAR official and asked for the air gun that Ken Schrader ran over. "He said, 'You don't get it back.' I said, 'You don't understand, it wasn't our fault!' He said, 'OK, we'll see that you get it back.' " Don shakes his head and gets to work, pushing carts into position to be loaded on the hauler.

Before 45 minutes have passed, the only thing that says "Square D" in the infield is the hauler, and that's started and rumbling and ready to go. The side door is open, and one last cooler sits on the ground in a growing puddle of water. The postrace beers, and everyone has one. "Got any beer left?" someone asks, walking in from a last check of the pit area. "The round cooler," Dave Ensign says. "You know I always take care of my boys."

The team stands around, down to T-shirts and pants, wearing Square D hats and sunglasses. Newt's hat, instead of the plain blue with the logo on it, has a lightning bolt pattern, and for the moment it looks like he wears it not just proudly but happily. He sucks down a beer and looks around the asphalt infield, suddenly seeming bare as the haulers pull out, turning onto the track in Turn 1, circling once, and heading out the crossover gate in Turn 4. Seven haulers are enough to completely fill the backstretch.

The Filmar Racing team was wise. They parked the white van they drove up in from Charlotte in a parking area outside the track. They walk out to it and head home, fighting traffic. It's not as comfortable or as fast as Filbert's 10-seat plane, where they play poker and listen to Two-Can tell stories, but they're on their way home.

When they get back to the team headquarters outside Charlotte, most of the guys go their separate ways; the truck can be unloaded in the morning. Newt and Eddie get in a car and follow Two-can, who's got them all tickets for that night's Charlotte Panthers game. It turns out that they lose Two-Can on the highway (you should never have to try to drive behind a race team member immediately after a Winston Cup race) and never find him at the game. So they go home and go to bed. Just as well; the Panthers lose.

Frank Good has a last errand to run. He has to get an engine hoist, load the extra engine into the back of a pickup, and drive around to return it to the Robert Yates engine shop. That's how it is when you rent your engines.

He says he gets home before 9.

❖

The speedway doesn't exactly clear out at 4 P.M. either. For one thing, the fans let in from the grandstand are crawling over the garage area. They're looking for souvenirs: a tire valve cover, a piece of sheet metal loosed by a wreck, anything that was used during the race. People grab lengths of hose out of the junk piles left by the haulers and in the garage. They root for clipped wires and frayed belts in the trash. They look, especially, for lug nuts. Lug nuts used in a Winston Cup race are the foul balls into the stands of Winston Cup racing. A lug nut is the best souvenir you can bring home from a race. Lug nuts from the car of your favorite driver—the number 24 of Jeff Gordon, the 6 of Mark Martin, the 88 of Dale

Jarrett, the 3 of Earnhardt—from a race he won are more like the ball from a game-winning homer your favorite player hit in an extra-inning game.

"Rusty's my man," says a man rooting through the wash of clipped nylon cable zips and crushed Gatorade cups and auto parts boxes covered with oil and rear end fluid and film boxes and food bags and concession stand litter that has built up around every one of the trash barrels and cardboard trash boxes everywhere on the infield. He's not too happy about the black flag that cost Rusty the race, but he knows that Rusty likes to jump the green flag on restarts, and once in a while he gets caught. Rusty only finished 15th, but he led the race, and in fact led the most laps, at one point keeping his car digging into the corners in first place for 150 laps in a row. If it's going to be a lug nut, it's going to have to be Rusty's, and he walks slowly along pit road, trying to determine which pit was Rusty's. "But don't think I don't root for his brothers, man." That would be Kenny and his brother Mike, who in the Saturday race at Martinsville (sort of the weekend's undercard), raced the number 52 Chevy truck to 22nd place in the NASCAR Craftsman Truck Series race.

In a crowd of fans, kept away by the omnipresent Winston Cup flag tape wound around trash barrels, several cars are receiving postrace inspections: The number 99 Ford that won, the number 3 Chevy that came in second, and the 43 Pontiac that came in third. NASCAR inspects the winner every race, and usually the top finisher of every make. The cars receive an inspection as detailed as the one every car got several times before the race.

Along the front of pit road, a hauler with a Racers, Inc. logo prowls along slowly, with three guys loading in the piles of used tires the pit crews left out front. Racers, Inc. is one of two companies that, by contract, recycle the tires. They pick up the used tires after the race, remove them from the rims, take the rims to the Goodyear race shop for the next race, and dispose of the tires. Some, of course, end up in the hands of fans, where they become planters, mirror frames, coffee table bases.

Those grasping hands can be a frustration to the guys trying to finish their jobs and go home. Anyhow, so says Vince, a radio frequency camera technician who works for Broadcast Sports Technologies, which supplies remote cameras to the network televising the race, in this case ESPN. He shakes his head as he winds cable around his arm, wrist to elbow, to spool it. "Digging through the fucking trash," he says of the fans. When the cable is spooled, he cinches it with nylon strips and tosses it into his golf cart. "That's the worst part about it. The people come out here picking up lug nuts, tire caps, going through the garbage."

His friend, Lorne, is a pointer. He's one of the guys who follow around the camera guys wearing a backpack with a transmitter in it and holding a metal rod taped to a broomstick with a tiny dish broadcast antenna with a foam soccer ball on the end of the center spike. He gets paid $75 a day to be a pointer at Martinsville. He points that spike at a collecting antenna on top of the home stretch grandstand. No benefits, no nothing. Just this year pointers started getting their hotel rooms paid for; people like Vince demanded they get at least that.

"We said, we need these guys," Vince says.

Vince's job is to sit in his little golf cart, parked behind a junction box that connects about a dozen pit areas. He controls video feeds from the overhead pit cameras from cooperative crews as well as feeds from a couple of remote cameras used by the pit reporters. Not every team allows their overhead camera to provide a live feed. The number 3 team of Dale Earnhardt always says no, "and no tobacco teams," he says, showing the uneasiness beginning to develop between NASCAR, its broadcast partners, and the tobacco sponsorship that has made it what it is.

They arrived in Martinsville on Wednesday, two days before the haulers and the Winston Cup teams. They arrived this morning at 6:30, same time as the Winston Cup teams. They'll be going home around 9 tonight, around five hours after the Winston Cup teams.

And not only do they have to spend hours after the race retrieving shotgun microphones and ripping up cables duct-taped onto the ground; not only do they have to get covered with tire goo and brake dust and asphalt fragments all day while they do their jobs; not only do guys like Lorne get paid barely enough to make air fare to their next assignment, whether it's another Cup race or an Indy car race or a basketball game, but they have to put up with "these fucking race fans," Lorne says, who get stuff on them and trip over their cables and engage them in endless discussions of why ESPN doesn't show their favorite driver more often and ask if they can look through the cameras and want to take pieces of the cable for souvenirs.

Then Lorne smiles a wan smile as he washes his hands with the ice from a soft drink cup: " 'Course, I used to be one of them race fans I'm cussing."

By 4:30 or so, even the fans clambering around pit road are straggling toward the crossovers back to the grandstands and parking areas. The lines of cars are moving now, and the camps are being struck. As the cars filled with tired race fans wearily grind up the just-not-quite-too-slippery grass slopes, if you look out over the camping or parking areas, you don't necessarily think "Woodstock," but you don't think anything too far from it. It's been a long, wet, hot, and satisfying four days for these folks.

But it's over now. The sun is setting in a blue sky whitening toward the horizons. No stars are visible yet, but just a hint of peach, of pink, is starting to seep into the light above the shadows of the pines. It's time to go home.

❖

The last image of Martinsville Speedway in the rearview mirror, as the sun sets among the Piedmont hills, is that tiny road leading out of the speedway, with the cars rolling out and kicking up just a little cloud of that famous red dust. Traffic this late isn't bad on Route 220, heading south, down a big hill and then back up again, following the hills southwest into North Carolina. Toward Charlotte.

And you'd never believe it in the rapidly suburbanizing South, where cul-de-sacs are replacing tobacco fields and choking the land like kudzu, but rolling through the countryside from Martinsville back to Charlotte, you drive two-lanes through some rural stretches where you still don't see too many lights. In fact, if you take North Carolina Route 87 all the way over to U.S. 29—if, on the map, you stay on a gray line for a while instead of getting right on a double red line—you can stop at a yield sign at the top of a hill, in the middle of the night, where a gravel road angles in from the forest and through some cleared pasture to meet Route 87. And you can pull your car over onto the wide part of the gravel road so you're not in the middle of the road in case another car comes by, even though you know one won't. And you can turn off the lights of your car, but not the engine, because if it doesn't start up again there's nobody around.

And you can stand outside and look up at the stars. There isn't a streetlight within miles; you can see millions. And it's still a day or so before the new moon begins rising, so even Venus and Mars, on a line slightly sloping downward in the clear sky of the west, barely draw your eye. And then you can notice.

Your car is still running. It's a motor, and it's running, cycling over and over, thousands of times a minute, working. Driving.

You like the sound.

Chapter 3

AIR WRENCHES AND ETOUFFÉ

Tuesday, September 30

In the Filmar Racing shop on Zion Church Road in the town of Concord, North Carolina, a few miles up the road from Charlotte Motor Speedway, fabricator Aaron Brown leans over, hands on his knees, inspecting the Martinsville car that the crew has just unloaded from the hauler, and he asks the only question he can ask about a race car the day after it's raced.

"Are we going to fix this car?" he asks, of nobody in particular. "Or is it done?"

It's done. It'll be ripped apart and started fresh, from the chassis up.

What is at first surprising is that in the big picture, that doesn't mean much to the Filmar racing team. You remember the old Peanuts cartoons where Lucy would smash the bust of Beethoven on Schroeder's piano and Schroeder would calmly walk to his closet and get another one? For anyone still laboring under the impression that a race team runs a single race car, the first glimpse of a Winston Cup shop provokes the same surprised laugh as those dozens of Beethovens lined up in Schroeder's closet.

Yes, sure, you see the blue-and-yellow Square D colors the minute you walk in—and yes, there's the race car. And there, and over there, and there again, and over there, too. On a smooth, gray coated-concrete floor under long, hanging fluorescent lights in the huge brick-and-metal two-story shed that houses the shop, lined up in two long rows, are nine nearly identical race cars in various stages of completion. They're arranged in two rows: On one side, parked diagonally almost like cars in a mall parking lot, are the Martinsville car that just came off the hauler, the car being prepared for Charlotte next Sunday, several sets of tires, a car with no body at all, just a chassis and a roll cage, and one of the cars used for road courses.

Across a wide, clean aisle from them, parked straight in, are the backup car that just came off the hauler, a car being prepared for the Talladega superspeedway race coming up in two weeks, another backup, and the car that won the pole and then ran terribly at Bristol a month before. Its future is uncertain. Then there's a group of tables and metalworking tools and a welding booth with a ratty military green curtain. Finally, at the end of the row, almost at the back of the long shed, sits a clean gray steel chassis: the first of the Ford Tauruses the team is building for next year, when the team is changing from Thunderbirds to the Taurus. It's got wheels and some of its brushed steel sheet metal, but still no roof, no rear deck. Occasionally its flimsy metal hood is laid on top of the body frame; more often it's laying nearby on a table.

"That's the Daytona car," says fabricator and shop foreman Andy Johnson, a wiry, slim-hipped guy in his early 30s, with shaggy black hair and a moustache and, almost always, a cigarette dangling from his lips. As for the other cars, Andy manages them like the head of any repair shop, keeping everything moving along, rushing one out when needs change or an emergency comes up, when suddenly the Bristol car becomes the Richmond backup, or the Rockingham backup gets pressed into duty as the Dover car. It changes hour by hour, depending on parts, on decisions Newt and Eddie make in the offices in the front of the building.

And by the way, another car is at the chassis shop, and one other is in the paint shop right now, a little building out back of the main shop, getting its coats of blue and yellow.

Eleven race cars in all.

Andy explains. "Two superspeedway cars. Two road-course cars. Three short-track cars. And four intermediate cars." Superspeedway cars (for Daytona and Talladega, 2.5-mile tracks where aerodynamics are paramount) have their hood hinges recessed and their bodies hung for minimum aerodynamic drag. They'll have soft springs and shocks to enable the down force the air resistance generates to push the car as close as possible to the track to diminish wind on the spoiler and let the car cut through the air as smoothly as possible. The short-track cars are set up with more of an eye toward brakes and steering than aerodynamics. Turning left is all they do, a thousand times per race at Martinsville, so the A-frames that hold on their front wheel assemblies are set up to encourage that. The road-course cars are the only cars in the shop set up to turn both left and right. There are two road courses, so one car is set up to favor each course. Instead of leaning to the left on flat ground, they're designed to look neutral, almost like a car in your driveway. The Watkins Glen, New York, course has a lot of right turns, so that car is set up to turn right well; the Sears Point, California, course is more equal, so that's the most neutral car in the shop.

The intermediate cars—for Charlotte, Darlington, Dover, and the great run of tracks on the circuit—get the most attention, and the most use. But cars get shifted around due to changing race shop needs, and you'd best keep your head up.

"That's why I stayed up all night getting that New Hampshire car done," Andy said one night after a race in Richmond. "Figuring I didn't want to get that Bristol car done and then lose this car and be looking at no car for Dover." He took a car raced at New Hampshire and prepared it for the Dover race that was coming up the next weekend, that is, instead of taking the Bristol car and reworking it for the upcoming Martinsville race. Martinsville was a week after Dover—first things first. This week the focus will be on the Charlotte car and its backup, and the Martinsville car, the Talladega car, and all the other cars in the shop will get attention when it's available. The building is about 60 yards long by 30 wide, and it's full of race cars.

Before 8 A.M. comes, Frank Good is already running full-tilt for the morning. "I have to take that Martinsville engine out, take the engine in that one and put it into that one, and get the race engine for the Charlotte car and put it in," he says, gesturing all over the garage at blue-and-yellow race cars. "All today." Other crew members either squat in front of the Martinsville car or begin eyeing their own jobs—replacing carbon fiber brake calipers or adding the power steering assembly or replacing a windshield—when Newt emerges from the office.

His cheer of the afternoon before has vanished entirely, replaced by stone-faced calm. The Martinsville race the day before was a welcome respite, but it's Charlotte week again, and he's bracing for the pressure. He looks like a man placing himself under the end of a lever currently held by someone else, and he's getting ready to stand up and assume the burden. Part of him appears anxious for the feeling, anxious to assume the familiar load; the rest of him seems to eye the guy leaving, the man shrugging off the load, with jealousy. It may be that the two parts of him are at war. If so, the worker wins. It always does. He takes the weight.

He leans over to speak with "Suitcase" Jake Elder, a member of the crew who's recently had health problems. Then he chats with Two-Can a moment about Kenny's brakes from the day before. He nods, his hands on his knees as he examines the brake rotors still mounted on the Martinsville hubs.

Then he stands up and sighs heavily. "Well, let's get this done and over with," he says, not necessarily an announcement but loud enough to be heard around him. He picks up the phone and calls out to the paint shop. "Let's do this deal," he says. A moment later the entire Filmar Racing crew, in black Filmar Racing T-shirts and pinstriped mechanic's shirts with name patches sewn on the right breast and "Filmar Racing" on the left, in jeans and in blue work pants, gathers around the silver slab of the surface plate.

The surface plate is a rectangular steel platform at the front end of the shop, just across from the rolling garage door. It's raised a few inches from the coated concrete floor, and it's checked and plumbed to be perfectly level. There are little outcroppings on the long sides for equipment or mechanics as they work on the car that will eventually sit there. This is where the race car for the upcoming week will be set up, where it will get its chassis adjusted so that the right amount of weight sits on each wheel, so that the back and front wheels point where they need to, so that when tires with the proper stagger are mounted on its hubs it sits with the correct angle down toward its left side determined by years of experience at the track, maintained in meticulously updated three-ring binders.

But no car sits on the surface plate now. They're still an engine, springs, shocks, and a sway bar away from even having a car to *put* on the plate for its final setup. That car will have to be ready tomorrow morning, but for now it's time for the obligatory postrace morning meeting.

"I looked the shop over this morning," Newt says, unfolding and folding his arms, "and it looks excellent." It's been weeks since the team lost a part due to failure in practice or during a race; he congratulates them about that. He introduces Ricky Turner, who's been pushing a broom since he showed up in the morning, trying to get busy. "He's got the burning thing inside like everyone," he says of Ricky, who glances up, trying to look unfazed.

Then Newt quickly switches to the race report. "You guys would've been proud of us," he says. "We unloaded and didn't change a whole lot, kept calm and cool. We learned a lot the other night what not to do." He's referring to the previous Tuesday night's testing effort at Charlotte, where the car had looked unimaginably bad and the team had suffered a sort of meltdown, routinely pulling the car in from the track to make changes—not a slight tire pressure adjustment or small change to the track bar or a spring, but four new shocks, two or four new springs, a completely different tire pressure program, and maybe even a different rear end gear. "We were kind of just throwing shit against the wall to see what sticks," Eddie said later. "It was terrible." The car had never improved much, and its times were still much slower than most of the others' at the end of the test. Just one more reason for Newt—and everybody else—to worry about this week's race.

But truly, at Martinsville the team had unloaded the car, got it inspected, and started running practice laps with a clear program in mind. They ran a few laps, then changed tire pressure, talked about how the car was handling, rubbed their chins, changed rear springs or maybe front shocks, sent the car back out for another few laps, and asked Kenny some more questions. Their process looked orderly and purposeful; they used the endearing term "clusterfuck" to refer to the exploits of NASCAR officials failing to put cars in line where they belonged, not to each other, which they had been known to do.

Newt goes on for a moment about the Martinsville race, mentioning Kenny's sixth-place finish again: "You guys at the track really did something this week," he says. "I'm just tickled to death." Then he introduces Eddie.

"I just want to reiterate, the car was set up perfectly," Eddie says. Then he turns to Andy: He wants some new pads to take to the track to stand tires up for examination after they've come off the car. "Can you make those for me this week?" Andy nods. Eddie shifts to business concerns, where mail bins will be, how travel itineraries will be distributed. "Office paperwork, stuff like that," he says. This is the kind of stuff Eddie thinks about, the kind of stuff Eddie likes to think about. "I really enjoy the business aspect of all this," he says. "Sponsorship, the guys in the shop, all of it. There's so much that has to go on."

Speaking of which, he gets serious.

"This weekend, this is Charlotte, and you know what that means," he says. "The CEO, the CFO, everybody and their wives will be there. We want to see you in decent, Square D attire, a Square D shirt, all the time. That's so important that they see that. That's what they're paying for." Everybody shuffles their feet; Duze snorts and overtly rolls his eyes. Duze, not content to merely light a smoke and hunch over a stack of tires during the races, when the pit has been reset and the crew has nothing much to do, fairly often unzips the top of his jumpsuit, revealing either a ratty T-shirt or a thick mat of hair. That's probably one of the things Eddie specifically doesn't want to see, and that's something Duze doesn't care for. He mutters something low about what that has to do with racing, but he's not looking for a fight.

Eddie glances at Duze and goes on to more mundane topics. "When we load to leave, if Frank and Buddy and Dave take the toolbox and go back to the truck and start loading, . . ." he starts, suggesting a procedure that might save a few minutes after the race. He talks for a moment about the pit stop that resulted in the flat tire. "We probably let the car down early," he says, "but we need to check the tape."

Newt mentions that the team had an understanding NASCAR official during the race. There's a NASCAR official for about every two pits; he checks to make sure the pit stops follow the rules, that pit road speeds are observed. He'll also answer any questions teams have during the race, say, whether their driver shouldn't be ahead of someone else during the lineup for a restart after a caution, or whether someone a lap down shouldn't be getting out of the way of two cars racing for position. A good official can mean position during a tight battle through lapped traffic; a bad official can miss something in a pit stop and even assess a penalty. A bad official can mean a bad race. They had a good one at Martinsville, which meant that Ken Schrader running over their air gun ended up being something to laugh about, not a mistaken 15-second penalty that would have destroyed their race.

"We know Andy is short-term," Eddie says about the crew during pit stops, "but starting very soon we need to start practicing, at least every three days, eight stops a day. That's what other teams do." And if that's what it's going to take, that's what they're going to have to do. The meeting, with 15 or so guys quietly sitting around the surface plate, doesn't so much end as wind down. Two-Can and mechanic

Buddy Cram wander over toward the Martinsville car, discussing how the car handles in the turns: "Say you got 100 percent traction," Buddy says, using his rigid palm to roughly represent the rectangle of a race car as mechanics always do, "when you're turning, that takes away 50 percent. When you're braking, that takes away 50 percent. So if you want traction to get going off the straightaway, you can't be turning if you're braking." Two-Can nods. "That was my point coming home yesterday in the van." Then attention turns back to the Martinsville car, and its brakes, as they squat down for a last look before the car gets dismantled.

"What's the deal with that hat there?" Buddy asks, looking at a section of the hub that has a groove scored into it, about an eighth of an inch deep. Two-Can laughs and rocks back on his haunches.

"He was on 'em so hard that the caliper come over here; the pad dug into it," he says. Then he narrows his eyes, noticing that the brake rotor is not only scored, it's actually cracking from the wear. More than that, it's got a black residue that on closer examination turns out to be not merely brake dust—it's soot. He barks out a laugh.

"This shit was black," he says. A standard picture shown during the broadcast of a Martinsville race comes from a tiny camera mounted in the wheelwell of one of the cars. The camera points at the brake shoes, and when the driver puts on the brakes going into the turn, the brake pads heat up so much they turn bright red. By the end of the race, when they've been blinking on and off like Rudolph's nose for 500 laps, those pads glow like taillights on a rainy night.

Here's proof that they do more than just glow.

"Look at this," Two-can says. "This bitch was on *fire*." He smiles. How much longer could Kenny have driven on those brakes. "Oh," Two-Can shrugs, "30 laps?" He thinks a moment, shakes his head. "Twenty?"

Interesting enough, but that's last week's car. Two-Can and Buddy go over to a tool chest and open a drawer full of wrenches. An hour later that car will barely be recognizable. By the end of the day it will barely exist. Frank, already bent over the engine disconnecting hoses by unscrewing their shiny blue and red aluminum couplers, looks out from under the hood.

"Buddy?" he asks. "Jeremy's coming over in 45 minutes, and he's gonna pick up this engine." It's got to be disconnected, hoisted out, and ready to go in 45 minutes. "Can you help me with it?"

Buddy can, and the work starts in earnest.

❖

Newt, meanwhile, heads back into his office, expecting his postrace morning call from Filbert.

It's Filbert's team; it's Filbert's toy. Filbert lives and works in Nashville, but he checks in on Newt every morning after a race. He's around all weekend during a race, but at the track he keeps his distance, watching and listening rather than offering much advice. He mostly saves his comments for Newt during those morning calls.

Sitting in his simple, rec-room paneled office, Newt seems almost uncomfortable at his desk. He's a guy comfortable touching cars; he doesn't think of himself as a desk guy, and it shows. When Filbert decided he had to change crew chiefs, Newt told him immediately that he wanted the job. But still, in the office, with its big magic-markered calendar ("testing, Charlotte"; "Talladega"; "testing, Atlanta"; "Las Vegas?", all in four-day blocs, cover the calendar from February to November) and a simple wooden desk standing kind of starkly in the middle, he looks like he feels a trifle out of place. Getting a race car to go fast is something that comes naturally to him; dealing with the stresses of running a team is a different deal. His desk is covered with paperwork, with pamphlets from supply companies, with forms to sign and send to NASCAR or Square D or Filbert. He's got to think about travel arrangements and expenses, about personnel and turnover and tire budgets. Sometimes it looks like the whole business can overwhelm him.

Then he remembers why he's there. He thinks back to his days as a driver at Nashville. "The driving," he says, leaning forward, "the driving is the easiest thing you can do.

"You gotta love it, and you gotta have the knack for it, you gotta work at it, but that's the easiest part. You just know the feeling, going into the turn—right front, left front, right rear, left rear, *plant*." Using his hand, stiff, to show the car. "I can talk to the driver."

He leans back in his chair. "Now I'm more the coach. A crew chief's gotta be a coach. We call the wrong play, the wrong stop, that can wreck a whole race." He thinks back to Monday's race. "Track position is everything, driving up front." In an important way, he says, Eddie's preparedness kept them in the race. "We had that blowout on the left side, and we had to work with that deal." What saved the race, he thinks, is Eddie having a set of left-side tires planned for just such an emergency. "We put on a matched set, two on the left side, and we were good to go. A tire man is the crew chief's right hand man. Up until this week, I didn't have one. I was airing the tires up, which I've done before, but now I do not have to be doing that. That helps."

He's almost looking forward to Filbert's call. It's been a long season, and it's nice to have something good to discuss, especially after the previous week's disaster at Dover. During that race Kenny had been running so badly (he started 19th and was running in last place almost immediately) that Filbert actually shouted over his radio, "Newt! Something has to be done about that car! Now!" Newt pulled Kenny behind the wall, into the garage, and had the team scramble to change shocks and springs. Kenny finished 38th, 37 laps off the pace. You don't like to run 37 laps off the pace when you didn't at least get collected in somebody else's wreck. It means you never figured out what you were doing that week. "You race the track, not the other cars" is a racing truism drivers still repeat with intent. If you finish that far off the pace, it means the track kicked your butt.

"Dover almost shut the door on this team," Newt says, cringing at the memory, mercifully a week older now. "The driver went crazy. He went and got shocks from Rusty; I went to other guys I know. We didn't know what we wanted to do. Then we went to Charlotte and tested and went crazy." He shakes his head. He feels profoundly responsible. When the team pushed the awful Dover car toward the hauler after that disappointing race, there was some talk of some kind of equipment failure, maybe a tire equalized and caused some shimmy that caused something to break, that sort of thing. Newt wouldn't have any of it: "I think what you call that," he broke into a headset conversation, "was a badly missed setup." That's the crew chief's responsibility, and he won't let anybody else share the blame, a blame he seems to feel powerfully.

The Martinsville finish gave the team a gulp of air, going into their biggest race of the season.

"Now we've got a better deal here. We're gonna go out and change one thing at a time, one step at a time. It's like golf. If it's a par 4 and it's got an elbow there at the corner, you can't try to hit it all in one swing. These other teams got a lot more experience. But little steps, little steps. I'm learning that."

The phone rings, Newt answers it and grins. It's Filbert.

"Yes sir," he says, smiling. "Thank you very much."

❖

While Newt listens to Filbert on the phone in his office, in the shop the Filmar crew is going about the business of being a race team.

Frank, Buddy, and Two-Can clamber over the Martinsville car. Two-Can has the brakes off and he's working on the rear end gear; all four wheels are long gone. The axles will be next, and then the A-arms—or A-frames—that hold the hubs on. The power steering needs to come off.

Frank and Buddy disconnect motor hoses; the carburetor is gone, ready to be disassembled, cleaned, rebuilt, and ready for another race. Jake sits underneath the Charlotte car, bolting on the power steering and putting on the upper and lower A-frames. Like everything else about the car, those are chosen and adjusted for each racetrack. Upstairs in a storage area above the offices, Filmar Racing has a few dozen A-frames hanging around. "We used to have twice as many but it was driving us crazy," Andy says. "We threw about half of em out."

All over the shop, with a country station playing in the background, crew members lean over cars. Rich Vargo works on one of the back-up cars, preparing a template from which he'll cut out a right-side window for the Charlotte car. On tracks of 1.5 miles or longer, like Charlotte, the cars run with right-side windows. At short tracks like Martinsville they leave the right window open to keep the driver cooler, but once aerodynamics become a factor at the higher speeds on longer tracks, the right-side window keeps the car moving faster.

In the back of the shop, Andy and Aaron work on the chassis of the Daytona car they're building for next year. Andy, leaning over the chassis, looks around the shop, then gives a practiced nod of his head, tilting the welding helmet down over his face. Then the sparks fly, as another piece of steel tubing finds its home.

The activity is constant, but smooth. Occasionally a crew member shouts: "I'm going over to BSR; anybody need anything?" BSR is one of the parts suppliers that have sprung up in the area to service the teams. The suppliers deliver ordered parts to the shop, but there's always something missing, and guys come and go constantly. Other people cycle into and out of the shop as well: representatives of Safety-Kleen, a recycler and waste disposal company, come in to empty the drums of used gas, oil, and fluids. Guys come in to keep the team supplied with clean uniforms and gas rags. Occasionally, fans stop by, and Gloria, the team secretary, walks a few people into the shop. They stop and gawk at the buzz of activity, take a picture or so, and disappear unnoticed.

If you stand around for a moment, you can feel overwhelmed by the amount of activity. Newt walks up and down the shop, checking over guys' shoulders, but he's not really supervising so much as making sure they've got what they need and that they know about any changes—which shocks are supposed to go in the backup car, what needs to happen to the Talladega car, even today, when almost everything is focused on Charlotte.

❖

Sitting quietly in front of the Charlotte backup car is Tom Emery. He's the one-man paint shop. He's already painted this car, and he's applying decals. "Everything from the number forward is a deal with NASCAR," he explains. "They've got a deal with each company, where it goes, how much money they give to the series." He's got about half the stickers on the front, the Goodyear sticker right above the wheel, 3M, Mac Tools, Stant radiator caps, and on and on. Some of the small stickers are optional. You choose which spark plug company you're going to use, they give you spark plugs, you put their sticker on your car. And rest assured, somebody will check during the race weekend to make sure the stickers are there.

Tom stands up and wipes his hands. Some spots on the front fender are still marked by masking tape instead of stickers, and he walks upstairs to a suite of unused office rooms. There he keeps boxes of the decals every company provides for the cars. He's also got piles of the huge "81" decals for the side and the roof of the car, the Square D logo for the hood, the seat posts, the rear quarter panels, and the rear deck, and the little "Kenny Wallace" signature that goes above the door. There are even tiny little Square D logos for placing on the bumper, the dash, and anywhere else an in-car camera might point when one of those is mounted in the car.

They're the final part of his job, yet he applies the decals patiently, a seat of Zen concentration amid the maelstrom of shop activity. His paint shop, in a small building out back, is itself an oasis of calm. In a shop filled with guys working together to make the car go fast, Tom works alone. And his job doesn't necessarily make the car go fast. His job is to make the car look *cool*.

Well, maybe that's an overstatement. He's the guy who repairs torn fenders and stove-in noses after short-track races like the Martinsville race. "If it doesn't get tore up real bad and we're going to a place like Martinsville where it's going to get beat up anyway, we just repair it. But everything that's on the car we keep in stock upstairs. We get what we need and replace what we need to."

He's been with Filmar Racing for about a year and a half, but this is his 12th in Winston Cup racing. He's worked for the Hendrick teams, for Junior Johnson. But for the body man the routine is the same everywhere. "They pull the motor and gears out of the car. You knock all the dents out and wash the car up. Hopefully, it doesn't need a new front clip." That's the whole geometry of the nose of the car, hung on the chassis exactly where the team has determined it ought to be for a particular type of track. A quarter of an inch to the left or right can mean the difference between a car that handles perfectly and a car that barely makes it around the track. "Then you go in the body shop, get it all prettied up. Paint it up nice. Back into the shop for wheels and wheel bearings, A-frames, springs, shocks, new gears, new motor, and go at it again."

His shop is cool. It's temperature controlled so the body filler and paint set just right, and it's got industrial exhaust fans to keep the filler dust and paint fumes he generates when sanding and spraying from poisoning him. He likes the blue-and-yellow design of the Square D car, especially because it's easy to paint—

long, simple borders, straight lines. "The Tide car, that was tough," he says of his days working with the famous bright orange Tide target. "You had to apply the orange, fade it into the yellow, put in the white, then cover the whole car with a clear coat." Nothing that complicated on this car.

Outside, sitting in the harsh sun in the shop parking lot, is the car he painted that morning. It's a sight: bright red frame covered by a blue body with a thick yellow slant angling from the front of the roof to the back of the door panel. A red stripe follows the base of the car. Everything else will be applied with decal, from the number 81 on the fake headlights to the blue-and-yellow fading square pattern along the color border.

Around the back of the shop is a little junkyard: bodies from cars that, like today's Martinsville car, are done. Once separated from the chassis with reciprocating saws and power chisels, the entire steel body of the car can be lifted off the frame by two guys and carried out back as easily as a canoe. There it's used, for a while, for cannibalizing. Parts might be sold to collectors or racers in lower series—"restaurants, ARCA guys," Tom says. (ARCA, the American Race Car Association, is a kind of single-A national race circuit that runs Winston Cup-style cars on large speedways, like Charlotte. It's not a NASCAR series.) But mostly, the discarded bodies just sit, like the discarded, broken toys of a gigantic child. Hoods, wheels, aluminum pans, split hoses, and brake rotors lay beneath the couple of complete bodies, lending an air of true junkyard to the pile.

But that's junk. Here in the parking lot is a fresh-painted body, all bright red and brilliant yellow and deep blue, seeming to almost buzz beneath a crystal clear sky. Tom stands a moment, enjoying his handiwork. Then he hooks up a power washer. On the end of the hose it looks like a lean submachine gun. He approaches the car with a purpose.

❖

Back inside the main shop, the pace hasn't slowed down. Frank and Buddy have disconnected the Martinsville race engine, hooked it up to a hoist, and removed it; it sat on a little roller near the garage door for all of five minutes before Jeremy Anderson, the Robert Yates employee who kind of baby-sits the engines Yates rents to Filmar, came and got it, dropping off the Charlotte engine. Frank and Two-Can have been busy on the Charlotte car ever since, connecting the transmission and the drivetrain, hoisting the engine into the new car, and connecting the fabric-covered hoses and zipping them to chassis pipes with nylon ties. They work together beneath the red-painted underside of the hood, with its own Square D logo. (If the car malfunctions during a race and the hood comes up, chances are TV cameras will come by to show what's going on, and that's one more opportunity for the Square D logo to show up on viewers' screens.) With guys doing work under the hood, the Charlotte car finally starts to feel like it's on its way. It may have a long way to go; it still needs springs and shocks and brakes, it has no wheels, no carburetor, but it's got an engine in it, and suddenly it feels like a race car.

Other cars all over the shop get attention from other guys, and watching from the balcony of the shop at the back end is fabricator Aaron Brown, a guy of about 30 with a thick five-o'clock shadow, a flyaway mop of brown hair, and a sarcastic view of racing.

He's up in what functions as a sort of race shop parts pile, looking to see whether he can find a finished piece of sheet metal to save him and Andy from making a new one for the Taurus they are building. Old car noses, new and old windshields, and painted and unpainted pieces of sheet metal lie scattered up here, along with air hoses, templates, a couple of race seats, exhaust pipes, and countless other car fragments. All the balcony needs is a dressmaker's dummy and an old lampshade to look exactly like somebody's attic. When he gets up top, Aaron often takes a moment to look down at the shop. Racing flags—checkered, green, white, red, yellow, black, and blue—hang from the shop ceiling, and Square D Racing banners and blue and yellow banners line the outside walls. Below him the guys buzz, just trying to keep up.

"When you're a $4 million-a-year team trying to keep up with $11-million-a-year teams, you don't stop," he says. "We're trying to bail out a sinking battleship with a 5-gallon bucket. If this was an honest-to-God business where you had to make a profit, we'd've been out of business by Daytona." Still, he's worked for other race shops. "I've worked with the Bodines, with Jimmy Spencer, with Hut Stricklin," but he's happier here than he's been before. He's been with Filmar about a year.

"I don't usually last long," he laughs. "I get pissed off and pack my shit up and go home. Take a vacation and start all over again somewhere else." It's behavior like that that got "Suitcase" Jake Elder, who is working underneath the Charlotte backup car down below, his name. It's pretty common in racing. There are about 50 teams trying to run Winston Cup cars regularly, and once you've made your contacts, you kind of stay up. You move around, but you're part of the gang. It's around 1,000 guys, the size of the senior class at a large high school, playing an endless game of musical chairs. It's part of the deal.

"It's all the politics and shit," he says of what keeps guys jumping from team to team. He then makes the comment most often heard among Winston Cup team members, a comment that might be tattooed on their biceps: "It's not racing anymore," he says. "It's a traveling circus." The sponsors, the money, the television coverage, the collectibles, the overwhelming festival of a Cup race, all have conspired to take away the sort of hike-up-your-pants-and-climb-in-your-car feeling that drew most mechanics in racing to their local racetracks as young guys. Winston Cup racing is so big that it's almost no fun anymore. "All the shit," Aaron says. "The race is like an aftereffect of race weekend now.

"No, I ain't for that hoopla horse shit. I'm here to race. I want to be left alone in the back room to build race cars. It's a way of life, really. It's not like a regular job, that's for sure."

But he's happy with Filmar, even though it's trying to run a shop on about half the resources he's seen elsewhere. "We've got 6 guys in the shop, including Tom out back," he says of the fabricators at Filmar. "At the Bodine shop, we had 15 guys in the shop doing the same workload. Still, we stay pretty caught up. The deal is, they get their cars done a week in advance. We're struggling to get our shit ready to go in the hauler." The Charlotte car, scheduled to unload at the racetrack at 9 A.M. tomorrow and still without brakes, shocks, or springs, stands as testimony below him.

"But this is a great place to work. These guys in here are the most dedicated group of guys I've ever seen. They stay until the job gets done, these guys. You won't see a harder-working road crew than ours. That Frank Good? He's the hardest-working guy on the circuit. I drive an hour to get here every day. I wouldn't be here if I didn't think we could win races." Other teams haven't been so dedicated. "One time we were going to Phoenix, when I worked with the Rick Mast team. We were loading the hauler, and the truck driver told me we couldn't take a radiator to test because they couldn't fit in their golf clubs."

Nobody at Filmar worries more about golf than racing. Racing is what they love. In fact, the overwhelming feeling in the race shop is just that'not so much the intense competition of Winston Cup racing, but that above all, this is one cool place to work.

In the clean, well-swept, and well-lit shop, everything you look at is a feast for the eyes and ears. Aaron, Andy, and the other guys in the fabrication end of the shop sand that new Taurus, sending showers of sparks flying; the sanders themselves, powered by retractable hoses from a shopwide air system overhead, add a satisfying whine. Tires come on and off cars all day long, the air-wrench sound becoming a kind of high timpani. Wrenches clatter to the ground and clank against bolts and tubes. Guys shuffle from car to car, working on several projects at once. It's not unusual to see guys working on seven or eight different cars, someone installing a window on the Talladega car, someone else spot-welding the new chassis. Aaron and Andy leaning over the Taurus, Frank standing actually inside the fender of a car as he works on the engine, leaning so far into the engine cavity that you feel you could close the hood and he'd disappear, visible only if you looked under the car and saw his legs. Lathes run, drills spin, air wrenches whir and whine from every angle. Frank Good especially is teased even by his teammates for constantly running among three or four cars, his pockets full of wrenches, connecting a hose here, running a line there, inserting a plug somewhere else. Here Duze works on a metal lathe, replacing steel control arm bushings with aluminum ones. ("We'll save maybe a whisker," he says, in the team's never-ending quest to control weight in the car.) There Aaron or Andy slides a piece of sheet metal several times through a roller, giving it the curve it needs to become a front fender, a rear quarter panel. And then again out back there's Tom, fixing bodies and painting them into race cars. Ricky Turner uses a cardboard template to cut a panel out of sheet metal. Guys walk back and forth to a half-dozen 7-foot blue cases filled with little cubbies of different parts. Several different red tool carts roll around; tools go where they need to, but they're always replaced in the drawers they came from. Templates for the cars—full-length metal silhouettes of the car from nose to tail; curves for the hood, the roof, the rear deck, the spoiler—hang on the walls.

At one end of the shop are half a dozen shiny, full race cars, with or without engines and tires, but race cars. Each, somewhere in the shop, has its own four-tiered gray cart, about 4 feet tall. It's marked with the car number (FM-1 through FM-11), and it carries extra hoses, brakes, hubs, seat pads, A-frames, maybe shocks or springs—any number of parts that fit the car but aren't on it at that moment. In a way, the chassis, parts, and engines make each race car seem kind of like a giant model. "We were racing that car a few days ago," Buddy says as he walks by one cart. "And look at it now, a pile of parts."

"Yeah, a big huge model kit," Aaron says. "Only they don't give you any directions." Those carts either stay with the car or stand in file at the back end of the shop, waiting for use. At that end of the shop, on a surface plate of its own, sits that shiny skeletal Taurus, with a pink string running between two standards through what will eventually be the windshield and the rear window. That pink line determines the centerline of the car, and plumb lines hang from each end, hitting a groove scored in the surface plate. Every measurement as the car is built comes off of that centerline. Eighths of an inch are consequential here; millimeters are consequential. Sometimes Andy crouches inside it to weld something and he looks like he's in a cage.

If you like cars, this is where you want to be. At the office end of the shop, near the surface plate, there's a series of white dry-erase marker boards, showing the information for the cars most currently in circulation: which chassis the car's based on (FM-5, say, or FM-8), which track it will run at, which engine will be used, which rear end gear, which drivetrain, and which transmission and steering box.

There's also plenty of space for larger comments, and Newt has written above the Martinsville data, "Sixth place! Excellent!" More important was something there some weeks ago, written by Kenny Wallace: "There are only 500 mechanics in the world who get to be Winston Cup mechanics. You guys are the best!"

Kenny shows up at the shop around 3 P.M., wearing a Square D golf shirt and his ever-present oval Oakley sunglasses. He has a deal with Oakley to wear them. He shows up most days at least for a while, he says. Today he's brought his three girls—they're 10, 8, and 6—who push each other around on under-car creepers and low rolling stools, filling the shop's center aisle with squeals. Duze teases them and sometimes comes out from his corner in the fabrication shop and chases them. They enjoy it; when he ignores them, they torment him until they get his attention back. Finally he lights an acetylene torch and roars at them, acting the monster. "Back off! I've got fire! I've got fire!" They screech with delight until he gets a little too close, then they cry. After the manner of too-aggressive uncle-figures everywhere, Duze rolls his eyes and returns to his lathe.

Kenny barely pays attention to the girls while he's in the shop. He's met with Newt, and now he's just checking in with the troops. "I like to come to the shop because it's my responsibility to debrief Newt and the crew," Kenny says. "Stay in touch, baby . . . Stay . . . in . . . touch. . . ." He trails off as he walks around, looking over the Charlotte cars as they get ready. The main car is almost set. It's got springs and shocks in it, and Frank is working on the carburetor. Newt is no longer pacing the shop checking up on people; now he's working on the Charlotte car. He's had Vic Kangas, a consultant working with the team, out in the hauler on the shock dyno all day building shocks, and they're installed now. He's working with them and the springs, closing in on the setup of the car. His intensity has increased during the day to the point where even Kenny leaves Newt alone, talking instead to other crew members. With the terrible testing results the team had last week and their history of bad performances at Charlotte, the car is worrying Kenny, though he's still interested in talking about Monday's race a little.

He wants to talk about trying to get by Jeff Gordon, who finished fourth. "I terrorized him," he laughs. He passed several cars on the outside, and he enjoys talking about how he did that. "You'd take that left front, root 'em in the right rear, and just push 'em up the straightaway," he says. "If I'd've done anything different, I've already thought what I'd do. I'd have more wedge and have the track bar a little bit higher. I'd go into those turns and I'd get perfectly sideways. . . ."

Frank interrupts to ask him whether he ever hit the rev limiter on Monday. That's a tiny chip the engine builder puts in the engine to keep it from revving too high, which could cause it to blow. "Nope," Kenny says. "Not once." Frank smiles. The Yates people put rev limiters on the engines they send to him, but he takes them out and replaces them with limiters a couple of hundred rpms higher. If the driver pushes the engine to the maximum and the limiter kicks in, it can make the engine feel like it's missing on a cylinder or so. It'll make a kind of popping sound that drivers can also mistake for a failing ignition. But it didn't happen at Martinsville, running at more than 9,000 rpms.

Kenny brings his attention back to Charlotte. "What my problem is now, once I go in the corner, it goes low, and I think it's gonna be OK, then the left front goes up," he says to Andy. "I told Newt I didn't know what to do. Maybe cut off some right front fender?" The car does have a kind of hippy fender, compared to the Martinsville car.

Andy shrugs; Aaron walks over. "We used to qualify with a smaller right front fender there," he says, but Andy doubts that will help.

Kenny nods, leaning on the rear deck of one of the cars. "It's like this," he says. "We gotta do something. Because right now, we're a second off." Every other car at practice was running lap times in the 30-second range for Charlotte's 1.5-mile quadoval. Kenny was running more like 31. That's not going to work. "I just can't get that left front to stay down," he says over and over. "We were talking to put a whole shitload of right front spring there, but I don't know."

He's convinced that the nose of the car is hung a quarter inch or so too far to the right, and that's making him roll over too far in the corner. Andy doesn't think it's an aerodynamic problem, and he goes to his corner and gets a pink carpenter's line and runs it across several points on the car, trying to prove to Kenny the nose is where it needs to be. He sets up standards and draws the line across each side of the car; then he drops plumb lines at each side of the nose, each side of the roof, and each side of the spoiler. Kenny's not convinced, but it doesn't make much difference. It's too late to rehang the nose of the car no matter what they determine. Somehow Newt is going to have to use shocks and springs to find a setup for the car that Kenny can drive.

❖

Much work is done in silence, listening to the country station, but the guys talk, like guys do anywhere people work. The surprising thing is how little they talk about the previous week's race. The guys who went to the track have said all they need to on that topic. The shop guys weren't there, and they probably didn't even watch the race on television. "You have to go to church, you have to keep the grass mowed, you have to spend a little time with your family," one says. Many guys either race themselves on the weekends or help friends race on the weekends. They're competing at the highest level of their sport at the shop, and they may race themselves on Saturday night at the local tracks. But when Sunday comes, they're often not even spectators. Their job is done, and their only respite comes at home. "I'll listen to it, sometimes," a crew member says. "But I get enough of that here during the week." These guys work 10- or 12-hour days, anywhere from five to seven days a week. At some point, they've all had to decide how much of their weekend hours they're willing to devote to racing.

Frank, though he has a baby at home, still goes to the track every weekend. If you try to estimate the hours he works each week, he just laughs. He probably puts in 14 a day Monday through Thursday, getting in before 7 A.M., leaving after 9 P.M. Then he tapers off to only 10 or so at the track Friday through Sunday, including travel time home from the race on Sunday. So if you start anywhere below 80, you're probably insulting him.

Aaron has gone the other way. He puts in his 10 or more every day at the shop, possibly including Saturdays, but he doesn't go to the track. "I used to change a tire" on the crew when he worked for another team, he says. "But I decided I had to get a life." He spends at least a day a week home with his family, but when he gets a minute to talk to you about his kids, what he shows you are pictures of his son's favorite activity. Along with Andy's kids, he races a go-cart.

❖

As the day winds down, on an unspoken signal, a few guys walk over to the Charlotte car and push it forward toward the door, then backward and up onto the surface plate. Perfectly level, the surface plate will allow Newt to set the car up according to the specifications he's determined through years of practice at Charlotte, through years of data compiled by Filmar Racing, through discussions with other crew chiefs, and other crew members.

Pushing the Charlotte car onto the surface plate breaks the mood in the shop just a little, and the tension eases. The Charlotte car will be ready tomorrow morning. That was job one, and it's done. Newt will set the car up tonight and tomorrow morning it will go on the hauler to the racetrack. There's plenty more that has to get done before 9 A.M. tomorrow when the hauler unloads, of course. The backup car needs to be set up too. The war wagon, the tool chests, the carts, the coolers, the entire hauler, and everything that goes with it has to be resupplied and cleaned. Dave Ensign has been working on that out in the parking lot all day long, while Vic's been puttering in the shock dyno. Uniforms have to come back from the dry cleaner; air tanks have to be filled and ready to run air guns. Everything has to be washed and ready to go. When the Charlotte car rolls off the hauler in the morning, it has to be ready to get its first technical inspection and then get on the track to practice. Every second of practice is precious, especially to a team with a car running a second off the pace. So everything has to be ready.

But with the Charlotte car done, at least the team won't be showing up without a race car. So as the mood eases, chattering begins. Andy, looking at the car sitting on the surface plate, begins free associating about what might help the car and different ways he's run cars at different tracks. "Oh, jeez, here it comes," Aaron says. He drops his own cigarette lower in his mouth, letting it dangle, and launches into a dead-on impersonation of Andy. "Ah, I remember, ah, one time, one time we were racing in Stafford Springs, we was running a car and the wheel fell off the car. Ah, the car went faster, and we won the race!"

It's getting late, though, so the guys are starting to clear up their workspaces. Everybody pushes brooms, making little piles of brake dust, belts, clipped nylon ties, and parts boxes. By 5:30 a good half of the guys, who arrived by 7:30 in the morning, are at least getting ready to leave.

Not that everything's done and everybody's cheerful.

The car that ran at Dover two weeks ago was slated to run at Rockingham a month from now. At some point during the morning it was decided that the Dover car (the one that ran so bad Newt pulled it behind the wall during the race to change the springs) was the one they ought to give up on, and the Martinsville car had another race in it. So Two-Can, done with the Charlotte car, is now working on the brakes of that car, which will be cleaned up and turned into either the Rockingham car or its backup. It's far too soon to know. The person most upset by this is Frank, who early in the day learned that he had one more engine to disconnect and reinstall, since the Richmond car now turns out to be the Charlotte backup.

"It sucks," he says, wrenches bulging out of his pockets. "There's no need for it." But it's racing, and he's doing it. He knows he won't be going home any time soon.

❖

Not that Frank would be going home soon anyway. Around lunchtime, the shop received a visit from Hank Ausdenmoore, who grabbed Frank, Duze, Rich, Buddy, and Ricky Turner and led them out back into an extra shop that used to be the shop for Kenny's Busch series car when he ran one. Now it's full of extra tires, an old Busch series race car, and a Cup car that doesn't race anymore. The war wagon and other carts that come off the hauler are stored here while Dave cleans up, and the shop is filled with other car pieces and fragments of a race team. With junk. It looks like your garage, or mine.

In one corner are a bench press machine, some free weights, and weight standards. Hank is the team's pit-stop coach and personal trainer, and he's trying to get the guys who go over the wall to beef up some. "We work on speed, quickness, the relationship between the tire carrier and the tire changer," he said. He tried to get them to go through some weight reps, but the day was just too harried. Moments after he led them into the shop, Hank turned his back and Frank disappeared. "He just found out they're changing the backup car, and he's got another motor to put in," Buddy explained.

Hank just nodded, then went into his coaching routine. "You guys were a top-10 team this week," he said. "You finished top 6, but you guys *looked* like a top-10 Winston Cup team all race long."

He didn't get much of their time at lunch; the day was just too hectic. But now, at 5:30, it's time for pit practice. Hank is back, and he leads the pit crew into a room in the office that has a VCR. They play back the tape of the Martinsville race. They watch all the stops several times. They still can't quite determine why the tire went flat in the midrace stop. It may be that the jack dropped early, while Andy Thurman was still tightening the nuts on the left rear. It may be that the tire landed on a lug nut, which was enough to pop the tire, running at extremely low pressure at Martinsville, off the bead. "I want to take it home and study it," Ricky Turner says. "All right," Hank says. "It's show time!"

The gang—including Andy Thurman, who's shown up after his day's work at a race car driving school at Charlotte—heads out back. Aaron gets in the old Winston Cup car and drives it away from the garage into the parking lot. Four tires are lined up along the front of the garage, behind a painted rectangle to suggest the pit stall.

"You guys ready?" Hank asks, stopwatch in hand. An associate of Hank's stands in the middle of the team with a long broom that he'll wave like the pit road sign—that extra person is part of the choreography of the pit stop. "Let's go!" Hank cries. And Aaron guns the motor and squeals in front of the team.

It's amazing. The intensity instantly rises; hearts race, guys scramble. Maybe it's the sound of the race car rumbling, even out in a parking lot next to a scrubby field with the sun going down. It may only be practice, but it's a pit stop. They race around the car, changing all four tires. Andy roars off, in a circle, and gets ready to come back in.

"You kinda let up a little early and left the tire dangling here," Hank says, going over the first try. "He had the gun going the wrong direction and spun that nut off." He turns to the tire carriers. "Just stay with your man and be patient," he says. "OK, let's do it again."

Duze swears and bellyaches, but when the car comes in he runs around, a fierce scowl on his face. Frank, with another engine to install in the shop, just works patiently. After two or three tries, their faces are as black as they get at the racetrack. They run eight stops, Hank analyzing each. When they're done, Frank hustles back inside, and Duze sits and has a smoke. Hank asks whether they want to practice again the next day. "Andy, we've got that ARCA race," Ricky Turner says. Frank and Buddy will be at the racetrack with the car. Still, there are some good points, Duze points out: "We won't have no boss people around." They agree to try to practice at 4:30 the next afternoon.

By 6:30, they're done.

Inside the shop, Two-Can, Dave Ensign, and Eddie talk about loading the hauler first thing in the morning. Frank and Buddy are back at work on the engine of the Charlotte backup, deep under the hood. The Charlotte car, on the surface plate, has an air both of technological mastery and of plain menace. String stands, made from poles welded to old brake rotors, are set up, and parallel lines are run alongside the car. Newt, using metal angled rulers and tape measures, checks clearances from the plate to different points on the car. He measures from the strings to different points on the wheels and sides of the car. He's entering a zone. He's the crew chief, and this is his race car to set up.

Two-Can refills some oil and fluid containers. He's replaced the Charlotte axles with ones that have been worn in a little. "They don't bind so much, save us a little speed," he says. There's nothing that might get this car going the smallest bit faster that they want to overlook. The car's on the bubble and they know it. This is Charlotte.

They don't want to miss the race.

The country station no longer echoes around the shop as guys leave for the day. Frank and Buddy work quietly; Eddie goes back to his office. Newt, his binder on the work table next to the surface plate, looks at his race car.

He concentrates.

❖

Kenny's been gone from the shop for a long time, but his day is far from over. That video game that Danielle had put into his hands during the Martinsville rain out is making its debut for a crowd of press and invitees. So if you drive up to the tony Cajun Queen Restaurant on East Seventh Street in Charlotte at around 8 P.M., you barely have to slow down before you know something special is going on. There are people at folding tables, checking your name against a list and putting plastic Mardi Gras beads around your neck if you are allowed to go in.

But long before you get to the door, you see that bright blue-and-yellow number 81, hood up and floodlit, out on the front lawn of the renovated house that is the Cajun Queen. Winston Cup points leader and wunderkind Jeff Gordon is here; reigning Winston Cup champion Terry Labonte is here. But the car slowing traffic in front of the Cajun Queen isn't Gordon's rainbow number 24, or Labonte's yellow number 5 with the Kellogg's Corn Flakes rooster on it. The show car out front belongs to Kenny Wallace, 34th in the points race, waiting to win his first Winston Cup race, and leader of exactly zero Winston Cup laps in the entire 1997 season. Danielle Randall, floating through the Cajun Queen like the bride at her wedding, explains.

"Kenny's my client," she says. "So is EA Sports," who produced the game. She bats her eyelashes.

Simple as that.

The restaurant, a maze of Big Easy–themed rooms, is choked with people in purple and gold and green plastic beads. TV cameras from the local news glare into the eyes of Michael Waltrip and several of the NFL's Charlotte Panthers who have been invited to race against the drivers. An AM sports talk show broadcasts live, pulling drivers and ballplayers over to talk to fans. Purple, green, and yellow stars decorate the walls, and red beans and sausage, etouffé, and free alcohol keep the mood high. One radio guy interviews Michael Waltrip and thinks he's talking to Panther quartback Kerry Collins. Venerable racing writer Chris Economaki makes an off-color joke about wide receivers and tight ends. It's so crowded that if you're trying to hold a drink it gets jostled enough that you give up and put it down.

Kenny Wallace's unmistakable laugh leads to a small room filled with couches and chairs, where drivers and football players are running "NASCAR 98," the new game. Michael Waltrip is racing Panthers tight end Wesley Walls on one screen, running the Atlanta track. Jeff Gordon races Collins next to him.

ESPN broadcaster Bob Jenkins is supposed to be doing a live call of the racing, but Kenny has sort of taken his position. Standing behind Waltrip, he's shouting out events in his race with Walls. He was going to race Gordon, but he handed the console to Collins: "No, I race him all the time—I can't beat him. *You* race him."

He looks over Waltrip's shoulder. "You can tell he likes that high line already," he says, as Waltrip goes high into the turns. "Look at him go! Michael's high, wide, and handsome!" Gordon glances over to Waltrip's race. "Michael, that's the line I been learning," he says. Waltrip laughs. "I usually get that line blowed off on Saturday in the Busch race."

Going into the next turn Waltrip spins. "Why'd I spin out?" he asks in his high, Kentucky twang. "They got a reset button here?" Kenny's tickled: "Listen to Michael," he laughs. He imitates Waltrip's accent: " 'Ah don't know what happened! Ah spun out!' "

On the other console, Collins beats Gordon, in what turns out to be a trend. The football players regularly beat the racers. "They hit hard, those football players," Kenny says. Collins stands up and addresses a news camera: "I had a real good car there. I just want to thank my sponsors and my team," he says, provoking a roar of approval from the drivers.

Cornered by a TV guy, Kenny talks up the game. "I think they did an excellent job of R&D," he says. "You can get behind another driver and make him loose, you can adjust the steering, you can draft. They got the thing race car drivers know as reality. When I win a race, it will be all because of EA Sports and the NASCAR game. When I get to victory lane I'll thank them."

Upstairs, in a small room with a bar, Kenny's wife, Kim, dressed in a black pants suit, sits quietly with Julie Post, the wife of Steve Post, who works for Danielle, almost exclusively with the Filmar Racing team. Kim is relaxed, enjoying the evening, especially after yesterday's strong finish.

She doesn't spend a lot of time around the track. "I won't be there tomorrow," she says about qualifying at Charlotte. She kind of steers clear of most events like this, but tonight, buoyed by the team's performance at Martinsville, she's just enjoying being around racing.

"I'm real impressed by the new team manager, Eddie D'Hondt, " she says. "I'm happy for all of 'em. We've struggled for let's say the last 10 races. You can't get excited over just one race, but it feels good to have a decent finish." She doesn't try to keep up with Kenny, whether at places like this or in the Winston Cup garage during race weekend.

She comes to the track and stays in the motor home to be with Kenny, but she doesn't spend much time at the garage. "That's his thing, that's his time," she says. "We were married seven years and on our third child before anyone there even knew he was married. Last weekend I cleaned the cabinets in the motor home. I'm not in it for the glory. I'm in it for him." There's a special radio channel on which Kenny can talk to her and driver Eddie Jarvis, so she keeps up during the day that way. She's occasionally in the pit during a race, but not always. "I listen," she says. "I used to never like to listen to the radio, because he'd get angry, and I used to pace, because I get very, very nervous."

But years of racing have worn the edge off that worry, and now she listens for more practical reasons. "So I can kind of brace myself," she laughs. "Do we have to tiptoe tonight? Can we be happy? Can we go eat?"

She turns back to Julie Post, and the two relax. It's a racing do, no doubt, but there's still an element of girls' night out. They're just having a nice time.

A nice time it is. The crowd stays late, everybody getting golf shirts from the EA Sports people to commemorate the occasion. A Winston Cup race is the shit-for-free capital of the world—shirts, hats, tote bags, key chains, all distributed to everyone within reach, inside and outside the racetrack. It's Tuesday night, so this is a little early for the start, but then again, this is Charlotte.

Danielle Randall, with EA Sports and Kenny Wallace as clients, stays in constant motion, checking to make sure everybody talks to everybody. Steve Post chats with Bob Jenkins, Panthers and drivers talk, Kenny talks to everybody, his laugh echoing through the restaurant.

And even that's not it for Danielle; she leans forward a little conspiratorially.

"See that guy?" she points to Regan Smith, a 14-year-old kid, wearing an RSR Team Racing golf shirt. "He's a go-cart racer. He's a client of ours too. He's trying to follow in Jeff Gordon's footsteps." Regan smiles a big smile. He's 14. He's wearing a NASCAR 98 hat and braces. And he's got a public relations company. With his parents footing the bill and driving the truck—he's too young to actually drive—he's raced all over the East Coast this year, he says, winning 10 out of 50 starts. Danielle, he hopes, will help him make his way to the top. "I'm trying to learn just how to talk and get up through the ranks of racing and get experience. Media relations, career planning, how about that?"

How about that.

❖

Back at the Filmar Racing shop, the guys whose career planning has already got them to the Winston Cup level are still hard at work. Eddie can't do any work with the tires until he gets the tires at the track tomorrow, so he does paperwork. He's working on sponsorship deals for next year; he's working on making sure whoever needs to be at Charlotte is on the sponsorship list so they can check in at the NASCAR trailer. Most important, the team is deciding at the last minute it wants to run a race in the Winston West series, a small, almost-Winston Cup level series of 14 races all in the West. The race is in Las Vegas, the week after the Phoenix race, a little more than a month away. Las Vegas will be a Winston Cup track starting next year, so several teams are running the Winston West race, considering it a sort of testing weekend. Since the Square D racing people will be in town for the Charlotte race, Eddie's taking the opportunity to present them with a proposal for the race—how much it would cost them to keep the team out west for another week. He works on numbers at his desk and clears out at around 9:30.

Frank Good finally gets the engine hooked up in the back-up car around 11, cleans up his workbench, and heads for home.

That leaves one man in the Filmar Racing shop. With the Charlotte car on the surface plate, the lines strung, and the shop empty, it's just Newt and the race car. He's got the white three-ring binder with every piece of information Filmar Racing has about what works at Charlotte. Tire air pressures. Shock pressures. Spring weights. How much duct tape ought to cover the grille for prequalifying practice sessions. How high off the ground the chassis ought to sit measured at various points.

Armed with a tape measure, his numbers, a few wrenches, and his wits, he faces down the car. Clambering underneath to reach the A-frames and hubs, he makes minute adjustments to caster, camber, and toe—settings defining the angle and placement of each wheel. He makes tiny half-cranks with long wrenches to raise or lower the springs, shifting the weight of the car from wheel to wheel. He adjusts the track bar in the rear and the sway bar in the front, which help place the car's center of gravity and its roll center.

He adjusts; he fiddles. He checks his notes.

Under the tiny buzzing of the fluorescent lights, alone in a room full of race cars, Newt works alone. Tomorrow is qualifying at Charlotte. The car is a second off the pace. His team is 34th, almost 200 points out of the all-important 30th spot. From somewhere, he's got to find the starting point that will get them a second faster around the 1.5-mile track.

He's never willing to admit what time he goes home that night.

Chapter 4

THE CIRCUS COMES TO CHARLOTTE

Wednesday, October 1

PART 1: THE CHARLOTTE GARAGE

If Martinsville is racing's Wrigley Field—cheap food, homey accommodations, free parking, racing family style—then Charlotte is its Oriole Park at Camden Yards, the big glitzy new theme park that has changed everything. Martinsville holds around 73,000 people. Charlotte holds more than twice that, in about 150,000 bright new plastic seats. Bob Latford, the mustachioed man who publishes *The Inside Line* and chatted with Dick Thompson in the Martinsville press box, called the passage from Martinsville to Charlotte, "from a fan-friendly track to a hassle track. Qualifying at 7 P.M. Wednesday for a 1 o'clock race Sunday"—on a cool, fast evening track for a hot, slower afternoon race. He shook his head. "Because the fans spend more at dinner time." You mean Humpy Wheeler, Charlotte track president and the sport's reigning Barnum, doesn't just want to make a better show, get you in the stands? Latford snorted. "He wants you at the *concession* stands." A three-day race weekend will do anywhere else. For Humpy at Charlotte, it's got to be five days.

And at Filmar Racing, this is what comes of that. A sleepy-eyed group of mechanics, finishing the job of scrambling two race cars into readiness in less than a day. Dave Ensign spent all day yesterday cleaning and restocking the hauler, but he isn't pretending everything's done. "We may not get the dry cleaning until we get out there," he says. "We don't have our nitrogen tanks filled yet." Nitrogen tanks are used to fill tires and to power air wrenches, but in the space of his day yesterday he couldn't make sure they were filled. He'll have to catch up with that at the track. In the meantime, he's filled every cabinet in the hauler with tools and parts. He's also already filled the hallway down the center of the hauler with everything else in the shop that's on wheels: the track tool chest, the war wagon, the crash cart, with its extra axles, A-frames, and rear-end assemblies, and the countless other carts, coolers, tanks, and tools the team will use over the next five days. And now he's backed the hauler to the door, dropped the lift gate, and he's ready for the team to load up the Charlotte car and its backup.

But the team still has a little hustling to do. Fabricator Jerome Aho, hanging around the door because he knows he'll be needed to push before long, takes a moment to clean the Martinsville car, even though most of its body will probably be cut off and replaced before it races again at Rockingham. "So people don't get so greasy just *looking* at it," he says, but that rings false. Say rather because he can't bear to stand around not doing something.

The Charlotte car is still on the surface plate, though the strings are gone from last night. Newt and Frank measure the rear spoiler angle, adjusting the little aluminum struts that secure it. Newt walks around and bangs the air dam, which hangs down from the nose of the car. Two-Can, with an air wrench, takes the lugs off the left side of the car and changes tires, putting on an old practice set that will do for rolling the car to its spot in the garage. Newt has the hood up and adjusts the front springs. He uses a long-handled ratchet to control a screw that sits atop the spring, determining how much pressure is on the spring, and as a result, how high the car sits. He adjusts until he gets the car to the height he wants it and marks it on a piece of yellow tape that stands out sharp against the bright red chassis tube, along with his initials: "5 rds 18 in. NM." Which means, 18 inches from the ground to this spot, with five rounds, or turns, in the jackscrew. That's base camp. That's where this car starts, on that corner, anyhow. Above the wheel, on the fender, another piece of tape. This one just says "25." Newt measures, grabs the car, gives it a shake, measures again.

As Newt, Frank, and Two-Can make final adjustments, a couple of guys work on the other cars in the shop, but most everyone seems to be hanging around the front. Finally Newt sets his face, jerks his head, and a bunch of guys push the Charlotte car off the surface plate, into a cleared space next to it. Then on goes the back-up car, and it goes through a 10-minute mockery of the setup Newt gave the main car last night. Two-Can climbs in the window and flicks the ignition switch; the car starts. Frank tops off the water and steering fluid, flicks a few switches on the dash, watches the water and oil temperature gauges to make sure nothing bizarre is happening.

They jack up one side of the car and slide two low square boxes underneath its wheels, then do the same on the other side. Behind the boxes they then place the four pads of an electronic scale. They roll the car backward onto the scale, then watch the readout. The car has to weigh at least 3,400 pounds; that's NASCAR rules. They check the cross-weight. The percentage of the car's weight on the left rear and right front wheels or the right rear and left front, also called wedge. The usual practice is to have slightly less weight on the left rear and right front, and Newt checks. "What's it got now, Two-Can?" Newt asks; "49.8," Two-Can answers. Newt reaches in with his ratchet, adjusts: "49.3 . . . 49.1." Newt grabs the car and shakes it. "OK," he says. "That's good enough. It's just a backup car."

The crew rolls the backup onto the lift gate and up it goes to the top of the truck, where a low space awaits the cars. The cars have to be 51 inches high, from ground to roof; the car compartment at the top of the hauler isn't more than 54 inches high, if that. Space is too important. There's enough space along the sides for the guys who strap the front of the car down to sidle out past the car. Barring an accident during practice—that is, with any kind of luck at all—that's the last anybody will see of the backup car until it's pulled back off the hauler next Monday.

Dave brings down the lift gate, and the guys get behind the main car. They lean, and moments later Dave is closing up the gate and preparing to leave. He pulls out at 9 A.M., just as the gates open for the Winston Cup haulers at the Speedway five miles down the road. Inside the shop, work on the other race cars doesn't even slow. Two-Can awaits a ride to the racetrack. "Go over and change your clothes while you're waiting," Newt tells him, remembering Eddie's exhortation the day before. "You can't go like that." Two-Can will have a clean uniform on by the time he gets to the track. Andy and Aaron drop plumb lines and make 1/16th-of-an-inch adjustments on the Taurus. Two guys have got started on the Martinsville car with power chisels and reciprocating saws. "Suitcase" Jake is already putting together the car that will run at Phoenix in four weeks. He complains to Newt that he couldn't find the car's jack screws on its cart. Newt just nods. For the next five days the shop will have to find missing jack screws without him. He's got a race to run.

❖

"That's pretty, when they all line up like that."

That's Gloria, the team secretary, talking about watching the team haulers assemble at the track, awaiting the sign that they can enter the speedway and race weekend has officially begun. At Charlotte, the moment loses much of its charm—it occurs at 9 A.M., since qualifying doesn't start until 7 in the evening. For Dave, behind the wheel of the Filmar Racing hauler, that's just as well. It gave him a few more minutes before he had to get away from the shop.

He had a few extra minutes built in, because the haulers enter according to their point standings. Like almost everything on the Winston Cup circuit, points standings determine where your hauler gets parked. That doesn't mean too much at Charlotte, where there is plenty of space for 50 haulers or more, and 50 separate garage stalls for the teams entering the race. But at places like Richmond or Martinsville or Dover, where infield space is cramped, a low points standing—say, 34th—can have you parked in a kind of adjunct row of haulers apart from the points leaders. The unfashionable end of Winston Cup row. Sink far enough back in the standings, that is, and you end up at the little kids' table. Filmar Racing has parked its hauler among the have-nots all season—the number 8 car, the number 42 car, the number 90 car, and the number 75 car are its usual neighbors. And those are also the cars the team is fighting for points. Those are the guys the team has to beat if it plans to reach that magical 30th spot in the points race.

But regardless of where you are in the points standings, Gloria is right. When the haulers all line up, it's pretty. At Charlotte it isn't so much to look at, with trucks kind of nonchalantly filing in and latecomers just fitting in where they can, but the week before, at Martinsville, the scene was magic.

At 6 A.M., in the dark of the morning on the first Friday of autumn, the track was filled with brightly painted Cup team haulers. With orange running lights along their tops, with red lights along the sides, with brushes of orange lights glowing like mustaches across the bottom of the semitrailer grilles, the haulers, slowly massing around the half-mile track, looked like a herd of some great beast gathering at dawn at their watering hole. The drivers arrive overnight and sleep in their cabs, parked three-wide on the backstretch. Their motors purr all night long, their yellow and red lights keeping new arrivals apprised of where they are.

Then at 6, with the sky just beginning to lighten, NASCAR officials join the troopers at the track gate. Late-arriving haulers can enter, but nobody else. Other officials cruise the track in pickups, sipping coffee from Styrofoam cups. A couple of officials take up positions on the infield, and at exactly 6 A.M., they usher in Terry Labonte's hauler. As reigning Winston Cup champion, Labonte has first spot at every race. Then comes Jeff Gordon's hauler. He's leading the points race this year. The remaining truck drivers, knowing where they need to be, slowly grind their gears and lurch into position. "We try to do it with a minimum of shucking and jiving," Dave Ensign says later. "We all know the drill by now."

Hauler after hauler comes in, with NASCAR officials guiding them into their parking places, only a few feet apart, with clipboards and flashlights like airport ground controllers. In description it sounds like synchronized swimming, or like those hippos in *Fantasia* dancing ballet; but it actually looks much more like a procession, like the launching of an ocean liner, say, or a Memorial Day parade of fire trucks and troop carriers. In any case, it's big, it's loud, it's choreographed down to the smallest detail, with huge, humming trailers moving slowly, inches apart, through the dawn. There's something stately, something majestic about it. And even at 6 in the morning, there are a few fans there to watch it.

It's NASCAR.

Getting the parking orders to the semi drivers is handled pretty simply. Sometime during race weekend, usually on Saturday, a NASCAR official comes to each hauler and hands the truck driver or some other team representative a big manila envelope. Inside are parking instructions for the next week's race, a schedule of events—when the haulers can enter, when the gates open for the mechanics, when practice starts, everything up until the start of the race—and parking passes and any other paperwork the team will need at the next race. At Charlotte, the garage, with 50 separate bay doors, sits in the center of a big U of haulers. The teams leading the field are down near the track and the tech inspection bay of the garage. The garages are assigned in exactly the same manner as the haulers. They're numbered from 1 through 50, following the U. So 1 backs up to 50 at the head of the garage. Labonte's in 50, Gordon's in 1, and the rest of the teams alternate their way down.

This means the number 81 Square D Filmar Racing Ford Thunderbird will spend its weekend having its gears, springs, shocks, engine, and tires constantly changed in garage 33. The trucks mass in Turn 3 of the track. One by one they glide into the garage area, angling in as neat as CDs in a rack. Dave pulls the huge hauler, glinting blue and yellow in the sun because he washed it from top to bottom yesterday with Tom Emery's AK-47 power washer, slowly into position between the bright red hauler for the number 8 Circuit City car, driven by Hut Stricklin, and the black hauler for the number 11 car, driven by Brett Bodine. At the same end of things are the usual gang of stragglers: Joe Nemechek's number 42, in its rainbow colors, and Dick Trickle's green-and-black number 90. The little gang at the end of the pack, the guys desperate to keep up. One by one, the lift gates of the haulers flap backward, the motion moving its way down the row of trucks like dominoes.

Time to open up. It's nine o'clock on Wednesday at Charlotte. It's race weekend. And everybody's here.

❖

If you've ever watched the circus come to town, or the state fair, or the touring production of a Broadway show, you know exactly what it looks like to see a Winston Cup team begin setting up shop for a five-day stay in a new garage. First, those lift gates flop down off the back of the trucks, slowly ratcheting down to horizontal, then levitating to the car space. The crew clambers into the crawl space, and out rolls a race car. It hovers slowly down as crew members lean on it casually, surveying the multicolored hubbub of the garage. If you look down the row of haulers at the right moment, you can see eight or ten race cars making their slow descent as crew members wave at each other and holler greetings.

Then the number 81 car hits the ground and the Filmar crew hunches into the car and pushes it to garage 33.

Team members park their cars in the infield and pour into the garage, separated from the infield by an iron picket fence. Equipment spills out of haulers, filling the empty garage almost instantly. At 9 A.M. the asphalt was empty of even a single hauler. By 9:45 it's filled with purpose and motion. Railings for viewing platforms go up atop haulers, ladders angling first up to the lift gate, sticking straight out, and from there up to the roof of the hauler. The lift gates become canopies, buttressed on each side by chains connected to the hauler corners. Clanking up or down on their chains, they look like drawbridges, or portcullises. The platform railings look like ramparts, and on some haulers, outlined against the empty, gray seats of the sun-drenched home stretch of the speedway, umbrellas go up. Here the blue-and-yellow Lowe's Home Center logo from the 31 car, there a black QVC above the number 7. With the fences, the chains, the gates of the haulers surrounding it and the bright colored fabric of the umbrellas and the team uniforms within, the garage looks like the encampment inside a castle courtyard for a jousting tournament. Which, of course, is basically what it is. On the first day of October the sun in the crystal blue sky is still bright enough for the shadows cast by those umbrellas and lift gates to look inviting.

Setting up the individual garage bays for a five-day stay takes moments. By 10 A.M., if you stand on the yellow-painted center aisle that runs down the long, low garage, you'll see 50 cars surrounded by 50 teams. Each bay is set up about the same. The team's tool chest—about 6 feet by 4 feet by 2 feet, with a central workbench, often with a light above the workbench—sits along the center aisle, keeping a measure of distance between the team and the crowds of people that develop as race weekend progresses. The tool chest tends to be the only large piece of equipment not painted in team colors. Tool chests are red, just like the one in your shed, with the team's name painted on somewhere and the team's tool supplier—Mac, Snap-on, Craftsman—getting huge play. They ought to; they supplied the chests for free.

The tool chest functions as the command module of the team's garage area, and not just because it holds all the wrenches, springs, extra shocks, extra axles and track bars, spark plugs, gauges, cleaning fluids, and rags the team will grab again and again. Notes to the team are posted there just as they are on the hauler bulletin board. "Pit 29," a note will say after the team has chosen its pit, or "meet lobby, 6:45" scribbled for a day when the team is staying at a hotel and needs transportation to the track.

Most important, taped to the side of the tool chest—and to the wall in the hauler—is a photocopied schedule of the weekend's events, with key times highlighted in green: when the garage opens each day, when Winston Cup practice sessions begin and end, when the drawing for qualifying positions takes place, and when the race starts. In Martinsville, the information for the entire weekend occupied a single sheet of paper, including events for Thursday, when the Craftsman Truck Series teams got started.

The Charlotte listings take up three full sheets of paper, taped one above the other. They start with two days ago—Monday—when the ARCA cars first showed up. They include everything from what time the track is closed for lunch each day to how much customers are paying to come and watch the practices: It's free on Monday to watch the ARCA guys nurse their cars around the track. Tuesday, when the Winston Cup teams haven't shown up yet (the Busch teams haven't shown up yet for the Saturday race, for that matter), it's $5, a buck for kids 6 to 12. Parking is free, though.

Not by Wednesday. To watch qualifying on Wednesday night—tonight—it's going to cost you $15, $20 if you want the commemorative ticket (you can save by buying in advance). Parking is $5 a car. It goes on like that, listing when the corporate suites open, which gates to the track, and across the track, are open and when.

Of course, it's not just detail that makes this weekend more complex. Martinsville followed the usual race weekend rhythm: Haulers in at 6 A.M. Friday; garage opens at 7. Practice starts at 11:30, ends at 2. Qualifying at 3, more practice starting around 5. Saturday, practice in the morning, second-round qualifying, one more practice, then race day. Four practices, then the race. The Charlotte weekend has no fewer than six practice periods, one of them lasting almost four hours. The fun never stops.

That informative tool chest is the only makeshift wall between the team and its competitors. And the only barrier between the teams and the thousands of fans, corporate types, salespeople, and hangers-on who overrun the garage, especially at Charlotte. Still, the people won't overrun the team's workspace. Not that they wouldn't if they could; there's just no room.

Apart from that tool chest, the team's garage, about 10 feet wide and 15 feet deep, will hold not only the race car and five or six guys climbing over it. It'll hold four floor jacks, to hold the car up off its wheels; two hydraulic jacks, to lift it; a pressurized water tank, for radiators, about the size of a hot water heater; a recirculator, about as big as an air conditioner (called "the regurgitator" by Frank Good, it rapidly cools water in the radiator); several piles of tires; water cans; pumps; hoses; and whatever rear end gears, brake rotors, axles, wires, spark plugs, filters, radiators, and other equipment happens not to be attached to the race car at a given moment. Fans will pay attention to and even generally respect the used-car-lot-style pennants strung from trash can to trash can outside the garage, but even if they didn't, they'd cause so much mayhem knocking things over that they wouldn't stay underfoot for long.

Like any traveling troupe, the teams quickly make the garage into home. They do this every week, and they're at Charlotte twice a year. They know the drill. Nobody has to be told what to do. The car numbers have been chalked onto the concrete of the garage posts. Some teams replace that with a sticker or decal, or even with their team number made of colored duct tape. The Filmar guys have more important things to do.

❖

One important thing to do is to get ice: A race team needs ice the way a race car needs gas. They put ice in the pressurized water tanks they use to cool down engines, and they use ice to keep drinks and food cold in the round or rectangular orange Gatorade coolers that every team has in abundance. So first thing, somebody from each team takes a gas cart or a three-wheeled cart or a tire cart and goes off to get ice, usually from some sort of truck making its way around the garage. Not here. There's supposed to be a vendor with a little shop set up somewhere. So when a guy in a black uniform pulls a bright yellow cart from the number 4 Kodak car, he looks like he has a purpose, and people start following him. A guy in a red Circuit City uniform joins in; soon a black Goodwrench uniform from the number 3 car follows, then a red-and-yellow McDonald's guy, and a bright orange Tide guy. Then they're stopped by a guy in shorts, a navy blue golf shirt, and a headset. He says he works for speedway catering.

"Guys, you have to go by the Wendy's hut this year," he says, pointing to a frozen drink stand run by Wendy's. "Everything's changed for race week."

The little gang heads there and finds a machine, but no ice. A DuPont crewman joins in. He's wearing not the rainbow colors of the 24 car but the gray shirt with red sleeve cuffs worn by his team, the number 5 team, and the number 25 Budweiser car, all owned by Hendrick Motorsports. At least until race day, for these guys, team identity is more important than sponsor identity.

The troop of ice hunters doubles back and splits. Half of them end up behind The Pit Stop, the little restaurant that serves the infield. The Pit Stop has ice, and so what if it's for food they plan to sell. It's race week, and these guys have jobs to do. A clerk there looks confused, and things threaten to turn ugly. Then the Goodwrench guy comes back, gives the high sign, and the whole gang heads off behind him. They find a truck and a big ice machine at the fence gate they walked through moments ago: A 40-pound bag of ice is $8. Each team gets four, and they help each other load up and toddle off, pulling their wagons.

❖

In the garage, each team performs the same tasks. They quickly fill the car with oil, water, and coolants, doing little more than tightening bolts. If anybody has nothing to do, he reflexively polishes the car with SD-20, an all-purpose spray cleaner, cans of which infest the garage area like roaches. While they're working, an official, in red-and-white Winston attire, comes by and checks engines, using a little vacuum measuring tube to check the car's compression and cubic inches of displacement. Compression is limited to 14:1, and it comes up exact. Another official wriggles under the car to have a look and to place a little transponder, the size of a pack of cigarettes, into a compartment on the chassis trailing arm. That will enable NASCAR to keep track of the cars' lap times during practice, so that the scoring computer can show teams the speeds of all cars on the track.

While the official is under the number 81, Newt asks him about their air wrench that got tangled in Kenny Schrader's car at Martinsville. The official gives a noncommittal grunt and heads off.

Frank Good, meanwhile, applies a layer of weather stripping to spark plugs, gluing spacers to their ends. That's to affect the placement of the spark in the cylinder? That's to change the way the gas-air mixture explodes, subtly altering horsepower and torque, making the car faster on straightaways or stronger in the corners?

"That's a Band-Aid for a fuck up," he says. "They made a mistake when they machined the motor." It's great renting motors from another team. He sighs and sets the plugs, in a little block of wood with eight holes in it, on the tool chest to dry. Jeremy has shown up from the Yates shop. He'll be around all weekend, helping (and Frank would say keeping an eye on his engines). He's part of the Yates engine deal. Jeremy is a smiling young guy in his early 20s, pale and slightly round, with a perpetual grin that sometimes looks dazed. He wears high-top tennis shoes and gives off the impression of someone's kid brother who hangs around without getting in the way and eventually turns out to be kind of cool. Frank has shortened "Jeremy" to "Germ" and somehow he's ended up "Squirm," which stuck. He's Squirm, and he seems always to walk in on the end of a conversation.

"You talking about how to take the rev limiter off?" he asks Frank, and Frank smiles. "Typical engine guy."

❖

Eddie heads with a cart to the Goodyear building to get tires.

Goodyear, the only company providing tires for Winston Cup races, has its own building inside most speedways. In recent years Hoosier Tires mounted a challenge to Goodyear, but after a fractious—and dangerous—period that people refer to as the tire wars, NASCAR decided to stick with Goodyear. When two companies were competing, NASCAR believed, the companies were trying so hard to come up with composites that would provide stickier tires—which would give better traction and more speed, though they wouldn't last as long—that safety was getting lost in the shuffle. After many accidents that drivers blamed on tires wearing out too quickly, NASCAR chose Goodyear. Goodyear designs tires for each track: for how fast the cars are going in the turns, for how the cars tend to be set up. For example, the track at Rockingham is in the North Carolina sand hills. The asphalt there just has more sand in it, which makes for a more abrasive surface. Which means a stiffer, less-sticky tire.

Right-side tires are a little larger than left-side tires. That's called stagger, and it helps the car keep turning left. The seams are in different places so that the force of the car doesn't separate the parts under the two Gs or so of force the cars undergo in turns. The crews replace the air in the tires with nitrogen, which expands less under pressure. Plus, when you fill a tire with air from the atmosphere, there's always moisture in there. When you fill a tire with nitrogen from a tank, there's no moisture. Just one more tiny variable the team can control.

But that's only the beginning. Tires, as Newt says, are a specialty in themselves, and every team has a tire guy. Eddie talks about someone else taking over for him at Filmar, but it's clear that at the moment, at least, nobody can provide the experience he's got.

Each team gets three sets of tires for use during practice and qualifying; teams that have to requalify on the second day are allowed to purchase a fourth set for their second qualifying run. Teams can purchase as many sets as they like for the race, and they can buy additional sets even during the race—from Goodyear or from other teams—if they want to. But the limit to three sets during practice and qualifying is a way to keep the well-funded teams from getting a little extra speed by having set after set of new tires to keep practicing for the qualifying run. Thus, during practice, the teams have to keep one set of tires ready for qualifying, either leaving them smooth or taking a lap or more on them if practice shows that tires that have a lap or two on them run faster. This means that the teams have to confine their entire practice, basically, to two sets of tires.

At the Goodyear building, a simple system is underway. Goodyear has received the teams' rims from the companies who retrieved the tires after the Martinsville race. Two semi-trailers of tires back up to the building, and Goodyear guys, in blue-and-yellow Goodyear mechanic's shirts and heavy aprons, roll tires, consisting of an outer and an inner tire, into the shop. There, rows of about 10 guys pop the tires onto the rims with automatic rimmers, use long steel tire tools to run the beads inside the rims, and then fill them with air. Complete sets are stacked outside the building, in order, of course, of Winston Cup points. Piles of tires grow like a forest behind the Goodyear building, and the tire guy from each team shows up early with a chest-high two-wheeled cart that can take a full set of tires at a time. Some teams have two-tiered rolling carts, like the ones gyms use for basketballs, but most use the two-wheelers. One set of tires is all the tire guy can work on at a time, anyhow.

Eddie stands over his tires, marking them up the minute he gets them. He measures the circumference of each tire, figuring out which lefts he'll put with which rights to give the stagger he wants. He also checks the codes Goodyear uses on the tires to mark date and time of production. "See, this one's a week old, this one's three weeks old," he says. "You don't want to pair a new tire with an older one." Goodyear assures the tire guys that the codes mean nothing and that the tire guys are wasting their time. The tire guys don't listen.

He uses a bright pink marker to circle tiny lead weights on the rims, which the Goodyear guys have put on during balancing. If a tire develops a vibration, he'll be able to check to see if any weights are missing. He'll let the air out of the tires and refill them with nitrogen once he's got them back at the hauler.

If a bunch of guys in the same-colored shirts pushing a car around is the most common species of fauna sighted in the garage, the pile of tires is the ubiquitous flora—the crabgrass of racing, but surely a beloved crabgrass.

They're stacked alongside the cars in the garage when there's room. Otherwise they go where they may: under the lift gate, somewhere else near the hauler, in any corner of the fenced garage area. By the middle of the weekend, tires (new ones, called "stickers" for the Goodyear stickers still on them, or "scuffs," which are worn to one degree or another on practice laps) will sprout in chest-height piles of four throughout the garage like mushrooms after a spring rain.

❖

A short few minutes of organizing the car and the guys drop it off the jacks and push it toward its first technical inspection of the weekend.

As the cars line up for that first inspection, the garage starts to lose its feeling of newness. Again, groups of guys in blue or orange or red or black lean into cars. First they push them through the Unocal gas pumps and fill their 22-gallon tanks with the 110-octane leaded gas that the cars run. Then the cars roll down a hill back toward the Tech Inspection bay, quickly backing up into a line of 10 or 15 cars, each car surrounded by five or six crew members like a queen bee surrounded by workers. This is greeting time. "Hey bub, how you doing?" and tossing a wadded-up piece of duct tape or newspaper. Shop time, goofing around time.

Leaning on the number 81 car, Frank reads *Winston Cup Scene*, the sort of trade paper of the circuit, published under NASCAR's watchful eye and distributed free to haulers and placed in piles in press rooms and information centers. He's found this week's only mention of his team, and he's annoyed. "For the most part, Kenny Wallace has had one of those seasons one would just as soon forget," begins a five-paragraph brief. "For the most part?" Frank asks, disgusted. "We won two poles!" He gives the paper another five minutes then hands it off. It's time to get the car inspected.

Inspection, of course, is how NASCAR officials make sure that the teams stick to the rules of racing. The teams don't complain about the inspections. When Bill France founded NASCAR in 1947, one of the first orders of business was to let people know what the rules were and to enforce them. In fact, after the very first NASCAR race in the series that would become the Winston Cup, on June 19, 1949, the officials changed the result when inspectors found the winner had used a block of wood to stiffen his springs—expressly against the rules. Team members talking about their early days in racing will talk about running at little county tracks where "they make the rules up as they go along." Genuine rules and actual enforcement are part of what has brought stock car racing out of the backwoods and onto ESPN.

The first inspection is simple. Even before the cars get into the inspection bay, officials work their way down the line and use huge templates—exactly like the ones hanging on the walls in every Cup shop—to make sure that the cars aren't bigger, smaller, wider, narrower, lower, or higher than they're allowed to be. The slit in the back of the spoiler of a Winston Cup car, in fact, is there to let the silhouette template fit in. The spoiler angle and size are checked; a gauge drops a metal rod above the rear deck lid to make sure it's the right height. An official takes a little wheeled aluminum block on the end of a pole and runs it underneath the car's front air dam to make sure it has the minimum clearance. The officials have dozens of different templates and probably thousands of checks they can make, and they can make them whenever they want to.

The cars have to clear initial inspection before they're allowed on the track for the first practice. There'll be spot-inspections all weekend long, and each car has to go through inspection again before qualifying and again before the race. If a car qualifies or finishes strong, it will be inspected again, as will other cars chosen at random. A car going through second-round qualifying (a car that isn't among the 25 fastest on the first round) will be inspected again, and possibly after the second qualifying run as well. A car that had to qualify both days could get complete inspections from NASCAR officials up to seven times during a race weekend.

And even so, the officials figure they're only doing part of the job. One official says, opening his arms wide, gesturing around at the open garage, "Our best check is the other teams." With no place to hide, teams can get creative, but not too creative.

Filmar public relations guy Steve Post agrees. He shows up at the track early, walking around the garage, just to be around. With the sponsor paying close to $4 million to keep the race team running, Square D wants to make sure it's getting what it's paying for. Here at Charlotte they've bought a suite above Turn 2, and they'll have a few guests in tonight for the qualifying. Then they'll have more guests around all weekend. Steve needs to make sure that everybody gets what they need, that Kenny's up in the suite if he's supposed to address a group of people, that he makes it to the Sunday morning hospitality on time, that anything the team needs from the sponsor is taken care of.

But if there's one thing that Steve Post doesn't mind, it's walking around a race track garage. He's been watching stock car racing since he was a little kid in New York state and built Popsicle stick stands for his Matchbox car race track. He looks around him: cars up on jacks, hoods up, wheels off. Arms and legs of every color seem to have sprouted from the cars, and tools are placed in empty hands. You rarely see an entire crew member. Here, two arms wave out of a window as a mechanic fixing a pedal gestures for a tool, there legs bend from underneath an exhaust system, as somebody changes a rear end gear that a crew chief changed his mind on before the first lap of practice. The air is filled with the sound of wrenches clattering on concrete, air wrenches whirring, and the occasional roar of an engine. The first engine that's cranked up on a weekend seems to change things. Its sound rattles off the garage walls, echoes off the other cars, kind of shakes around the garage, announcing that race weekend has started. Before long, like a lion answering a call, another car responds, a rev, a lull, two more revs, and then more silence. Things are getting started.

And Steve gets to walk around in the middle of it. And so do, already, hundreds of other people who aren't on race crews. Reporters wander everywhere, and there are never fewer than two television cameras visible. People placed on lists by the sponsors, by the race teams, by NASCAR itself, have passes that will enable them virtually unlimited access to the garage—and the pits—from the moment the gate opens until the end of the race on Sunday. That inconceivable access is one of the things that makes NASCAR racing different from other kinds of racing and keeps it competitive. "Indy cars each have separate garages," Steve points out. "They can hide," from fans, from the press, from each other. "We're all together. And we're closest to the guys we're fighting in points. The best inspectors we have is each other. Guys see somebody do something they're not allowed to do, they're going to narc." True, though crew members don't often squeal so much as ask pointed questions of officials: "That spoiler—we're allowed to have ours that low?" "Them valve springs, that's a new-looking deal. What are they made of?" Walk through the NASCAR hauler during any race week and you might find any number of parts laying on the counter, with a tag saying where they came from. If it looks wrong, it won't go on the car. Crew members think of reasons to walk through the NASCAR hauler just to glance at what might have been snatched up. And not just to see who got caught. "I get ideas that way," Frank Good says. He also looks over the shoulders of one official as he checks compression and displacement on other cars. "He likes me," Frank smiles. "He lets me."

The officials finish checking the number 81 car with templates; they roll it under a bar that drops a plumb-bob to check its height. Then they roll it onto a scale exactly like the one that Newt used back at the Filmar Racing shop. It has a little screen with red dots making its numbers: "Let's check out that little R2-D2 and see what we got," Newt says. R2-D2 says the car weighs 3,459 pounds—more than the 3,400-pound minimum—and that it has 1,606 of those pounds on the right-side tires. That clears too. An official leans over the car and sticks a fluorescent green dot at the top of the windshield. Pass.

And another lean, and another push back to the garage. They've got less than an hour to tighten and check everything before the first practice starts. For the first time all weekend they plug the car into the generator, and they get to work. Engines sound in earnest now, not just revving but idling to warm up. Generators putt, but their sound is overwhelmed by the engines from every corner of the garage. The first practice session hasn't begun yet, but every team has its game face on.

Qualifying is only six hours away.

❖

PART 2: MAKING THE SHOW

To understand the intensity of concentration around the car before qualifying, you have to understand that the teams aren't thinking so much about where they're going to start as *whether* they're going to start. There are 43 starting positions in a Winston Cup field, and anywhere from 46 to near 60 cars show up for a given weekend. If you've licensed a number from NASCAR, if your driver has been approved, and you want to spend the money, you can show up with your race car and give it your best shot. At Charlotte there are 50 cars wrestling for the chance to race. That means after second-round qualifying on Thursday, seven will go home, seven haulers slinking out of the speedway before the race, before even the Busch race. Before they'd even *show up* for most races, for crying out loud, guys will be driving home from this race in defeat.

Think about this hard. You're working 100-hour weeks. Your team is spending millions of dollars to field a race car. And then you travel away from your family every weekend, and it might turn out that the officials just tell you to go on home. It's kind of like playing for, say, the Yankees and showing up in Cleveland for a game, only after batting practice the umpires walk into your locker room and say, "Sorry guys, but today you just purely suck. Looks like Seattle's going to play today instead of you. See you next time, though, and good luck."

So job one in qualifying is to make the race.

Qualifying is simple: Each car runs a single lap for time, alone on the racetrack, as fast as it can. Fastest guy starts first, on the pole, the inside front-row spot. He also gets $5,000 from Busch Beer, which sponsors the Busch Pole Award for each race.

During the first day's qualifying, the top 25 cars make the race. Everyone else has a decision to make: Requalify or stand on time? If you requalify the next day, your time is erased and you try again. If it turns out your first time would have made the race and your second time doesn't, too bad. If you stand on your time and track conditions change and people who had no business going faster than you go faster and you miss the race, too bad. The driver says, "Just one of them racin' deals" into the ESPN cameras, you load up, and you go home. Just one of them racin' deals. And after second-round qualifying, when anywhere from 3 to 15 haulers slink out of the Winston Cup paddock, out through the infield and home, every crew member watches them pull out. "The worst feeling in the world," everybody says. "I just wish everybody could make the race," everybody says. And then everybody vows to stay just that little bit more prepared next week so that it doesn't happen to them.

So yeah, everyone wants to qualify well. But just qualifying will be enough, especially when your team is running 34th in points. Just making the race is something, especially with the sponsors' CEOs, the CFOs, everybody and their wives in to see the race.

Qualifying order, by the way, is competitive, so it isn't determined by points standings. It's too important. Track speeds change over the course of a day. On a sunny day, for example, you'd want to qualify first: The track gets more slippery—"greasier," they say, pronounced with a "z"—as a sunny day goes on. Tires grip less, so laps get slower. On the other hand, if the day starts out sunny and the forecast calls for clouds, everyone wants to wait until late to qualify. Allowing the points leaders to choose the best qualifying positions would simply give the leading teams too much control. So instead of giving owners or drivers any choice in the matter, NASCAR runs a little lottery. According to the schedule of events, the drawing for Busch Pole Qualifying here at Charlotte is at 1 P.M., right before the first practice. It takes place at the NASCAR Winston Cup hauler, which is parked against the garage area wall near the tech inspection end of the garage.

The NASCAR hauler is, of course, where the power sits during race weekend. That's where competition director Gary Nelson is, when he's not running technical inspection or looking over the shoulder of team mechanics to make sure they're not carving tenths of seconds off their lap times by breaking any of the rules they've got in the gray Winston Cup Series Rule Book sticking out of their back pockets. That's where NASCAR President Bill France is, when he shows up. That's where the information is.

The NASCAR hauler has a back door, like all the other haulers, but it also has a side door, and that's where the action is. A white dry-erase board keeps teams and officials abreast of anything they need to know: which cylinder officials will be testing for compression ratio, what time the driver and crew chief meeting is set for on Sunday, what time teams have to announce whether they plan to stand on their first-round times or to requalify. There's a bulletin board on which the entry blank for that week's race is posted, along with a photocopied sheet of the points leaders and whatever piece of race-weekend information is most current: the qualifying order when it's chosen, the practice speeds from the most recent practice, the qualifying results, the sign-up sheet where crew chiefs indicate whether they're standing on their times, the second-round qualifying order, the results, the final lineup of the race. There's plenty of space for anything else. One team is selling an old race hauler: "$175,000, great condition." It'll probably go to a competitive Busch Series team, or to a Winston Cup team starting up. Someone else is selling a house on Lake Norman. When Kyle Petty is organizing a Harley ride for charity, he tacks a flyer on this board. When Motor Racing Outreach, the NASCAR church and bible study group, plans an event, it tacks a flyer on this bulletin board.

At the moment there's not much there beyond the listing of events that's already taped up on every tool chest and every hauler. The bulletin board is almost empty, next to the little stairway leading into the hauler, with two potted yellow and orange hardy mums on either side giving that nice sense of family that everyone in the garage always talks about.

But the first piece of information for that bulletin board is about to go up. At the back end of the hauler, a woman in her 50s with red hair and a bright red Simpson Race Products straw hat is helping NASCAR official Morris Metcalfe perform one of the first official tasks of race weekend: They're drawing lots for qualifying position. To keep qualifying position unbiased, teams send a member or two—usually the owner—to the NASCAR hauler to, basically, pull a number out of a hat. Like everything else, teams pull numbers in order of points standing, though that's only done out of respect here. This is truly the luck of the draw. Morris, a smiling man in his late 60s who is NASCAR's chief scorer, loads 50 tiny red bingo balls into a little round red cage on a folding card table, and he begins turning the crank. Because the engines in the garage have begun roaring in earnest now, the entire operation is done in silence, a pantomime of a drawing.

One by one team members walk up; Morris cranks, opens the door. The guy sticks a hand in, looks at his ball, shrugs, hands it to Morris. He grins a big grin, and slowly turns from one side to the other, his arm held out, showing everyone: The number 24 team picked position 18; and the woman, Nikki Taylor, writes the number down on a legal pad, which she's got lined with numbers from 1 to 50. Morris writes the numbers down too, on a photocopied sheet listing the cars by points standings. They look over each other's shoulders to make sure they've both got the same outcomes going. When no team member emerges to crank or draw, Morris looks around a couple of times, making the car's number with his fingers. No takers? He draws himself, showing the ball just the same.

When it's the 34th car's turn, nobody walks up. Filbert still has to tend to his business interests in Nashville. He hasn't arrived yet to blow on his hands, like a dice player, and draw the number the way he often does. Morris draws: 31. Good. The track will be cooling down all evening and speeding up as it cools. The number 81 car, already on the bubble, can use the late slot.

When all the numbers are drawn, Morris and Nikki check their numbers. They agree, and the bingo balls and the cage go in a torn cardboard box, the card table is folded up, and Nikki and Morris go into the NASCAR hauler to photocopy the qualifying order on the copy machine that slides out of one of the hauler's cabinets. Moments later, members of the different teams clamor at the side door for copies. Nikki knows them each by face, and is strict: one copy per team, and none for writers or hangers-on. Those will be available, in a much more professional-looking, computer-generated format, in the media center in a few minutes.

For now, these are for the people who need them immediately. Dave Ensign, sent from the Square D hauler, grabs one and hustles back along the row to hand it to Newt, who reads it, slowly nodding his head.

❖

Qualifying has been an issue for the Filmar Racing team this year. Kenny has won two poles and qualified in the top 10 five times. On the other hand, 14 times the team has had to go home from the track after the first day of qualifying still not knowing whether they'll be running the race on Sunday. They've only missed one race, the inaugural California 500, but second-round qualifying takes a lot out of a team. That means out of 27 races so far, 14 times they've come to the track the day after qualifying, and while 25 teams were starting work on their race setups, the Filmar guys had to either spend practice time working on improving the setup for another qualifying run or stand on their time and sweat out the second round of qualifying, hoping they didn't get bumped from the race. Jeff Gordon, for an example of how the other half lives, has failed to make the top 25 in the first round exactly once all season. If his cars look better on the track, one of the many reasons is because his team gets to use every second of practice working on race setup.

Those couple of poles they've won are nice, but Filbert Martocci doesn't put much stock in winning poles. "We've shown we can make drag cars," he said wryly before a recent race, climbing up to the top of the hauler to watch the practice runs. "We need to figure out how to make cars that go fast for a whole race. You can make anything go fast for two laps." Qualifying at Martinsville and shorter tracks is a two-lap affair. Here at Charlotte it's one: The car will take off from pit road, build up speed once around the track, and have a single lap to qualify. So today it would be nice if it turns out that his guys *can* build a drag car.

That's what they're trying to do. While Morris and Nikki were pulling the bingo balls out of their cage, 50 race teams were pushing their cars into a long line waiting for 1:30 to roll around and the NASCAR official at the gate to start letting the cars on. Kenny Wallace sits in the number 81 at the head of the line: Every practice lap is important to a car running a second slower than everybody else. Eddie, Newt, Vic Kangas, and Dave Ensign climb to the top of the hauler and take up positions. Headsets are on against the noise that will start in a moment. A laptop computer up there is connected to the scoring program. Its screen surrounded by a blue metal glare shield, it will keep the guys posted not only on Kenny's speeds but the speeds of every other car on the track. Just the same, Newt and Vic have stopwatches; Eddie, like dozens of crew members atop dozens of haulers in the garage, has a clipboard with two stopwatches at the top. He can clock Kenny and any other driver he wants, or can clock Kenny on a full lap and a partial lap (how long it takes him, say, to cover the backstretch, or to clear Turns 3 and 4). At 1:45, the official steps out of the way and Kenny runs the first practice lap of the weekend. Alone on the track, the car makes a hollow, almost plaintive whine. Echoing off the mostly empty seats of the speedway (the first gates opened at 1:30, the moment practice started), the car sounds in a way like the world's largest, angriest bee. Even just getting started, even at far from full speed, the car looks fast.

It's a race car.

By the time he's finished his lap, the NASCAR official at the head of the line on pit road is letting other cars on, and the track is filled with race cars. Buffeted back by the banked track and the stands, the noise begins to build in the garage.

Kenny's first comment is comforting: "Man," he says after only a couple of laps, "this thing feels a *ton* better. Like the tires are sticking better. The car's real reactive. It's real neutral all the way around the track right now; I just need to get tightened up all the way around. I'm coming in."

Newt nods, as though he could see Kenny, then hits the talk button on the side of his headset. "Well, we changed a ton of stuff on that car. Nose weights, springs, shocks. I'll fill you in on it. You guys get a tire sheet? And Two-Can, let's put that 375 in the left rear." That's a 375-pound spring. It's a little lighter than the one the car started with. That lighter spring will resist the pressure the car places on it slightly less, keeping the left rear a fraction lower, which will tilt more weight off the right front and the right rear. A little more weight in the left rear of the car, which will shift onto the right rear in the turns, will help keep the car from losing traction in the turns, keep the rear from wanting to slide out from under the driver. From breaking loose.

Kenny goes low in Turn 3, slides down pit road, and turns behind the pit wall into the garage. Buddy stands far out from the garage, pointing him in like a guy parking cars at a football game. Kenny gets out of the car, takes a swig of Coke brought to him by Eddie Jarvis, his motor home driver. Buddy has the car jacked up in an instant, and Two-Can gets busy underneath it, changing that spring. Eddie, down off the hauler, takes the temperatures of the tires and checks wear, looking for clues to the car's handling. Frank pulls out the spark plugs, takes a look, puts them back in.

So that spring is the first tiny adjustment to the car in this practice session, which lasts until 5 P.M. The first of hundreds.

This first practice session is running, and every car follows the same routine: a few laps out, then back to the garage for a few cranks on the jack screws, a pound more or less air pressure in a tire or two, a crank up or down on the track bar, a new sway bar or shock absorber or spring. Cars duck into and out of their garages like actors running to stagehands for props and clothes between scenes. A dozen hands grab it in a dozen places, making changes and adjustments, and then someone from the garage stands out in the asphalt to make sure another race car isn't coming, signals the driver to pull out, and the car darts back to the track.

In fact, the whole practice has the feel of standing backstage at a late dress rehearsal of a play. It's noisy and busy, and everybody's rushing around in costume, but it's not show time yet and the intensity of performing isn't there, even if nobody's spending much time goofing off.

The roar in the racetrack builds to odd effect. When Kenny glides down the garage asphalt, the outside roar and the dampening effect of the headset make him seem to do so silently. In fact, the whole garage has a strange, silent feel during practice. Whispering gets a child's attention faster than shouting; just so, the constant battering of engine noise makes your ears, in a way, just ignore it. And since it drowns out everything else, the noise simply takes sound out of the picture. So your perceptions shift, and your world becomes principally visual. A car sliding through the garage under the glaring sunlight goes smooth as a shark; a flash of green, a burst of red, a sudden glint of yellow as a car pulls into a slot in the garage, or backs out of one and jerks suddenly, like a jet taking off, back toward the entrance to the track. With very few corporate types and hangers-on in the garage yet, the cars speed around, and you have to watch closely. In the silence, a car cruising up at 30 or 40 miles per hour may not get your attention quickly, and drivers despise applying the brakes in the garage for daydreaming onlookers.

When the car's back on the track, the guys in the garage light cigarettes and stand outside the door, watching the flashes of color barely visible between carts, haulers, and infield structures like the media center. Still, Frank carries a stopwatch and expertly clicks it when the blue-and-yellow 81 car zips by, clicks it again the next time.

So far the news isn't great. His fastest time after an hour of practice is 30.803 for a lap. The fastest guys out there are going less than 30 seconds a lap. Nobody expected the car to be among the leaders. But Kenny's running 42nd quick. That's not going to work. Plenty more adjustments to make.

Looks like nobody at Filmar Racing can expect an early dinner.

❖

Adjusting a race car is either the simplest or the most complex thing in the world, depending on whether you just did it right or just did it wrong, according to mechanics. Vic Kangas, when he isn't standing atop the hauler clicking a stopwatch and appraising the cars, stands down in the hauler, in a 2-foot-square office in the back, working on shock absorbers. He's got a complete shock dyno set up there. It measures the force the shocks give on compression—the bump—and on extension—the rebound. A computer screen displays graphs of the force against the speed of the shaft at different settings. The shock works by having the shaft displace oil inside the housing, and he can control the shape of the holes the oil travels through, the size of the holes, the shape of the piston, and the bleed valve through which the piston travels, among other things. He cranks up the dyno over and over, watching graphs and building shocks.

But he admits that he's not quite sure about all this computer equipment. Vic, a short, round man of around 50, says he's been building cars since he was 12 years old, and his philosophy is simple.

"You can't race a dyno," he says. "This is not a real complicated sport unless you want to make it that way. Racing is compromise. You gotta have the least amount of compromise than the guy in second place. It's a very simple philosophy." At the track, almost all the work is done to make the car handle as well as possible for the track and its conditions. But as he says, everything you do to gain one thing costs you another. Something done to help the front stay smooth may loosen the rear; something that adds stability may scrub off speed.

In handling, he says, "the right front is kind of the dominant wheel." To understand, instead of a race car roaring into a turn, imagine your own car on a suburban street corner, slowing down and turning left. When you brake, the weight shifts forward and the nose drops, and as you turn left, the weight of the car shifts to the right, which you feel as you push slightly against your shoulder belt. So since most of the car's weight shifts to the front and the right, the right front is the first wheel to pick up that weight. Since the front wheels control the steering, that right front has to grip the track just right. If it's got too much weight, the rear of the car will be too light and will probably want to fishtail. Drivers say the car wants to break loose. If there's too little weight on that right front, the car won't respond as well to the steering, and the car will want to keep going straight. They say the car is tight, or pushing.

That shift of weight to the right in the turn is why Winston Cup teams want as much weight as possible to be on the car's left side, and why NASCAR has rules that at least 1,600 of the car's 3,400 pounds must be on the right, so the cars don't get dangerously out of balance. The name of the game, of course, is turning left. Races are won and lost by how well the car turns left. And so all the adjustments in the car, as Kenny zips in and out of the pits on practice laps, respond to his comments on how the car feels in the turns. That's what the team talks about over and over on the headset.

That conversation, Vic says, is far more important than any shock dyno. "You gotta go by driver feel. That's what you're aiming for. And the better he is at explaining stuff, the better you are." Kenny is good at explaining, he says, "but sometimes you have to dig it out of him." Sometimes he'd rather tell you what he thinks you should do to fix it than what the car is doing. Kenny started out as a mechanic for his brother, Rusty, who's been a Winston Cup champion and is considered not only one of the best drivers on the circuit but one of the best mechanics. Kenny is sometimes accused of thinking too highly of his own skills as a mechanic. Being Rusty's crew chief meant doing what Rusty said, people often say. And the team has been working hard on getting Kenny to stick with describing what the car is doing.

Inside the hauler, where the roar of the practicing race cars can be heard even through the sliding glass door at the rear, Vic returns to his dyno. He's got more shocks to build.

❖

Stepping out of the quieter, air-conditioned hauler is like stepping out of a movie theater after a matinee. The assault of bright sunlight and overwhelming noise feels physical rather than merely sensory. The headset goes back on, and Kenny is doing exactly what Vic hopes he'll do: describing, not suggesting.

"The body attitude is good," Kenny says. "The front end is turning like a motherfucker. The ass end still feels a little stiff." Newt suggests new shocks and calls him in.

The team checks more than the tires and the handling, of course. Newt talks to Frank and Jeremy about the engine, asking about timing and carburetor jets, but he rarely makes suggestions: "You're the engine geeks," he says. He also constantly asks Kenny to check his oil and water temperatures while he's on the track, so that he can adjust how much tape is on the front grille of the car. More tape means less air going through the grille, which means less air resistance and higher speed. But more tape also means less air through the radiators. There's the main radiator for engine coolant, a special oil radiator, and even a radiator for rear end gear coolant. Air flows through ducts that cool the brakes, too. During qualifying—a run of less than three laps total—the entire front end will be taped up because the car won't have time to overheat. But the team has to find the spot where, for the long haul, the least amount of air enters the front of the car without the engine running too hot.

"Add a quarter on the oil cooler, and a half on the opening," Newt says once, and Two-Can and Buddy take out rolls of blue duct tape (racers use a brand called Shur-tape) and rulers. They measure and add exactly what he asked for. "Just a little at a time," Newt cautions. "Ten-four," Two-Can says.

Practice continues. Eddie runs up and down the ladder between the top of the hauler and the garage, taking tire sheets when Kenny comes in, checking tire wear and temperature for clues to how the car's running. Buddy, Two-Can, and Don, who's already at the track from his job in Pennsylvania, change tires and springs. Sometimes Kenny just stops on pit road, so the team can check his tires or make a slight spring adjustment. On pit road, groups of three or four guys from different teams sit along the pit wall, clipboards and stopwatches and tire meters at the ready. Three or four cars always seem to be stopped there. When they are ready to head out or head back into the garage, they have to pass by a NASCAR official who controls traffic with a whistle, like a crossing guard. In the garage, the long yellow strip down the middle, the aisle between the rows of cars, is filling up with PR people and guests. Charlotte people. Danielle Randall has shown up, in a white sheer blouse and nail-head check pants, and as the qualifying show draws nearer, people dressed like Danielle are beginning to outnumber people dressed like mechanics.

At the hauler, Vic builds shocks or stands on top with Newt, watching cars circle the track. He was crew chief for Joe Nemechek when he won the 1992 Busch Grand National series championship, and he still looks at a race car with a crew chief's eye, watching the line the driver chooses around the track.

Mark Martin, in the red-white-and-blue number 6 car, follows the white line along the bottom of the track, smooth and even as luggage around an airport carousel; Dale Earnhardt, in the black number 3, probes and investigates, looking for different spots on the asphalt that feel comfortable. Dale Jarrett, in the 88, takes a higher route through turns 3 and 4, but his car doesn't waver. He's finding what the drivers call the line, the groove, the best way around the racetrack for their cars, their setups, and their driving styles. Look at a racetrack and you'll see a deepening gray line as practice or a race wears on: down at the bottom in the turns, angling out to the walls on the straightaways, then diving back low into the turns. That's the line the drivers are following. It gets deeper as the drivers follow it, laying down more rubber from their tires. Of course, the rubber changes the groove, as does the air temperature, as does the humidity, as does the sun going behind a cloud. The groove changes over the course of a weekend, of a race, of a practice, of an hour. The drivers follow that ephemeral groove, looking for the setup that will mesh with the changing track conditions. They say they're chasing the track.

In early practice, cars share the track but remain almost unaware of each other except to avoid wrecking. Race strategy is far in the future. Right now, they're just trying to find a way to get their cars to go fast all alone, and the quicker they can get in and out of the garage to try different setups, the more successful they're likely to be.

The number 81 car comes in and out more than most. Every lap Kenny has more comments: "I'm pushing going into the turn, then loose coming out," he says over and over, almost regardless of what they try. "I'm pushy loose. I'm coming in." "We oughtta put that rubber back in there," Newt will say, of a rubber bushing that will stiffen one of the springs. "And somebody who's not doing nothing, let's put 5 degrees of spoiler from the middle of the car to the right." The changes are made in three minutes, and Kenny goes back out. "You still got that feeling of being too soft down there?" Newt asks.

Sometimes Kenny answers quickly; sometimes he's concentrating too hard and waits a second. Newt will tell him to go hard for a couple of laps, and then Kenny will ask for his times. "You had a 31 on the first lap, a 30.83 on the second, Herman," Newt says. "Oh," Kenny says. "I let off earlier in the second lap, so maybe I learned something."

"Ten-four," Newt replies. "Nobody ever said you had to go flat out all the way around this track to do good." Martinsville was a brakes track; superspeedways like Daytona and Talladega are aerodynamics tracks, where drivers tend to keep their foot on the gas the whole way around the track. Charlotte and most of the midsize tracks are handling tracks. Here, the drivers use little brakes but do kind of burp the throttle going into the turns to slow down the car. Finding where to do that—and finding the setup that keeps the car smooth when the driver does that—is the trick. Newt keeps an eye on Kenny's line and compares him to other drivers, gently coaching him. "Your Turn 3 looked just like the 24 car when you went through here," Newt says, " 'cept for he was on the line and you were 6 inches above the line. Otherwise you was exactly the same."

From the hauler, Newt and Vic can see when Kenny does anything or when he's driving, when he lets up on the throttle, when he touches the brakes. They can hear it, too: When Kenny gets out of the throttle, the buzz of the car takes a momentary tone down. Then when he's through the turn, it ratchets back up to that full-bore screaming whine. "As far as your releasing the throttle, that was the best you've looked all day," Newt says at one point. "That's how it sounded to me."

As the afternoon wears on, concentration doesn't decrease. Kenny's fastest lap has been 29.984, which puts him way at the back of the pack. "If I could just keep the right rear underneath me," Kenny keeps saying. "Right in the middle, the car's perfectly neutral, but getting out of the turn I get all floppy feeling, like my ass end is all loose on me."

At around 3:30, Filbert arrives at the track, in cowboy boots, pressed jeans, and a jacket. He climbs up the ladder to the top of the hauler and goes directly to the monitor to check the car's time, leaning over Newt's shoulder, an avuncular arm on his back. He looks for a long moment, then steps back and looks out at the track.

Charlotte Motor Speedway is something to look at. Where Martinsville, with its exposed skinny galvanized steel braces looked almost like a high school football grandstand—or, one fan said, like an old-fashioned roller-coaster—Charlotte looks like a *stadium*. Long rows of white and blue seats line the speedway from the beginning of Turn 4 all the way through the end of Turn 1. Several rows of concrete benches, traditional at racetracks, form the first 10 rows. At a racetrack, of course, the close seats are the worst, because you can see the smallest portion of the track and you get covered with tire goo and asphalt fragments. As Dick Thompson said at Martinsville, where they have added on to the top of their grandstands several times, "Every new seat we build is the best seat in the house."

A double-decker row of suites lines the top of the stands in Turn 1 at Charlotte, and next to them are actual condominiums, owned by drivers, teams, and fans. Several weekends a year they're the best seats in the house. The rest of the time they're a nice place to live, although kind of noisy during the day. Along the home stretch are the Speedway Club, where members can dine from a buffet during the race in air-conditioned comfort, and the scorers' and spotters' stands. Beyond them are the speedway offices.

In Turn 2, brand-new stands have been built, with plastic seats forming a checkered flag turning into a multicolored pattern; above it are two more rows of corporate suites. A low row of grandstands lines the backstretch. At Charlotte, only Turn 3 is still empty of seats. But everything at the speedway is new; everything is clean. Everything looks suburban-office-building expensive, with green-tinted glass and gleaming white concrete. With the stands almost completely lining the track, the speedway has a sense of place like any football or baseball stadium. It doesn't just give you a place to sit, it contains you. When you're there, you're somewhere. You're where it's happening.

It looks especially nice today. Fans have begun trickling into the seats. Only the front stretch is open, but the speedway expects 60,000 fans to pay the

$10 to $20 to come in the gate to watch qualifying and the ARCA race afterwards. During the afternoon practice, the sky has gone from crystal blue to flat, gray-bottomed, potato-pancake clouds. It's still beautiful, but a light, fresh breeze has come up; 10-foot vertical banners saying "UAW-GM" flap from the corners of the garage. Around the other haulers, just like on the Square D hauler, groups of five or six guys with clipboards and pens stand in sunglasses, turning slow circles and occasionally pointing as they watch their cars circuit the track. It's mesmerizing and beautiful. The sound buffets and almost embraces. The cars arc into and out of the garage, getting springs changed and air pressures adjusted. Everywhere little groups of guys stand together: along the pit wall, in front of the garages, atop or in front of the haulers. They smoke cigarettes, watch the monitors, drink Gatorade, bottled water, and soda in cans. You look around and you see one thing: guys together, trying to make something happen, trying to make cars go fast. It's a great day to just enjoy being in racing.

Or it probably would be if your car wasn't 34th in the points race and running like a dog in practice laps.

❖

Finally, as the minutes wind toward 5 P.M., when the car has to be as good as it can for qualifying, the trips in and out of the garage become faster and more tense. Two-Can and Buddy scramble underneath to change rear end gears, Newt, Eddie, and Don work on tires and springs, planning the next series of changes as they work. Eddie uses a scanner to listen to the communications of other teams to hear what they're trying. The regurgitator is hooked up between runs, cooling the radiator. Sometimes they lean a big blue fan on the fender of the car, blowing on the engine, and sometimes they revert to the old method, moving the car over a drain on the asphalt in front of the garage, opening a valve, and letting the water run out of the radiator while they replace it directly from a hose connected to their pressurized tank of cold water. When the steaming water hisses out of the car into a puddle on the asphalt from the middle of the car as it squats over the drain, it's impossible not to think of a race horse pissing.

The later runs become short mock-qualifying runs. Newt stands on the hauler with a stopwatch, and Kenny runs a couple of laps. The grille is completely taped, and they're trying final adjustments on the recalcitrant car. Eddie works with a wire brush on the used sets of tires, squeezing another lap of sticker-like handling out of them for the mock runs.

"I think we got her just where we want her," Kenny says after one run. "Just a little tight. Air pressure or something. Sometimes when you get those tires scuffed up it kinda makes 'em stand up. Gets the wiggle out of 'em."

Eddie says no. "I'm scanning everybody we can think of, and if you want to put more air in that tire you can, but you'll be going against the grain. You can adjust the air pressure to make you looser, but I think Newt's doing the right thing by changing that spring. We can change the air pressure in qualifying if we really need it."

Newt, from the hauler, says, "There's 11 minutes left in practice. So make this run, take the tape off, change the gear, then do the same deal: Try that spring, make a run, cool down, take the tape off, and make another run. Then come back in, we'll put that other one back in the left front and get ready to qualify."

All around the garage, the last minutes of practice spark a similar frenzy. Cars try to come back in and out for final checks, and guys who have hustled around all afternoon switch to running, carrying two springs or four shocks from the haulers. Finally, at exactly 5:00, the yellow lights in the turns and on the stretches—eight of them all around the track—start blinking, and the cars all follow in to the garage.

Every team gets their cars up on jacks, and they replace everything. They put in the rear end gears they've chosen; they load the springs and shocks they hope have the best lap in them. They replace the oil and rear end coolant, replacing it with special low-weight qualifying fluids (racing oil is 20 weight, for example; for qualifying it's 10 weight).

When it's all done, the cars come off the jacks and guys in team colors push the cars to the gas tanks to fill them up. Then they get in line, once again, for tech inspection.

❖

Shortly after 6 P.M., the show gets started. The sun is going down, and the speedway lights have gone on. Those lights won an engineering award when they were installed in 1993. A combination of lights atop the grandstand and ground-level can lights pointing straight up at angled mirrors, the lights make the speedway almost glow from the ground up. From a landscape of gray—gray track, gray tires, gray concrete in the garage—studded with bright colors, the speedway is transformed into a riot of color leaping out from an almost invisible background. Suddenly the mood isn't one of concentration and practice. Now it's electric.

This being Charlotte, a big part of the activity on the infield involves sponsors and teams announcing new or special deals. Early this morning, before the first practice, Hendrick Motorsports trotted out defending Cup champion Terry Labonte and a special number 5 car he would be driving this weekend. Instead of the usual Kellogg's Corn Flakes rooster, this one has a bizarre purple-and-green paint job and a "Spooky Froot Loops" theme, with Frankenstein's monster taking the place of the rooster. Labonte's in a purple-and-green driver's suit for the weekend, too. Kellogg's will like this, but the people who make die-cast collectibles will like it a whole lot more. Out in the trailers of souvenirs, die-cast race cars go for anywhere from $2 to $25, usually. But special collectors' editions—cars driven for one race by Dale Earnhardt or Jeff Gordon as part of similar promotions, and produced as die-cast cars in small numbers—tend to bring more in the $40 to $50 range.

Later in the morning but still before practice, Wally Dallenbach stood next to a number 46 car that was split down the middle. Half the car bore its usual green-and-black First Union paint job; the other half was painted to look like the NASCAR collectors' edition version of Monopoly that was released that weekend. Speedway Children's Charities was part of this promotion, and the strangely painted car stood in front of the media center next to a huge pile of Monopoly games, which the women distributing them would hand only to people with approved media credentials, turning away team members and corporate hangers-on. The little metal game pieces, by the way, were a helmet, a tire, a NASCAR logo, the Winston Cup trophy, a steering wheel, a checkered flag, and—you guessed—a race car. And no, not an open-wheeled one. A stock car.

But now, as the teams push their cars through technical inspection for the second time today, as a good 40,000 or 50,000 fans rustle into their seats, R. J. Reynolds PR people organize a special presentation on pit road. Wreckers move two sections of the pit wall, and RJR people put up a big plastic arch covered with a paper "No Bull" sign, the new logo of Winston cigarettes.

One of the two Miss Winston models who circulate around the garage all weekend distributing free cigarettes, claps her hands: "All right! Here we go!" she shouts. "It's show time!"

The public address announcer from the speedway, holding a portable microphone, demands the attention of fans and press alike. And in the deepening gloom, sparklers on the arch go off, fireworks come out, roman candles explode, and Jimmy Spencer bursts through the paper in his number 23. Only it's a 1998 Ford Taurus, the first one introduced to the fans. And next year his number 23 will be wearing the red and white of Winston cigarettes instead of the yellow Joe Camel colors it has this year. Press photographers come running across the grass infield like JFK is back. Flashbulbs pop, fans applaud, and the RJR crew hands out information sheets and starts dismantling the arch. A security woman by the door in the fence to the garage area takes a drag on her cigarette and says, "It's pretty, isn't it?"

❖

In line for tech inspection in the darkening garage, nobody's worrying about new paint jobs, least of all the Filmar Racing team. Their car has never really run well all day, and at the end of practice their car never got much better than it had started out. "The last run before this, we had 29.60, and we're 40th," Eddie says. "That's how competitive this is." Fortieth today ain't going to make the race, so nobody's smiling. But you don't run the races on the monitor times. "He might be able to pull a rabbit out of his hat," Eddie shrugs.

Inspectors run through their template checks, which this time include tire checks. Another official takes a little silver can with a screw-top lid to each car, has someone on the team crank the car to bring fuel into the engine, and fills the can. He puts a green dot on the side and writes the car number on it, places the can in a cardboard Lipton Tea box sitting on a ratty Formica table guarded by another official. Like athletes giving urine samples.

Cleared through inspection, the car hooked up to its little generator, they push the car up the incline onto pit road and into Charlotte. In other races, qualifying just means you push the car onto pit road, an official gives you the high sign, you build up speed for a lap, you take the green flag, you run the lap, you take the checker, and you come back in the garage and watch how everybody else does. Here, just getting onto pit road is madness.

In the first place, even under the lights you can see that the grandstands are filling. In the second place, instead of a couple of crew members standing around each car, pit road is swarming. Half the cars seem to have two or three PR types, though the Square D car is an exception, with only Frank and Buddy and Two-Can and Eddie pushing it to its spot in line, near the front of the second line of cars, then standing there looking like they have heartburn.

It's not just people on pit road, either. Lugnut, a sort of animated creature that is the Charlotte Motor Speedway mascot, is there, as are people in Tom and Jerry costumes, hanging around the number 29 car, sponsored by the Cartoon Network. "They go to six or seven races a year," says Patty Hopkins, working marketing for the sponsor. "We don't do hospitality at every race. We just do the biggest races," she says. For the Cartoon Network, race sponsorship is "a branding issue. We sell a lot of merchandise: shirts, hats, jackets, die-cast cars, all the little stuff. That's pretty much what it is."

And if it's cool that Tom and Jerry are here, wait until the race on Sunday, she says. "Scooby will be here, and Dexter. That's Dexter's laboratory on the car this year." Scooby Doo was on the car design before this one, and Fred Flintstone was on the car before that. And now, besides Dexter on the side, it's that Tom and Jerry. Oh, for the record, Patty, uh . . . "Tom is on the left, the tall one," she says. "And Jerry is the mouse."

❖

Then almost without warning, with no clearing of pit road, with no announcement you can hear, the fans cheer and an engine roars, and Kenny's brother Rusty, a previous Winston Cup champion, spins the tires of his number 2 car out of the pit road exit onto Turn 1, and qualifying has started. He builds up speed around the track, roars out of Turn 4 onto the bent front straightaway of the track, and takes the green flag. The Charlotte track is what's called a quad-oval. It's kind of like a big uppercase *D*, with the straight line being the backstretch and the start-finish line being the flattened front of the curve of the *D*. Rusty spins his lap, and takes the checkered flag at the start-finish line and slows down through the first and second turn. The big flashing scoreboard set up along pit road, visible to the fans on the homestretch, flashes his time: 29.845 seconds to travel the 1.5-mile track. That's just a hair under 181 miles per hour.

As soon as Rusty's through the turn, the official at the head of pit road gives the OK for the next driver—Brett Bodine in the 11—to start his engine. The official steps out of the way, and when Rusty is halfway down the backstretch and getting ready to turn onto pit road coming out of Turn 4, he pats Bodine's hood, and he takes off, starting his own qualifying run.

One after another, the cars run their laps. Rusty's time doesn't hold up for even a single driver. The track is cooling off, getting faster. The radio broadcast of the race is fed onto a channel that the scanners used by the teams can pick up, and driver after driver says he'll just be happy to make the top 25. None of the early drivers expect to have a chance for the pole.

Eddie listens to the broadcast, keeping count of the times of the cars and their order. He also scans other team's frequencies, listening to see who's using new tires—stickers—and who's using scuffs, trying to pick up any information he can about car setups that seem to be working. As the line progresses, as the times get faster, his face sets. The track is faster, which is good, but these guys are starting to run times Kenny never came close to during practice.

As Kenny creeps up the line, Two-Can and Buddy head back to the garage; Frank and Jeremy stick with the car, pulling its generator cart along with it as it goes. As soon as the number 75 car, qualifying 30th, right before Kenny, spins off pit road and onto the track, they unplug the cart and head back, too. Then Kenny's on his own, waiting to run the most important lap of his season.

The official nods at him; he flicks the dashboard switch and starts the engine. With the number 75 halfway across the track, Kenny's engine sounds loud, almost reassuring. Then the 75 goes by after taking the checkered flag. Kenny grips the wheel. The official pats the hood twice, almost affectionately.

Kenny slams on the gas and the car screams out of pit road into the shine of the floodlit Turn 1, his yellow-and-blue rear end fishtailing just a bit. He's off. The scoreboard, as he gets started, flashes that he was rookie of the year in the Busch Grand National series in 1989. As he starts through Turns 3 and 4 to take the green flag to start his lap, that seems an awful long time ago.

❖

His engine off, Kenny glides into the garage, a place of bright glare and stark shadows under the speedway lights. He pulls into his stall and gets out, pulling off his helmet. Hair mussed, face red, he puts down the helmet and stalks to the hauler. Newt will be there. Frank leans into the car, checking the rpm gauge, which tracks the highest revs the car ran. It's 8,300. That's fine.

But it's the only thing about the lap that was. Kenny ran a lap of 30.224, 178.666 miles per hour. That's almost nine-tenths of a second slower than the pole sitter. Kenny was the 31st car to qualify, and he's currently 28th quick. That's bad. That's real bad.

That's miss-the-race bad.

Two-Can lights a cigarette and turns to Frank, wondering whether to pump the gas out of the car. "Leave it full?" he says. Frank just says, "We gotta requalify tomorrow."

In almost unbearable quiet, the guys replace wrenches, stow tools. The garage still has to be neat for tomorrow.

Kenny comes back from the hauler and joins a little crowd watching the monitor hooked up to the tool chest of the number 42 car, in the slot next to his. He's changed into an Aerosmith T-shirt, his favorite band, from their "Nine Lives" tour. You've got to figure Kenny's down a couple of lives right now. He sighs, shaking his head slightly, a look of disappointed calm on his face.

"The track slowed down," he says. "A lot." He looks back at the monitor: "Fucking Geoff Bodine on the pole." He shakes his head again: Bodine, who's won 18 Cup races in his career, is having a terrible year. He's 27th in the points. This is a huge boost for his team. "Well," Kenny says, "We'll just have to chase it again tomorrow." He's talking out loud, to anyone. "My car just took off. Both ends were sliding."

Two-Can, who watched from the hauler, nods his head. "Just took off. Just slid. Didn't grab *nothing*."

A period of glum waiting descends on the crew, until Andy Johnson walks into the darkened garage, looking spiffy in a black-and-gray Square D shirt, nice slacks, and lace-up shoes. Andy came early to walk up and down the lines of cars awaiting qualifying to see if he saw anything new, anything he could learn from. Then he went up in the Turn 2 suite Square D has leased, and he watched with guests as the cars qualified. He saw something nobody else saw: "When he went through that turn, he hit the ground. I saw sparks. I mean, I thought a tailpipe had come off somehow. It was just, bump—chssssssssssh! Trailing sparks the whole way." He mimes the bump with his shoulders, showing the car's path with his hand. His eyes are wide.

Newt nods slowly. "Well, let's rack it up and do it again tomorrow." Two-Can pats the car, like it's a quarterback who's thrown a costly interception. "We might take those pipes and warm 'em up, try to squeeze 'em," he suggests. Newt shrugs. "We done the best we can, boys. We gave it a hundred percent. Come back and do it again."

Kenny's talking to Andy: "I wasn't tight, I wasn't loose, I just skidded. I'm worried I won't make the race." Two-Can agrees that something strange happened: Kenny sure didn't cause anything by, perhaps, accidentally tapping the brakes in the turn. "He didn't use no brakes. I just changed the brakes without using no gloves." They weren't even warm. Eddie says, "If anything, he probably drove in too fast, instead of cracking the throttle." Over the public address system a voice comes: "Attention Winston Cup garage: The garage area will stay open until 25 laps to go in the ARCA race, then open in the morning at 7 A.M."

Vic walks over. "Ernie Irvan stepped on his dick too," he says. Irvan, in the 28 car, was less than two-tenths faster than Kenny, qualifying 45th. And Irvan wins races.

Eddie shakes his head, looking at the car. "It's gonna be a different story tomorrow. The ARCA guys are putting down that Hoosier rubber. We'll have to qualify on stickers." Hoosier, the tire company that used to compete with Goodyear in Cup races, makes tires for other series that are softer, and they'll leave a lot more rubber on the track. "The pole sitter, the 3, other cars that run good, they used stickers." He watched every car get started. "That's part of my library," he says. "So next time we come back, we'll try on stickers."

Wives have shown up now. Frank's wife holds their baby; Frank puts his headset on him. Vic points out that Bodine, on the pole, never got out of the throttle in the turns. He could hear it. Newt opines that the gear was probably right, anyhow:

"Nobody said you need to be all the way wide open here." Vic took corner speeds like he usually does, timing Kenny's car from the beginning to the end of the turns. "He was three-tenths off what he needed to be."

Andy pipes up again, telling anybody who will listen about those sparks: "I mean, a *big* old spark. And then it just skidded sparks the whole way."

"I'll tell you who looked good was that 18," Two-Can says. "He just hugged that wall. That picks up about 300 rpm because he makes that straightaway so damn long." He's on the outside pole. The ARCA race has started, and the cars fill the racetrack with sound, but the guys keep talking. Eddie suggests they pack up and come in fresh in the morning, but Newt and Andy jack up the car and get underneath with a flashlight. They measure the chassis settings and discover the car was a quarter inch lower than they wanted it. Two-can is shocked. "We did that? Here?"

"The springs settle a little here," Vic says. Newt purses his lips.

"Well, we'll raise her up then." Then he turns to Andy, nodding grimly. "You look rather debonair," he says.

Eddie allows a smile. "He was at the meeting yesterday," he says. "He was listening. Dress to impress."

"I don't see you dressing so nice," Andy shoots back. "Maybe we should switch jobs."

"Hey," Eddie says. "I built chassis for five years."

Two-Can is still staring at the car. "A quarter inch. Enough for him to skate in there. You'd think he'd have felt that. . . . Shit. I don't know. We go on these streaks. . . ." Newt finally gives up. "Y'all go home," he says, picks up his clipboard and briefcase, slaps a few shoulders, and heads out.

Eddie still stands, hands on his hips, looking at the car. "Where's another second?" he asks. "Tell me where there's another second."

Two-can pats him on the shoulder. "It's there—gotta be. *They're* doing it. And you can't do big things. Little bitty things can make you go a lot faster."

They'd better.

❖

Under the lights, the ARCA cars speed by. In the winner's circle, Winston Cup pole-winner Geoff Bodine talks to the press and mugs with Lugnut for the TV cameras. The shining lights glint off the ARCA cars. There's that swarm of bees sound, and the speed, the color, the motion, the energy. It's racing, and the fans who have stayed for the ARCA show probably love it. It's not much fun for the Square D guys, going home to worry about whether they'll even make Sunday's race.

The infield is still virtually empty. A few drivers' motor homes have shown up, but no drivers are staying in them yet.

The drive out of the infield through the arched tunnel under Turn 3 takes you through the empty areas around the backstretch. A few little fires glint from the campers that have already set up. Around the front of the track, the souvenir trailers have set up, and fans who came only for the qualifying are filtering through the ones that are still open.

It still feels like the night before the fair. Campers, a few; trailers, a few. But tomorrow morning the infield opens for campers, buses, and anyone else who wants to come in. The ARCA cars do what they can to fill the air with the sound of racing, and it echoes around the empty air outside the racetrack. It's a little chilly, sweatshirt weather, maybe. The sky is clear, and the stars look down on the racetrack, lit up. It's not in full swing yet, but for the fans—those who came early—it's race week.

As for the Square D Filmar Racing team?

It's still too early to tell.

CHAPTER 5

A PIECE OF DYNAMITE

Thursday, October 2

The Winston Cup garage opens up at 7 A.M., and if you walk in a few minutes after that you can see that the teams have been divided into two distinct groups. The number 24 crew, fourth on the grid, and the 18, in second, are all smiles and slouches: We've made the race; we're just here for practice. At the garage areas of those still looking to make the show—the 5, which qualified terribly, or the struggling 81 crew—faces are grim: We've got a lot of work to do, and no guarantees.

Still, certain constants link all the teams, reminding you that tense or relaxed, this day is part of a cycle that goes on week after week, with a routine that provides comfort, if not security. For example, two or three orange coolers sit in front of every hauler, pulled out by the truck drivers the moment they got into the garage. Their drains open, they release the water from the ice that melted overnight. They sit in front of each hauler like some sort of ritual, like a water sacrifice to some god, made by each team in the hopes of doing well. From each cooler a little trail of water dribbles down to the drains in the garage concrete.

Dave Ensign has his coolers out front like everybody else, and he's ready to go get some ice to refill them. Sodas, beer, and bottled water need to be ready for the crew members. Today will be busy. There are practices from 9 to 10 and again from 11 to noon, and then second-round qualifying begins at 1:30. They won't have a lot of time for rest, so fluids and food had better be at hand. To that end, Dave is filling the coolers and getting ready to run out to the grocery store for food.

He keeps the Square D hauler like it's his home, and in truth, Dave is a kind of big-hearted den mother for the team, running from the hauler to the garage with parts the team needs, running to the Winston Cup hauler for information, and otherwise keeping the hauler clean and tidy. He keeps coffee brewing in the morning. They drink out of Featherlite Styrofoam cups, provided each week by Featherlite, the trailer manufacturer, which entertains people in its own show hauler at the end of the row.

Dave, a big light-haired guy with an open face who often wears a gas-station rag around his neck to keep him cool, loves his job. "You gotta love it," he says, "because the hours are long and the weekends are short and you have no life. When these guys head for the airport to go home, I'm headed for the interstate." Dave has driven the truck for a Craftsman Truck Series team and another Winston Cup team, but he's happy here: "This team, we got all the right pieces. It's all coming together. When we get there, we'll do it as a team."

Like most people in Winston Cup racing, he started out driving a car himself. "I ran super modifieds in New York" around his home near Dryden, he says. "It wasn't nothing fancy: Use your tires five or six weeks, just make it look good when you get to the track." He did well enough that he ran the car a second season, but he saw that his future wasn't driving a race car. Connections led him into the Craftsman Truck series, and now here he is, and he likes his role. "I try to do what they need so they don't have to spend those few extra seconds," he says. "I try to keep it orderly. Sponsors, salespeople, visitors, they all come here. It's gotta look nice." He keeps a stack of Kenny Wallace 8-by-10 postcards in a little easel on the back bumper of the hauler so fans looking for a souvenir won't have to bother the team. One project he has for this weekend is to unload a couple of extra truck tires he's come up with that don't fit his hauler. He had one option to trade them for new doors for the back of the hauler, "but I need a spare tire worse than I need those doors. So I brought these tires. The Close Call team has no spares," and they drive the kind of truck these will fit. "So I'm gonna go over and save some money." He drags the tires around on a little cart, checking different teams, seeing how he can do. "I'll drag 'em to the race next week if I don't unload 'em here," he says. "I've been working the pits lately."

He also has to go out and buy some groceries. Mostly, though, his job is to take care of his hauler. "This trailer oughtta last five years," he says. "It's state-of-the-art. It cost $212,000 new, with the shock room there, and the fancy lounge with the TV and satellite dish. As delivered it weighed 36,500 pounds, a lot more than a lot of tractor-trailer rigs weigh." Loaded up with race cars and engines and carts and tools and parts, it goes 80,000 pounds. Which puts it right on the edge of illegal on the interstates. "Since I've been here I've eliminated some of the things that weren't being used," he says, because being a Winston Cup hauler, "painted up and lit up like a Christmas tree," can make it hard to avoid attention.

Virginia is the worst about looking out for the Cup haulers after a race, he says. "They can be closed all week, but the weigh stations'll be open after a race." Then again, that Cup trailer has its benefits too. "Coming back from Dover once, a whole row of us had to get weighed, and the guy said, 'Do you have any spare hats?' We all coughed up a few hats, and we didn't have to cross the scales." And when a bunch of haulers traveling together were stopped coming out of Watkins Glen once, he says, "there were no scales in sight, but there were six troopers down there with hands out wanting free stuff. And they remember the guys who gave 'em stuff. So you play the game and you go on down the road." The best, though, was one night after a race at Darlington. "Coming into North Carolina, the first county you go through one of those skinny little two-lane roads we travel. They had road blocks set up for drunks." The trooper, as ever, wanted some hats, which are the recognized currency, sort of the Euro, of NASCAR racing.

"Then he said, 'Oh, by the way. These guys here with me? These are the only badges in the county.'" So after that road block, the drivers mashed the gas and the haulers fairly flew into North Carolina.

Dave likes that. He likes the way the rigs delight people. Slowly creeping out of the crossover gates of the tracks after races, he often signs autographs, and he keeps Kenny Wallace postcards up front with him to do it. These are kids, he figures, who just want to feel connected to the sport they love. "And everybody lines the streets in the little towns we drive through," he says. "They want to see the race cars and want you to honk your horn. Pennsylvania's got the most race fans on the streets. Across Route 81 in Pennsylvania, they line the overpasses, even after dark. You see a bunch of kids and you give 'em a couple of blips on the horn. They know you're not gonna stop and give 'em stuff, but they want to feel like you did something."

Driving and cleaning are his main jobs. After that, "it's just kinda maintaining," he says. "Being this close to home, the wheels are shiny, the chrome pipes are shining, the sun shines off all that bright aluminum. That in itself is quite pleasing, when your stuff looks just as good as everyone else." He'll never forget the way he learned to wash the top of his truck. He had gotten to a race fairly late in New Hampshire, and it had rained. He made sure he cleaned the sides of the truck for race weekend, and thought he was done. When he set up the viewing platform for the weekend, though, he saw that most of the other trucks' tops were spotless. His was covered with rain spatters and mud, which is not the look he wants to project, so that joined his list of things to keep track of.

He refills all the parts bins during the week at the shop, and he keeps track of what's there all weekend. The hauler—it's air conditioned—has a long central hallway, with fluorescent lights, electrical outlets, workbenches, and aluminum cabinet doors lining the sides. The shock dyno is in the back corner, by the stairs up to the office that Kenny, Newt, Eddie and Filbert use for privacy and relaxing. Each cabinet is labeled: air hoses, extension cords, gearboxes, hubs, brake rotors. Back by the shock dyno there are two large bays for engines. Everybody has a locker. Some haulers have bench seats at the back for relaxing, but the Filmar Racing hauler is just outfitted for work. Like every hauler down the row, it has "Team members only" stenciled on its glass doors.

And right by those doors there's usually food—doughnuts, chips, cookies—and cabinets for food to prepare for lunches and dinners. At the moment, though, the cupboard is bare. So he's off for groceries.

❖

The guys in the garage start the morning by pushing the car to the tech inspection bay to use the gauges. There's no line this time. They check the height to see whether the car is too low. It's not, and they push it back to the garage.

Not everybody who didn't qualify yesterday knows what they're going to do yet. So from the moment the garage opens, teams are sending guys down to check on the photocopied piece of paper hanging on the NASCAR hauler: It's the stand-on times list. Each crew chief who hopes his team's first-day qualifying time, even though it wasn't in the top 25, will hold up, has to sign his name and car number. Otherwise the car is automatically registered to qualify again. So the teams of the 96 Caterpillar car, the 77 Jasper Engines car and the 99 Exide Batteries car—it won last week and qualified no better than 28th this week—can be expected to stand on their times, since they qualified 26, 27, and 28 yesterday. At the back of the pack (Kenny qualified 47th out of 50) everybody can be expected to try another run, even on a track that should be significantly slower than the track last night. The decision, it seems, will be easy.

Not so fast.

Into the decision of every team you have to throw in provisional starts.

Today's qualifying will determine positions 26 through 38 of the 43-car field. Positions 39 through 42 will be awarded as provisional starts, based on the teams' points standings. The final spot is the previous champion's provisional starting position. The goal of the provisional starts is very simple: NASCAR recognizes that fans come to races to see the top drivers. They want to see Dale Earnhardt and Jeff Gordon, they want to see Mark Martin and Rusty Wallace and Terry Labonte. NASCAR wants the field to be open and to let the best man win. But if Dale Jarrett's car gets loose in his one-lap qualifier, he stands on his time, and the track speeds up and a whole bunch of guys qualify past him on the second day, NASCAR doesn't want his legion of fans to go home not even having seen their favorite driver. The provisional starts, awarded in order of points standing, are a kind of fail-safe to keep the drivers who are among the leaders—and can be expected to have the most fans—in the races. The previous champion's provisional is a further fail-safe, used often this year by Darrell Waltrip. It's just a way of figuring that once a guy's won a championship, the fans want to see him in the race. It's often called the Petty rule, since it was invented after series god seven-time Cup champion Richard Petty (he's called "the King") failed to make a race at Richmond one year very late in his career. The next time he didn't make a race on speed, he still drove his race car.

So even if, say, Dale Earnhardt qualifies terribly, stands on his time, and gets qualified out, and even if four guys ahead of him in the points standings are in the same situation, he'll still be in the race because he's won a championship. It's kind of like an exemption on the golf tour.

It's just good event management by an organization that has never forgotten for a moment that its sport has to be, above all, entertaining. It's got to have its fans to work.

So that stand-on times sheet looms large.

For the Filmar Racing team, though, it's not that important. The guys at the head of the second-day pack can be expected to stand on their times, and many of the guys who may or may not requalify are ahead of Kenny in points. If the times stand as they are and provisionals are distributed, Kenny would not make the race on time, and he would be sixth in line for a provisional start. That would make him the 44th car in a 43-car race.

In the garage stall next to the Filmar team is the number 42 car driven by Joe Nemechek, called "Front Row Joe" for his propensity to qualify in the first one or two positions—and then not win the race. He's been in the front row five times this year, and his best finish is 6th. Still, he's two positions ahead of Kenny in the points race. Much more important, yesterday he qualified 24th. Nothing to write home about, but he's in the show. Around his car the guys can take their time, get the car ready for practice, think about how they want to set it up for Sunday's race. No such freedom around the 81 car.

❖

Second-round qualifying is just a tough way to spend a day. Last week, at Martinsville, with his sixth-quick qualifying spot under his belt, Kenny stood in the sun atop his hauler, sunglasses on, in jeans and a Filmar Racing golf shirt and enjoyed the show. Right next to him, on the hauler for the number 42 car, stood Joe Nemechek and Wally Dallenbach, both drivers of cars owned by Felix Sabates. Nemechek, with his eighth-position qualifying run, looked pleased and comfortable, what Kenny would call high, wide, and handsome.

Dallenbach, pale and quiet, looked like he had a stomachache.

After a poor qualifying run, Dallenbach's team had decided to let the 46 car sit out the second-round. They chose to stand on their time. As the second-round qualifying started, Kenny and Joe chatted about race strategy and confidently discussed the next day's event as one after another the cars went by. "Jeremy says his qualifying setup don't work," Kenny said. "He runs these big old bars, so he don't get no roll." Jeremy Mayfield, driving the 37 car, was sitting out the qualifying too. But among the nonqualifiers he was highest in points, so he had first provisional. He would be in the race, starting 39th, at the worst. Dallenbach, on the other hand, was originally going to run only a partial schedule, so he didn't run seven of the first eight races. He hadn't done particularly well since then, so for him a provisional start wasn't even a remote possibility. He had to hope not too many cars beat his time. Dallenbach thought he had "fucked up [his] qualifying run" the day before. Kenny suggested he was being too hard on himself.

"I ran a 55 on the first lap," Dallenbach said. That's 20.55 seconds. Kenny qualified sixth with a 20.35.

"Oh," Kenny said. "You *did* fuck up then."

But Kenny went on. "Aw, this ain't one of them tracks that speeds up the second day," he said. "The turns are so sharp the rubber builds up, and it slows down." Dallenbach tried a grin. "As I got off the turn, I didn't get out of the brakes," he said of his effort. Kenny nodded. "Trail braking," he said. Dallenbach went on: "You gotta get off as fast as you can."

They watched the cars on the track to see if they did. The number 1 car, driven by Morgan Shepherd, roared around the track, looking strong into the turn. Then it had a little wiggle, a little bobble, coming out of Turn 4. All three shook their heads.

"He floated it through the corner, he was perfectly sideways, and he was ready to floor it out of the turn—and he lost it right there," Kenny said. "He's going home." Another car spun by. It beat Dallenbach's time, pushing him a little further toward that final 38th spot awarded for time.

They predicted who would miss the show: "Him, the 78, and the 71," Nemechek said, pointing at the number 1 car, but they all agreed, saying almost in chorus: "I wish nobody had to go home." They've all been there, and it's no fun. Kenny's made every race this year except the California race, but that one miss was enough. (He still wears the watch given to the drivers in commemoration of the inaugural event to remind him. "I don't like to try to forget the bad things," he said. "A lot of times when I'm reminded of a situation, I'll learn from it." He smiled. "Plus, it's a nice, thin watch.") As each car ran its lap, they glanced at the monitor on the 42 car's hauler. "Only two more, buddy," Kenny said.

A car ran, and Dallenbach leaned over the monitor. Then he stood up straight, took a deep breath. The car didn't beat him. Even if all the remaining cars ran faster than he did, he'd still make the race.

"There you go, buddy!" Kenny said, and suddenly Dallenbach was all chatter, listing with Nemechek the tracks they don't like to run. "Bristol, Dover, Texas, Martinsville, Darlington, Rockingham," Nemechek said, running down a list of tracks that he figured are either short and tight or poorly designed.

"We need to build a bunch more like California and Las Vegas," Dallenbach added. "Where you can *race*. All them others, if you're not in the bottom, it's single file. People get impatient." When people get impatient in race cars, bad things happen.

Kenny just laughed at the tracks they like. "All the tracks they do good at," he said. Then qualifying was over. The three—all racing the next day—climbed down from their haulers and got back to work.

❖

But that was last week. This week Kenny can't watch second-round qualifying because he's in it.

Yet in the Charlotte garage, surprisingly, this morning finds the Filmar crew not just calm but actually cheerful. They got the car set up for its practice quickly, and as they wait for the 9 A.M. practice to start they pass a little time hanging around the hauler. With the most important 30 seconds of the team's season a few hours away and the car about a mile from a good setup and only going in the wrong direction, they laugh in the narrow hallway of the trailer, Kenny sitting on the workbench next to a vise, sipping a cup of coffee, comfortable with himself. The car's going to have to run a lap under 30 seconds to make the race; everyone agrees. Can Kenny find a half-second in that car?

"I don't know," he says, calm and relaxed. "I'm ready to make the race, but I'm ready to miss it, too—up here, mentally," he says.

He and Vic start talking about different things drivers have done to make races. Soaking tires comes up. Soaking tires with a softening compound makes them grip the track better and can give a car a fast couple of laps. "Balough used to bring 'em into the trailer, with blankets on 'em," Vic says. "Balough would do it from the inside." Kenny laughs. "Old Gary 'Hot Shoes' Balough." Vic recalls "a hydraulic tie bar—so it'd shift the weight. Go this way on the scales to pass inspection, that way on the track." He reaches for a Fig Newton, which this morning is what passes for a breakfast table in the hauler.

Don adds to the little knot of blue-clad mechanics at the back of the Square D hauler, and Vic instantly begins riding him about his Square D hat, which is utterly filthy, covered with grease and oil and soaked through with stains from his days sweating at asphalt racetracks in the sun. "I'd throw it over the fence," Vic says. "Some fan'll love it. They'll wash it, at least. Either that or throw it in the dishwasher for a cycle. You got a lot of salt flowing through that thing."

Don shakes his head. "End of the season I can sell it. I can make $500 with the gas tickets. Sign Kenny's name to 'em." Those are the tickets the Unocal people slap on the gas cans when he gets them filled during the races.

Newt comes in, looking at the cluster of idle mechanics clogging the hall and gives his head a little shake in mock disgust. "Three-wide down the chute!" he says, aping the breathless call of an announcer as cars jockey for position on the backstretch. "Newt, I might be going to Japan and race," Kenny says, "but I don't want to go. Nobody does." NASCAR is putting on an exhibition race after the season in Japan. One last year was a huge success. Newt shrugs. "Nobody remembers Rusty won that race last year," Newt says. Kenny agrees. "The thing is, I mean, shit, why go?" When Kenny swears, the crew erupts in scolding. His brother Rusty was assessed a $5,000 fine by NASCAR because he swore on live radio when interviewed after the black flag on that final restart that cost him the Martinsville race.

Kenny just laughs at the swearing. "That don't make me bad, just because I use a cuss word," he says. "I'm a good kid who believes in the good Lord and has a fulfilled life. Like my mama says, I have so many wonderful qualities that it's easy to overlook my few disgusting habits." Talk shifts to the number 5 team, whose crew chief, Gary DeHart, has suddenly stepped down "for personal reasons." The story has spread throughout the garage: DeHart, notoriously quiet, snapped and threw an axle across the shop, whether directly at someone or not nobody can say. "An axle?" Kenny asks. "An *axle*?" An axle weighs at least 10 pounds and can be easily gripped like a baseball bat.

"That's when you don't care if you kill anybody or not," Newt says. "Who was he mad at?" Vic asks. Newt looks at Two-Can, who's just entered, coincidentally looking for an axle. "Obviously, the gear man," Newt says. Two-Can smiles, says, "Whoa! Watch out!" as he gets his axle, and leaves. The rumor is DeHart got into a dispute with another crew member at a previous race, and it apparently simmered ever since.

Frank tries to step into the hauler, but it's just too crowded. "You ready to go?" he asks. "I got the recirculator hooked up on there." If Frank calls it the recirculator instead of the regurgitator, things must be getting serious. At that moment, to complete the crowd at the door, Dave walks in with the groceries, at which point Kenny makes the morning's only general comment about the team's predicament.

"You should have waited to buy those groceries, Dave," he says, "until after qualifying."

❖

For the team, missing the race would certainly be a disappointment. "That's the worst feeling there is," big Steve Baker had said last week at Martinsville, watching the haulers of the unlucky cars snake their way out of Martinsville's cramped infield. Everyone remembers missing the race in California. Everyone remembers missing the Busch race they gave up a weekend off to help Kenny run in St. Louis. Nobody wants to miss a race at the home track, but undeniably there are those extra teams above them—the number 12 team, the number 27 team, the number 91 team—that haven't been running all year and now stand between them and making the show. Plus Tabasco Sauce has introduced a car, the number 35, driven by Todd Bodine, the third of the racin' Bodine brothers. Its team members wear bright orange-and-green uniforms that are the most fabulous uniforms in the garage. They'd be a welcome addition, only they qualified better than Kenny did. "It's those damn extra guys," Newt says at one point, looking at a qualifying results sheet. "See, all them fucking guys that ain't even supposed to be here are way up here." And there's that blue-and-yellow number 81 car, still not even close to making the race.

But guys who haven't had a day off in months can be excused for their belief that they'll weather the storm if they have to spend the weekend somewhere other than Charlotte Motor Speedway. "I have three days of work to catch up with at the shop," Frank Good says. "Plus I could cut my grass. It's only up to my knees."

Danielle Randall, owner of the Motorsports Decisions Group, in charge of every angle of management of the Square D-Filmar Racing partnership, is hardly so calm. She and Steve Post both show up at the garage early. They'll have plenty to do no matter what happens.

"I came to work last week after the Tuesday practice, and I said do we have a contingency plan for the worst case scenario?" Steve says, pacing the garage in a leather jacket, khaki pants, and sunglasses. Danielle is in the hauler; she has been taking over more of the weekend responsibilities for the team in recent weeks, and at the moment that suits Steve just fine. There are options, though.

"There's the possibility of putting the sponsorship on another car. With all those extra cars, there's some unsponsored ones," Steve says. Most notably the number 12 car and the number 11, both of which have already made the race. The 12 is driven by Jeff Purvis, and this is the third race he's started this year. Brett Bodine's number 11 was until recently sponsored by Close Call phone cards, but a dispute with the sponsor ended that relationship abruptly and on an unsatisfactory note. During testing at Charlotte last week on Tuesday night, one job the number 11 team members had to perform was peeling the Close Call decals off their car and covering the huge Close Call logo painted on the hauler with black Shur-tape. That means the team is suddenly trying to make it on virtually no money.

Danielle could offer one of those teams money to put the yellow Square D logo on its hood and quarter panels. "They could probably just decal it," Steve says. "They can do that right in the garage area," requiring no repainting. Bodine's number 11 is even a rich purple, not *all* that far from blue and yellow. The problem is,

Steve says, "That puts the car owner in a pretty good position." Sponsors looking to buy their way onto a car three days before race time have what you might call an emergency, and a car owner can kind of hold them up, especially since several owners will probably approach them. "It cost Graybar $50,000 to put its name on Kenny's car in a *Busch* race," he says. "So the car owner has a pretty good bargaining position."

But there isn't much else to do. "You could do nothing," Steve says. "That's not a good answer either. No matter what, you're battling a lose-lose situation. What is the least painful compromise? Quite honestly, I am glad I'm not making the decisions for our team right now."

Danielle is making those decisions, or having them made for her.

Early in the morning, she called Jack Carlson, vice president of marketing at Square D. He's the decision maker for Square D, and he might have to make a pretty tough call. According to the contract between Square D and Filmar Racing, if the team fails to make a race, it has to send money back to Square D. It's around $30,000, though nobody will say exactly. Square D might prefer to try to spend that money—and maybe more, depending on the negotiation—getting its logo on the number 11 car. Or it might just want that money back.

With Carlson himself planning to come to the race, a hospitality suite rented and paid for, and more than a hundred clients and corporate officers to impress, Carlson didn't need to think much.

"Oh," he told Danielle, "We *will* have a car in that race." She called Filbert, too. He had flown home to Nashville after Wednesday night's show. "I said, 'We need to think about taking care of the sponsor.' He said, 'Do what you gotta do,'" she says.

So Danielle, in a white linen jacket, black slacks, and brown pumps, leads Kenny into the back office of the number 11 hauler, coincidentally parked right next door. They don't come to any decisions. Bodine has to meet with his partner to make a decision, which can't be made before qualifying anyway, but he'll say that they're one of the first teams to express interest. If Kenny fails to make the race and Bodine accepts an offer, both he and Kenny will go to the Square D hospitality suites on Sunday morning, explain the situation, and give the guests a chance to meet two race car drivers instead of one.

When Kenny and Danielle emerge from the trailer she begins backing toward the media center outside the garage, he toward the hauler. Above the entrance in the steel gate from the media center to the garage is a sign, stenciled with simple Helvetica letters: "Through these doors walk the best drivers in the world." Whether Kenny will be one of those drivers this weekend is highly uncertain.

They share an awkward gesture that is almost a hug. "I'm going for it!" he says, his face composed.

"I know you are," Danielle says, looking at him and, over his shoulder, at two haulers: the number 81 and right next to it the number 11.

❖

Practice starts, and Kenny climbs into the car in good spirits. "Tell you what boys, let's run us a lap," he says, and he does. "When he comes in, you want a plug check?" Jeremy asks Newt. After the car has run a few laps, Jeremy and Frank often pull the plugs out of the engine and peer at them through the piece of equipment a doctor uses to look in your ear. If the fuel is burning incompletely, it leaves a green residue on the plugs, and they can get other clues about what's going on in the cylinders from the plugs. But in an effort to squeeze whatever power they can from the engine, the team has put in the biggest possible carburetor jets and advanced the timing as much as possible. If the fuel mixture is a little light on gas, it's said to be lean, and it certainly isn't lean today. So Newt looks disapprovingly at Jeremy. "That thing's fat enough now to sink a ship. What do you need a plug check for?" Newt swings his arms and rolls his shoulders. His back is bothering him.

Kenny comes in and everybody scrambles. Kenny to the monitor: He's eighth of 15 drivers on the track so far. From under the car comes Two-Can's voice: "That thing's still barely hitting on that pipe." He dabs paint on the bottom of the exhaust pipe so he'll be able to see if it's still bouncing after they readjust. "We can gain just a little bit by taking them washers out," he says to Newt. They're talking 1/32 of an inch here; then again, they're also talking about thousandths of a second. Everything helps.

Kenny's in and out, and the car doesn't look much better. His best time is 30.5. Though that's not on new tires, that still doesn't look good. He's complaining that the car is loose, mostly, but everything they try seems to unsettle something else. More than anything, though, Kenny keeps complaining about the right front of the car rolling over too far. It's the same thing he's been complaining about since testing at this track more than a week ago. The car just dips too far on the right side going into the turns, and nothing seems to help. Shocks come on and off. At one point progress stops because nobody can find a shock they want to put on the car. After a few minutes of looking it's discovered, already on the car. Newt takes a deep breath, and they back up, take all four shocks off the car, and start over.

Newt, over and over, tries to get Kenny to follow the inside line through Turns three and four, hugging the white line at the bottom of the turn. Kenny has trouble getting the car down there, and he tells Newt about it, but Newt keeps urging him on. "Is that the lowest you can get in the turn in 3 and 4?" he asks. Through Turns 1 and 2 Kenny rides the line nice and low, but in 3 and 4 his natural line is somewhat higher. He tries a wider swing, staying out at the wall and making a sharper left, lower into the turn, and Newt likes it. "That's the best you've looked, going into 3, that you've looked all week," he says.

The early practice ends with Kenny's best lap—a 30.456, 21st of the 44 drivers who've been practicing. Not too hopeful. "You know, if he's still loose, what do you think of that 8-inch A-frame?" Two-Can asks while munching some chips and a sandwich slapped together from Dave's groceries. The Busch cars practice from 10 to 11, and their droning doesn't quite drown out conversation at the hauler. Newt shakes his head. "Didn't do anything for us the other night," he says. "But it might be time to take some of that camber out of the left front." Camber describes the tilt of the tire, compared with perfectly perpendicular to the track. The left front is usually slightly positive—the top of the tire is tilted out a tiny degree—and maybe losing some of that will help get the car where Kenny wants it.

Newt stands up, looks around at the guys chewing their sandwiches in the shade of the hauler lift gate. "OK," he says. "Let's everyone stay focused here and find a way to get in this race. I'll be firing shit off, so let's try to do it as fast as possible." He turns to Kenny. "OK, buddy. You've raced this place a lot of times, you know how to go. Just race the way you know how." And then it's 11, and they're back out on the track for their last practice before their final qualifying run.

Kenny's first words from the track are bright: "Man, this sumbitch feels pretty good right now!" he says. Vic, keeping time on the top of the hauler in the sun, shakes his head. The stopwatch says 31.06. "Can you get in there a little harder?" Newt asks. Kenny comes in and out, as they try changing camber, changing shocks, lowering the track bar that stabilizes the car in the rear. Nothing works too well. "Seems to me what's helped the most is when you've held the right front up, kept the left front from unloading," Kenny says from inside the car. "That keeps me tight getting in." Kenny likes a race car tight: Tight, he says, "you can manhandle it." Loose, it's getting out of control. Newt, in his own driving days, preferred a loose car. The car just about sideways going into the turn lets the driver punch the gas the moment he's through it, without feathering until he gets his rear wheels perfectly behind his front ones. When he gets sideways, about halfway through the turn, he's headed straight down the backstretch. Their differing preferences might cause some miscommunication.

Whatever, Newt comes to a decision. Eddie is apprising Newt on tire temperatures he's just taken, comparing the inside, center, and outside temperatures on the different tires, another clue on whether the car is loose or tight. Newt breaks in.

"Aw, hell," he says. "Let's put this thing in right now. I got a piece of dynamite for the right front." He keeps talking, but he addresses Kenny. You can hear the change from the tone of his voice, suddenly directed, suddenly focused: "The more we get this thing to pushing, the more you can drive it in the corner, is that right?"

"Yeah, that's right," Kenny says.

"Well, we're goin' to make it push this time. Push, she should." And he walks over to Two-Can and tells him to put in a new right front spring, with a spring weight of 2,484 pounds. That's about 400 pounds heavier than anything else they've tried, which is already about 400 pounds heavier than anything anybody else is using. That's a superspeedway spring. But you gotta try whatever you got, and nothing has worked so far. Newt even cuts a spring rubber in half with a hacksaw, reaching under the fender to put both halves in the spring. They'll stiffen the car up even more, and they'll be easy to remove if the car is now too tight.

Next door, in the 42 car's garage, the car goes in and out in a leisurely way, the crew sweeping between runs. Nobody in the Filmar garage has time for that now. This is it.

"Feels good," Kenny says. And runs a time of 31 flat. Newt implores him: "Can't you get in the gas any sooner?"

"I can't, Newt: I got 30-lap tires on this thing."

Newt looks at the car from the top of the hauler. "Well, you think you got a second on it in new tires? You picked up two-tenths in the corner here just with that spring change." He comes in and they switch to the best set of tires remaining. Newt comes down to the hauler and leans over Jeremy. "Do you have anything left in that engine, Jeremy?"

Jeremy looks up from the engine. "A little," he shrugs.

"Could you give it to me?"

"Ten-four." Frank Good later admits that was a lie. "We just tell him that to make him feel better," he says. "We had it all out there already."

They put the car out on the track for one last trial—and Kenny feels good, following his own line through the middle of Turns 3 and 4, not trying to go low the way Newt wants him to. "You're not believing how much better this car is," he says. It's not showing up on the stopwatch. Kenny's best late practice time is 30.653, 40th of 47 cars practicing.

Newt talks to Kenny again. "You got your line, the line that works for you, don't you," he says. "You just don't listen to what everyone else, every Tom, Dick and Harry says about it. I guess I've been hardheaded, that's all, I guess I'm hardheaded."

"No," Kenny says. "You're just not in the race car."

Newt is on to other concerns. "Dave," he says. "Could you go down to look at the stand-on-times list?"

Dave does.

❖

Hanging on the bulletin board by those potted plants at the side door of the NASCAR hauler, the stand-on times list has been busy all morning. Guys in different uniforms come up to it, stare intently at it, and then walk off to huddle with their teams. The crew chiefs of the first few teams—the 96, the 77, the 99—sign early in the morning. Almost nothing could convince them to give up a position so close to the front to try to run a faster lap on a track that in the steady sun will surely be slower.

As the morning progresses, crew chiefs from other teams come by, stand for a moment, take a deep breath, and sign their names. When Dave goes to check at noon, when the deadline has passed, he gets a photocopied sheet from Nikki Taylor. It says what everybody expected it would. Everybody from 26 to 38 has stood, hoping that the track will be so much slower that nobody beats them. Darrell Waltrip, driver and owner of the 17 car, ran 48th quick in qualifying, but he's standing too, leaning on that previous champion's provisional. Everybody else—11 cars—is going to requalify.

In the garage, the team puts the car on jacks and cleans it up, putting in a qualifying gear, one that accelerates faster, since the car has only a lap to build speed and is running only a single lap for time. Jeremy works on the engine, and Frank takes a second for a smoke, leaning on a stack of tires, squinting into the bright noonday sunlight.

"See?" he says. "You go from a high like last week to a low like this. We won't even make the race."

He figures Kenny can't squeeze a lap out of the car? He shrugs. "If he can, where's it been? He ran a 30.10 this morning, but that's on the crew chief's stopwatch. The crew chief's watch is always quick. He's gotta run a 30 flat, but that's gonna be hard as hell. We ran a 29.60 last year. We'd be eighth with that." Goodyear has changed the tire composite from last race to this one, he says, and he thinks that's what's got them flummoxed. "Stiffer sidewalls," he says. "That's what's fucking us up." That subtly changes the way the car handles, the weights pushing back up from the track onto the springs and shocks. It's a little change. "But just one little thing throws a curve ball," he says.

But that's Winston Cup racing: thousandths of a second, fractions of an inch. "I knew it would be hard," he says, "But I never thought it would be this hard." He grew up racing go-carts in Wayne, New Jersey. Then he and his brother put their money together and bought a Late Model car. "He drove it because he put more money in," Frank smiles. "I wish I could do it again, what I know now . . ."

He came to Charlotte two years ago to attend Motor Sports Training Center in Mooresville, one of several schools and community college programs that have sprung up around Charlotte to train the people the race teams need. Then-crew chief Gil Martin called the school looking for workers, Frank says. "He called on a Friday, and I called him back. He said, 'I'm setting up the car for Bristol. Call back on Monday.' I said, 'I'll *be* there on Monday.' And I was—8 A.M. And I was lucky. They took me right into the Winston Cup shop." That's Frank Good; he's number one on the referral list at his school and he shows up at 8 A.M. ready to work for a guy who barely offered to talk to him. Then he gets hired and somehow he figures it must be luck.

His wife, Melody, came with him when he moved to Charlotte, of course. "She's supportive," he says. "I'm like, 'I want to do this.' And she said, 'Quit talking about it and let's go.'" She quit her job working as a hairdresser and making a lot of money to come down and help her husband pursue his dream. And now she sees him at 9 at night for long enough to watch him fall asleep, and that's during the week. On weekends he's not there at all. And she's OK with that?

"I don't know if she's OK with it," he grins, stubbing out his smoke. "But she lets me do it."

She's OK with it—she said so last week during qualifying—just another night at some damn speedway for her. She held the baby, 14-month-old Chad, while Frank worked. She was there just to find a few minutes with her husband. "Yeah, it's hard," she said, jiggling the baby on her hip. "I do get resentful. When he misses Chad's first birthday, misses his first Halloween, yeah, that's hard. A couple times he's had a really high fever, and I've had to say, 'You need to know I'm worried. You need to worry too.' Chad will be wearing a 101 Dalmatians costume this year for Halloween, while Frank's racing in Phoenix. 'Take a lot of pictures' is what I get from Frankie," she laughed. "He thinks racing 24 hours a day. We'll be in bed and he'll start mumbling something. I'll have my eyes closed and I'll know he's lying there with his eyes wide open, thinking about racing." But she shrugged and said the same thing every single wife of a Winston Cup crew member says: "He's happy, and that's all that matters." The money's OK, their husbands are happy, and that will do.

Newt's wife, Rhonda, was a little less certain one afternoon after a race at Darlington, as she stood around waiting for the crew to pack up so she and her husband could leave. "And I sat here four and a half hours this morning waiting for the green flag to drop," she smiled.

"If we'd have had kids, I'd have never done it," she said of her move to Charlotte from Nashville when the race team climbed to the Winston Cup level. "He gets to do something he loves, and I get to stay home," she said, which she enjoys. "When he became a crew chief, he told me that filled the void he felt from not driving. The money is good. But sometimes you wonder about it. There's nothing in my life that I love enough to put in the hours that he does." The stress level Newt endures worries her. "He will try to do it all by himself," she said of the problems Newt and the team faced. "No matter what you do, it's 'What could you have done to be better?'" But she doesn't try to calm him down, doesn't try to provide perspective. "Women sometimes can upset the apple basket," she said. "I let him handle it."

That weekend at Darlington, the team failed to qualify the first day, and that was about the worst she saw. "On qualifying day, everyone's stressed out and tensed up. When they don't qualify, it gets worse. But then like this week, when they qualify faster second round, it's like a thousand-pound weight is lifted from his shoulders." She sat back down on her yard chair, while the crew packed up and talked about schedules and she waited for her husband.

Today at Charlotte she's not here. She won't come until the weekend. But everyone's working like hell to lift that thousand-pound weight from Newt's shoulders, and nobody more than Frank Good, leaning on a stack of tires. "This is a second-year team," he says. Expectations shouldn't be too high. "Newt works really hard," he says. "I'll stand behind him to the day he dies. Eddie's cool too. I hope he stays for a long time."

At the moment, making it through this weekend would be nice.

❖

The car is ready. Tires are on, gears are changed, and springs are set. The key change is the "piece of dynamite" Newt had for the right front, the spring with a 2,484-pound response weight. Plus it's still got half a spring rubber in it to stiffen it further. If that can't keep the right front from dropping, can't keep the car from getting loose, Newt Moore doesn't know what can. The car comes down off the jacks and they push it back out of the garage. They fill it with gas. They go through complete inspection for the third time this weekend.

And then they push the car out onto pit road, hooked up to its generator, to wait in line for second-round qualifying. Crew members from other second-round hopefuls are scattered along pit road, watching their cars. Buddy and Frank sit down to watch their own. Several crew members come and go, speaking quietly, wondering. There's no hoopla surrounding qualifying like there was last night, no people in animal suits, nothing. "Just wait until race day, though," Patty Hopkins of the Cartoon Network had said last night. "Then you'll see something." Maybe; the frowning faces on the Square D crew don't bode well. Sure, the race will start on Sunday, and Jeff Gordon and Dale Earnhardt will be there. Tom and Jerry will even be there. But it doesn't look much like Kenny Wallace will be there. The next 30 seconds in the life of their car will tell whether they'll see that after all, and the guys in the blue-and-yellow shirts aren't too hopeful. "I think," says one, "that we're going to run one more lap, load up the car, and go home."

Kenny will go 6th of the 11 cars requalifying, and when the number 14 car takes the first lap and comes in at 30.186, frowns droop even more. That's a 10th slower than that car's qualifying time yesterday, and yesterday that car was a quarter of a second faster than Kenny.

The cars go one by one, and finally the number 81 is at the front of the line. Kenny, almost invisible under a helmet and behind the safety netting in his window, flips his ignition and the car roars to life. The official pats the car and Kenny roars off into the asphalt heat of Turn 1. He builds speed on the backstretch, takes the middle line he's comfortable with through Turns 3 and 4, and mashes the gas getting onto the straightaway for the green flag. The car disappears into Turn 1, but on the giant television screen set up to provide a better view for the fans in the stands, you can see Kenny driving deep into the turns. It's balls-out for one lap for Kenny Wallace, and he's challenging the car and the track. If he doesn't make the race, it's not going to be for lack of trying. He's going to fly or he's going to wreck.

In fact, that's what Kenny said that morning. "I talked to the car," he said in the garage. "I said, 'You're either gonna stand up for me or you're gonna wreck.'"

One way or the other.

❖

Only Buddy stays out on pit road to watch the lap; everyone else has started walking back to the garage. He watches Kenny buzz by, taking the checkered flag flat-out, then disappear into the turn again, all the way around the track to the pit road entrance in Turn 4 and then into the garage. Buddy turns, stares up at the scoreboard, the same one that yesterday had told about Kenny's 1989 Busch Grand National exploits. His face doesn't show the result. But as he turns to trot back to the garage, he faces a long row of shaking heads of members of the other teams lined up on the pit wall, and smiles, and outstretched hands for Buddy to slap as he runs by. Buddy smiles too as he runs toward the garage, speeding up as he goes.

If you don't see that, if your scanner is set to the frequency used by the number 81 team, you might think that something has gone wrong with the equipment. "Newt Moore! Newt Moore!" That's Eddie's voice, from the garage. "Did I tell you . . ." then a burst of static, as everyone talks at once. Frank and Two-Can and Buddy are all pressing their buttons and talking, all making their way back to the garage from pit road. Kenny's talking as he's coasting into the garage with one hand out his window, waving his index finger wildly. Newt Moore is talking, scrambling down the ladder from the top of the hauler as fast as he can.

Kenny found that extra half second. The time that flashed onto the scoreboard was 29.739. By far the fastest lap Kenny had run in two days of practice and qualifying. If he'd run it Wednesday, he'd have qualified 15th. Those shaking heads on the pit wall were pondering the same question everybody asks the rest of the weekend: "Where the hell did *that* come from?"

Around the Square D car, nobody is asking that question. Around the number 81 Square D Filmar Racing Ford Thunderbird, parked in tech inspection for a postqualifying checkup, the guys in yellow and blue have just won the Super Bowl. Frank Good stands happily, leaning on the car and opening the hood as Kenny scrambles out. Two-Can and Buddy slap hands with Don, with Eddie. And when Newt Moore makes it over, his face red, his yellow streak-of-lightning hat still on, he and Eddie grab each other by the back of the neck and scream into each other's faces, swinging around in a sort of mad, ecstatic jig, Eddie practically climbing onto Newt's shoulders.

Kenny, out of the car, hugs Don first, and then everybody else who comes up. "Can you believe that shit!" he screams. "I busted a lap! I busted a mother-fucking *lap*!

"I been telling 'em for two years to make the car tight, I'll go faster," he says, his sweat-streaked face in a euphoric smile, his helmet-mussed hair all over his head. "I think I got a Daytona spring in that right front, don't I?" He looks for Newt. His piece of dynamite for the right front turned out to be exactly right.

During the crew's dance and moment of celebration, the remaining cars have run their qualifying laps, so there is more good news. Kenny has run the fastest lap of second-day qualifying, good for a $500 Busch pole award and 26th spot in the starting grid. Danielle comes hustling over: "You are the *man*!" she shouts. Kenny nods, smiles, accepts the hug. Turns out that Brett Bodine isn't the man, at least not this week, and at least not for Square D.

Kenny starts walking across the garage to his hauler, but he can't get far. He's accosted at every step by well-wishers and reporters. "Man!" he tells a reporter. "We went out in left field big time. We did all kinds of measuring, we checked, and finally we said the hell with it." He stops, thinking of Rusty's fine. "I mean the heck with it, excuse me. And we put in a spring that's a Daytona spring. I told the car this morning: 'I'm gonna give you every opportunity to make this corner.' And the car delivered."

Danielle runs back up: "I spoke to Filbert!" she says. "I said: '29.739.' Filbert said, 'Yaaaaaaaaah!'" Kenny says, "Tell him I saved him $33,000!"

Kenny stops in the middle of the concrete, suddenly embraced. It's driver Ken Schrader, whom Kenny considers one of his best friends. "We were watching on TV in the office!" Schrader says. "Man, we were jumping up and down for you! You should have seen us!" Kenny and Schrader hold each other by the forearms, smiling and laughing. Kenny starts to tell him about the unusual spring setup.

"Whatever it takes!" Schrader says. "There are no rules in handling."

Then another reporter comes up. "I'm getting good lately at pulling the rabbit out of my hat," Kenny smiles. "We got a new crew chief, we were afraid to give the car everything it wanted. Then we miss the first round and go hog wild, and hog wild is what it needs. Our crew chief, he's laid a lot on the line and I'd hate to have us miss the race. One thing, I'm so proud of myself."

Danielle has been dialing her cell phone, and she pushes it into Kenny's hand: "It's Kim! It's your wife!" Kenny grabs it. "Honey! I made the race! I love you! Bye!"

Finally, as he nears the hauler, one last guy with a notebook comes up. "All the Square D people are coming, and now, hey, it's show time!" Kenny says. "You know what," he goes on, "I believe in the good Lord. I'm not super religious. I don't go to a whole bunch of church. But I told the guys, 'What are y'all nervous about?' I have that deal about me that I wasn't going to let it bother me. You have to go when the car is not ready to go in this sport. The track was slippery and our car has got a lot of down force and we just didn't have enough spring in it. We gave it the spring it needed and four new tires and laid 'em on the dashboard, and it was awesome. Only Kenny Wallace can pull off stuff like this. I'll tell you what, we've got 'Front Row Joe' and now we've got 'Big Balls Kenny.'" The guy stares wide-eyed, a little overwhelmed.

"Thanks, Kenny," he says. Oh yeah. How about the car?

"It handles great."

❖

After a shoulder-shattering high-five from Eddie, Kenny ducks into the hauler to take a breath, though the crew's doing no such thing. Buddy comes back to the hauler to find the crash cart, and with Frank acting as shield, he welds the exhaust pipes where they were cracked in Wednesday night's fiasco. The cars for the Busch Grand National race on Saturday are qualifying, and in the hollow roar of the single cars making their way around the track Newt is already giving directions over the radio. He's chattering happily about changing A-frames and springs and camber; from the sound of his voice, it appears that that Daytona spring lifted more than the right front of the number 81 car. That thousand-pound weight his wife talked about is, at least for the moment, off his shoulders. Something wonderful is about to start at 3 P.M.: practice for Sunday's race. Practice for a race that the number 81 car will run, starting in 26th position.

Inside the hauler comes Russell Wallace, Kenny's dad. A racer himself, winning championships on the tracks around St. Louis, he got all of his sons interested in stock cars. Rusty's won a championship, Kenny's a regular on the Winston Cup circuit, and Mike runs trucks and Busch cars, often running Cup races, too. Seven Winston Cup races have started this season with all three Wallace brothers in the field. When he talks about his team's struggles, Kenny often says, "It's not so much being a race car driver and not winning; it's being a *Wallace* and not winning that's hard."

But at this euphoric moment, Russell is talking to Kenny, but not about Kenny's remarkable effort. He's interested in the fine NASCAR levied on Rusty. "I could become a radical over it," he says.

"That's the problem when you got three kids racing," Kenny says. "One of 'em's always in a mix-up."

"I like rules," Russell comes back, "but I don't like a dictatorship, where the rules get changed every five minutes."

Kenny sighs. "I been through so much," he says. "Life on the edge. One week you do great and everyone tells you how good you are, and then you go to another track and everyone wants to know what's wrong." His dad leaves, and Kenny climbs to the top of the hauler to join Vic, watching the Busch cars qualify. Standing up there, sunglasses on, still in his driver suit—called a future suit by the crews—he looks relaxed and happy. He's high, wide, and handsome, at least until practice starts again.

"The relief," he says, "is like ecstasy. The feeling is so great to know that you did it. Now I'm so relaxed, it's easy." He thinks back over the last couple of days. "They were all wanting me to run the line that Mark Martin runs. If I'd run the line Mark Martin runs, I'd be Mark Martin. They kept trying to give the car what they wanted to give it, instead of what the car wanted. Then they gave it all that spring, and that made the car tight, and I can drive that sumbitch."

He sips a soda. "Today was a huge breakthrough, because now we can go to Atlanta and have a good start." Atlanta, owned by Bruton Smith, like Charlotte, has about the same track setup as Charlotte. Now they know where to start for that race. And he talked to more than his car this morning too. "It wasn't until I got in the shower this morning that I figured it out," he says. He heard the Tom Petty song "Turning Point," and it got his attention. Today was going to be a turning point for him, and he talked his way through it, alone in the shower.

"I said I could either get aggressive about this shit and be a man or I can sit and pout about it. Mark Martin, that line he drives, that's so pretty. The hell with being pretty. I want to be aggressive."

Looking over the garage while the Busch cars run, he notices the number 31 car's crew packing its gear. Mike Skinner, the car's driver, paces over to a white sport utility van and climbs in. "He don't look too happy," Vic says. "This is really amazing here. They have to go home."

"That ain't nothing," Kenny says. "Wait until you see DW pull out."

That stops Vic. Darrell Waltrip, three-time Winston Cup champion and after 25 years of racing still a huge fan favorite, did not qualify. Because three cars qualified for the race on the second day—Ernie Irvan in the 28 car and Lake Speed in the 9 were the only two others who made the show—the back end of the pack got pushed a little farther back. Defending series champion Terry Labonte's number 5 car, with its special Froot Loops paint job, got pushed back from 36th to 39th. That put him in the provisional pool, and because the most recent champion has priority, he got the previous champion's provisional that Waltrip was counting on. The remaining four provisionals were awarded based on the current points standings, and Waltrip, in 20th place, was beat out by four other cars. Everybody uses provisionals. Kenny's used two this year. And every previous champion leans on their special provisional, too; the only previous champion who hasn't used one this year is Jeff Gordon. So it happens to everybody. But two previous champions at the back of the pack is rare. That rarity has caught Waltrip, and he's going home.*

---

* This is even more complicated than it sounds; the planets had to come into a remarkable alignment for Waltrip to miss this race. For one thing, do not lose track of the fact that once you get past the 38 guys who qualified on speed, lap times are completely ignored. Thus Rick Mast, who ran a lap time of 30.016, went home, while Jeremy Mayfield, whose best time was 30.051 (35 thousandths of a second *slower* than Mast) ran the race, starting in 39th position. He got the first provisional spot because he was 11th in the points standings, highest among the nonqualifying drivers. Note further that while Mayfield started 39th, Kyle Petty, who also qualified slightly faster than Mayfield, started 40th. Petty was behind Mayfield in points, so he got a lower provisional. Then confuse matters even further by recognizing that the previous-champion provisional is assigned *before* the other provisionals, even though it's for the 43rd position. So Terry Labonte, whose 39th-quick lap of 29.997 missed 38th position by *one-thousandth of a second*, was assigned the 43rd (and final) starting position even though he was faster than all the other provisional starters. More, if you assigned the four provisionals first and then the previous champion, that's one way Waltrip would have made the race, because Labonte would have received the first provisional spot and Waltrip would have been the only remaining previous champion. Then Ricky Craven, in the 25, would have gone home. OK? Now listen to this: That thousandth of a second proved costly indeed for Waltrip, because if Labonte had made the field on speed, he would have displaced the 78 car of Gary Bradberry, who then would have gone home, since he's 43rd in the points standings. (OK, ask it: If their times had been *exactly the same*, then what? Well, it's obvious: Labonte gets the nod. He's ahead in points.) More important, with Labonte in the race on speed, Waltrip would have been the sole previous champion in the provisional pool, and he would have made the race. One last complication: Provisional spots are assigned based on *owner's* points standing, not *driver* points standing. The two are almost exactly the same—they're awarded in the same quantities by the same rules after each race. But if a driver changes teams in midseason, the owner—and the car—keep the points standing for qualifying purposes. It's a way of rewarding the sponsors and the team owners who put up the money—if you lose your driver, you've still got a chance to start the races. And in this case it did exactly that. Waltrip, 20th in the points standings, was bumped by Craven, who's 21st. The reason was because Craven had missed two races due to injury early in the season, but the number 25 car had been driven by substitute driver Todd Bodine. The car and its owner kept amassing points for those races, though Craven didn't until he returned in Martinsville. So while Craven was behind Waltrip in points, the number 25 car, owned by Rick Hendrick, was ahead of Waltrip's 17, which he owned himself and had driven in every race. Tough luck, Darrell. ("The point of having rules," a Cup official said to me, "Is that you follow 'em.") By the way, Greg Sacks, in the 15 car, also beat Craven's lap time, by about three hundredths of a second. Too bad—Sacks had started only 10 races all year and was 45th in points. He went home with Waltrip and Skinner and Mast—and Dave Marcis, and Elliott Sadler, and Steve Park. Craven got to sit in the bright red number 25 Budweiser Chevy when the guy said, "Gentlemen, start your engines." Hard old world.

Waltrip failing to make the race is momentous. It's the first time it's happened in his 25 years of Cup competition, and it briefly stops Vic from criticizing the lines the Busch cars are taking through Turns 3 and 4. Though three cars had to qualify in the second round for it to happen, Vic makes the obvious connection: "We sent him home."

Kenny shrugs. "See, I don't feel bad for him. Everybody knows the feeling you have when you miss a race. But they'd much rather it'd been you than them." That feeling, in fact, is part of what pushes a driver to do well—and to do better than he ever has. "As long as you know that feeling and you can remember that feeling, you'll win races."

And he's at least made this one, so he's thinking about only that. "See, Rick Mast has missed the race and Mike Skinner has missed the race, so if we can just finish in the top 20 . . ." Skinner and Mast are 29th and 30th in points, and Mast, the closest qualifier on time not to make the race, missed it by two-hundredths of a second. They're part of the group he's trying to catch to make it into the top 30 in points for that $7,000 a race next year. Before the Martinsville race Kenny was 126 points out of 33rd place and 240 away from that magical 30th. Now he's only 13 back of Dick Trickle in 33rd, and 184 out of 30th. With five races to go, he needs to pick up about 40 points a race, and last week he picked up 56. It's still a stretch, but it's still possible, and a top-20 finish is the first step. "We *want* more than that, but we just *need* to finish top 20." He climbs back down the ladder. Practice is coming up.

Vic stands on his own, watching the Busch cars, clicking his stopwatch, taking corner speeds. The Filmar team doesn't need this information. This is Busch stuff and they're not interested. Vic's doing it because it's racing, and racing is what he does. You can tell whether a car is loose or tight by watching. "If the driver drives in hard and they slide up, you can usually tell if the nose goes up first." That means he's tight. "Oh, look at that. That's Joe Nemechek [he's driving in the Busch race as well as the Cup race]. He's running a perfect line. He's going to be fast. He's got a shot at the pole." He clicks his watch. "Shit, he's 2 miles an hour faster than anybody else. I can't picture anybody beating that."

The cars buzz around the track, one by one, and Vic stays up there watching until Cup practice starts again. When the Busch race starts on Saturday, Joe Nemechek sits on the pole.

❖

As Busch qualifying winds down, the team gathers around the car for the day's last practice. A NASCAR official walks through the garage holding a sign on a photocopied piece of paper on a clipboard: "WC practice 3:30–4:15. Garage closes 5:15."

Kenny comes in and out quickly during the final practice. The race setup will be completely different than the qualifying setup. A car running in traffic for 500 miles and a car running all on its own for a lap might as well be completely different cars. By the time the race car takes the green flag Sunday, it basically will be: springs, shocks, tires, gear, engine, all will be different. So the late practice today is a first stab at what the car ought to feel like. They change springs and shocks and take the tape off the grille. Seconds of speed aren't the point now; long-term handling is. The crew of the 42 car next door is long gone. Nemechek, the driver, is spending the afternoon with his Busch car. They did what they could in the early practices, and their car sits quiet under its cover. The Square D guys, on the other hand, squeeze every second out of the 45-minute practice. With four minutes to go, Newt asks whether Kenny wants to make a final spring change or whether he's ready to give up for the day.

"I don't wanna give up on *nothing*," Kenny says. "That's the old days."

Newt clicks right back on: "New day, new deal." Then the red flag comes out and practice is over anyhow. "Well, come in here and we'll talk about it like civilized human beings," Newt says. "Guys, hell of a job today. Way to stick in there and believe."

As soon as Kenny's out of the car, Frank, Jeremy, Buddy, and Don are ripping the engine out. Teams use different engines for qualifying than they do for the race itself. The qualifying engine is set up with cams and a valvetrain that will maximize speed for an extremely short time. It's designed to go real fast for a couple laps. The race engine is designed to last the entire 500 miles of a race and to deliver its power over a longer period. "We won't have an engine until about noon tomorrow," Newt says. They're still waiting on their race engine from Yates, so removing the qualifying engine wouldn't usually be a rush.

But nobody's complaining. NASCAR needs the qualifying engine. Kenny was fastest in second-day qualifying. They'll take it apart as a natural part of tech inspection, and the Square D team doesn't mind that a bit.

Nor does anybody else. "The thing that's important to remember," one NASCAR official says, "is those other guys all went home. They missed the race by two-hundredths of a second, or whatever. That's part of our job, that all these guys who stayed are legal so that those guys legitimately went home. That's why we spend a bunch of time back here to make sure none of these guys are beyond the rules. That kind of intensive enforcement of the rules has made the series what it is."

By 4:45 the engine is on a hoist, and Frank and Two-Can are underneath the car. By 5 they're standing around the hauler for a quick beer or two, as NASCAR officials pace the garage, urging guys to close it up. Dave starts closing up the hauler, locking it for the night.

Two-Can takes his usual couple of beers and heads out. Would this be a good time to spill the secret of his name? "Got company coming, no time! No time!" he says. "No practice tomorrow, just around the garage all day. Plenty of time then!" and he's off through the gate to the infield and his car.

The number 81 car is under its cover in the garage, the door pulled down behind it. The late rays of a setting sun rake the racetrack, sparkling off the concrete in the garage as the end of Busch practice suddenly brings silence to the track. The stands are almost empty, and the officials stroll the garage, making sure nobody's hanging around late. They lock the gates behind the last guys to leave.

❖

In the infield, the paddocks reserved for the drivers' motorhomes are filling up, but the fans have not yet shown up much. The infield officially opened up around 7 this morning, but you'd have to be a pretty dedicated fan to come in Thursday morning to see nothing more exciting than second-round qualifying and a little bit of practice. So the infield stretches empty in the yellowing sunlight, the green expanses of grass studded with blue trash barrels. It's ready, because tomorrow it will start in earnest.

Outside the track, across Route 29, the trickle of fans into the campgrounds is picking up, and more than just souvenir trailers have set up. Food is available, and little curls of smoke above barbecue trailers, above spots where you can get fried bologna (the peanuts and Crackerjack of racing), fill the clear purpling sky with a sweet-smelling haze. A few fans wander, illuminated starkly by the light from the rows of souvenir trailers, but it's not buying time yet. These fans just got here. They may not even have been inside the speedway yet. A lot of the trailers have closed their awnings for the night. Starting tomorrow, they won't have a minute to themselves, and they're just waiting for the rush.

South of the speedway on Route 29, though, the party has started.

In front of a tired 1976 Winnebago parked on a vacant lot is a telephone pole, on which is attached a 4x4-foot banner. It's bright blue, and it's got that big yellow D in a square in the middle: "Square D Racing," it says. Standing in front of the banner in red shorts and a blue shirt is Shane, from Columbia, South Carolina, a young guy of about 25. Next to him on a piece of plywood is a big sign: "Buy/sell Tix."

"I'm hustling tickets!" he says brightly, offering a beer. Cool. How'd he come to be a ticket hustler? "I have a master's in drama," he says. "Doesn't mean anything. They gave me a masters in how to teach drama, but they didn't teach one course in how to teach drama. I call that a money racket." His wife is at home, pregnant, and this is his current living. "Racing's enough, if you do it right," he says.

On the door of the Winnebago is a cardboard sign: "Open, please knock." Inside sits Shane's friend Dave, who characterizes ticket hustling thus: "It's better'n driving nails." With him sits a woman who identifies herself, with a glance at Dave, as "your lawyer." She's drinking a beer and smoking a cigarette, so she might not be. "We've been here all week," Dave says. "Since Tuesday morning. The guy who owns the property lets us be here. We kind of protect his building." They talk about the Square D banner. Someone in a truck came by earlier in the day and asked him if he could put up the Square D banner, Dave says. "I said sure. It's racing, right? Every organization has their group that runs up and down the highway putting out banners. They saw a place where a lot of people were going to see it, and they put it up."

Friends and fellow partiers—and, occasionally, someone who wants to buy or sell a ticket—roll into and out of the little brown dirt parking area. Dave and Shane are free with their beers, and friends line up in lawn chairs in front of the Winnebago. It's hard to blame them. The inside, with a plywood floor, two unmade beds, decrepit floral upholstery, and a chair that looks like it used to be brown, is probably best reserved for Shane and Dave.

Another woman sits down with Dave and his lawyer. "We're trying to convince her not to go back to school," Shane says. "What'd it do for me?" He talks about race day traffic, which will build up past his booth—a mile away from the speedway—by 7 A.M., he says. "This is Charlotte, baby." But maybe that master's degree hasn't hurt him so bad. He's fascinated by the culture he's become a part of.

"It's a transient subculture, which I like," he says, slipping into a camping fleece shirt as the evening cools down. "They come together for an event. Next event, you see 'em again. It's actually a pretty small world. People are on the road, so they're stripped of their creature comforts, so you see the best of 'em. Humanity comes together. You rarely see TV at night [you certainly don't here, now that he mentions it] you just sit and talk. To me, that's neat. Any other sporting event, it's kind of a mad dash to the event and away from the event. Whereas Winston Cup racing, people take a year's savings to come for a weekend of events. You stay a while, so it's not so rushed."

He takes a deep breath.

"I like it."

It's Thursday night, two and a half days before race time. Traffic flows up and down Route 29, and occasionally someone climbs out of a car to do a little business or drink a little beer. It's warm enough to wear shorts during the day and chilly enough to wear a sweatshirt in the evening. In a southwestern sky utterly devoid of clouds, Venus and Mars stand out bright above the horizon, shifting positions in the little two-step they've been dancing all week. No TV, friends to sit and smoke a cigarette with, a warm place to sleep, and a buddy or five. "I like it," Shane says.

What's not to like?

CHAPTER 6

STAR GAZING

Friday, October 3

Dawn comes over the Charlotte Motor Speedway to the sound of tools. This morning, though, a new sound overpowers the clank of wrenches on the concrete garage floor and the nasal whine of air wrenches. This morning, under a blue-white sky on a day that promises to be hot, another sound echoes off the empty grandstands before 8 A.M.

Hammering. Hammers pounding nails into 2x4s and plywood. Hammers pounding tent stakes into the ground. Hammers whanging steel scaffolds together. Hammers knocking jacks underneath pickup chassis to stabilize them for the viewing platforms being built above. Everybody is building something. Overnight, the infield has started to fill up with fans.

It's not full by any means. You can still see the winding asphalt roads that cut through the packed grass and brown dirt, making the whole area feel a little like an airfield. Most of the blue trash barrels stand alone, and vast sections of unpopulated lawn still soak up the morning sun, showing the gentle undulation of the turf—lowest in Turn 4, a sort of hollow in the center below the backstretch, rising to a high hummock just before you're between Turns 1 and 2.

The Winston Cup garage is set off by black steel fence pickets, and other compounds. The Busch Grand National garage, the infield care center, the little angled roofs that were used as a garage by the ARCA cars Wednesday night are set off by chain-link fences. In the middle of the infield, close to the garages, clean concrete buildings, about as nice as those at a quality campground, house rest rooms and showers. The dark little Pit Stop restaurant, with a dozen tables, serves eggs and grits and fried chicken and mashed potatoes to both fans and crew members. If you don't want to sit down, you can go to the "Pit and Git" window or to another little walkup restaurant that offers hamburgers and hot dogs. A few flea-market-style tents, most noticeably one for Tabasco (unveiling its new Winston Cup car this weekend), provide shade for employees or sell track souvenirs.

But what's amazing about that infield now, what's amazing about this morning, is the campers. Motor homes and school buses populate Turns 1 and 2, where the ground is lower. Up on the higher ground speedway rules forbid the big vehicles (they'd interfere with sight lines and camera angles), so tents have started to pop up, with viewing platforms atop the pickups and vans that brought them in.

In Turns 3 and 4, on the long asphalt lane that runs the length of the infield and functions as a sort of fan main street, Mike Floyd, a well-groomed geologist of 38, is banging around on top of a big pale blue school bus, setting up a plywood viewing platform. "Let's see," he says. "We bought the bus about five years ago. Before that, my drilling company had a lot of box trucks. That was really cool, but they outlawed those. Now you either have to have a school bus or an RV. I think we paid $800 for the bus. We took it to our shop, ripped out all the seats and just hosed down the thing. One guy had some fun, and we were able to retrofit some of the old seats."

Barely. The seats line the inside of the bus along with two or three old couches. A coffee table makes the back of the bus into a little living room. Outside, a wooden shelf swings down from the side of the bus, holding a sink, fed from a barrel on top of the bus. A broad awning will shade the main street side of the bus, making a perfect place to sit and drink and watch streams of other fans parade by. "It's not like home, but it works for a place to party and hang out," Mike says. They pay $100 a year for the reserved space for the bus, and each person who comes in has to pay $45 for the whole weekend or $25 for just Sunday. He looks out across the slowly filling infield. A slow trickle of campers and pickups is coming in through the tunnel under Turn 3. By this evening the infield will be studded with campers. By Saturday night it will be filled. Mike knows who the neighbors will be. "Since it's reserved spaces, we see the same people every year. That's the biggest change in the infield experience; everything is reserved now. Seems like things have toned down."

We'll see. Infield stories are to fans what cheating stories are to crew members, the oral history of their sport, the proof that they are part of something. In Darlington, fans will tell you, there used to be a little hoosegow set up by the sheriff, where he'd toss people who got out of hand. At Charlotte, before every spot was reserved for every race, the weekend used to start unofficially at about 7 on Wednesday evening, when campers, vans, buses, and Winnebagos started lining up outside of the Turn 4 tunnel. Fans would sit in a long line, raising their Confederate flags and pirate flags and flags for their drivers, and they'd sit and drink and work on an early sunburn until at some point—never announced, or if it was announced never when they said it was going to be—some guard would open up the gate and it would be the Oklahoma land rush out there, the spots along the fences in the turns going first, then the spots high up on that hummock between Turns 1 and 2. That's called Redneck Hill these days, and the crown is held open so that fans can go stand there and watch the race. But the fans who set up along Redneck Hill tend to be the loudest, the drunkest, the rebel yellin'-est, the best fans at a Charlotte race.

Just outside that circle of open space atop Redneck Hill, three pickups—two with viewing platforms on top—and a van pulling a camper roll in at about 9:45 A.M. Out spill 11 people: three women, three kids, and five men. It's Rick Dohman, a smallish, light-haired 37-year-old office manager, and his crew. "We've been coming to the races 14, 15 years," he says, and then goes about the business of setting up.

Watching this group of fans set up their race weekend compounds is exactly like watching the race team unload the hauler and set up the garage. First coolers come off the pickups, one by one by one, then the poles for the flea-market-style tent they'll set up. The pickups, camper, and van are parked in a rectangle along the border of their area as if they're circling the wagons, and piles of stuff—blankets, sleeping bags, grocery boxes of food, cases of beer—migrate to the central area. "We've been buying groceries for two months," Rick says. "Looking at sales." They back the two pickups together, so their platforms, well-constructed scaffolds with 2x4s bolted as floor joists and triangle supports, fit together. A carpet remnant goes on top. Backing the pickup into the space barely inches wider than his truck, Rick looks like Dave Ensign expertly guiding the Square D hauler into the garage. Someone is dispatched for ice, pulling a little red wagon; those wagons are everywhere. Wander the infield and you've got to have your wagon, whether it's to go off to get ice, to carry your towel and gym bag to the showers, or just to carry a cooler so you're never too far from a beer.

The camper opens up on cranks. Grills stand to the side at first, the dome tents hurriedly constructed and popped anywhere they'll fit. Once in a while, a wind gust sends one rolling slowly away and someone has to fetch it and weight it down with a lawn chair. Quickly the instructions come out for the big flea market shelter in the center, and everyone works together on that. A little kid in a number 18 Bobby Labonte shirt separates the poles into lengths; a laughing girl of about 20 holds the instructions so the men can walk up and, frowning, peer at them. They've done this before dozens of times, and the shelter goes up in about 15 minutes. Immediately, expertly, everything else goes underneath it: Three banquet tables form an L; food boxes on that. The two gas grills extend one end of the L, next to a freestanding plastic sink. Then out comes a satellite dish. "I think we were the first ones out here to have a TV dish," says a heavyish, dark fellow named Mike Cenzer, setting it up. "We try to make an improvement every time," Rick says. "Satellite, we rig a shower on the Port-a-Jon." Mike smiles. "We're trying to think about a swimming pool."

Then Mike laughs again. "The first year we set up the TV, we had one of those drunken rednecks stumble up: 'Y'all are on cable?' I told him, 'Yeah, they hooked us right up. Aren't you?'"

Oh, those drunken rednecks. Even this morning, they're already out. Cars, vans, buses, and campers trickle slowly into the infield with people who took Friday off to set up, and the hammering and clanging are everywhere. People drag their wagons on errands to get ice, to buy souvenirs. Walk among the tents and platforms filling the infield before your eyes, and you quickly begin to notice a general sameness to dress: Among the men, shorts, flip-flops, no shirts, and skin already showing the pink of a quick sunburn; among women, much the same except a Terry Labonte or Jeff Gordon shirt added to the mix. Sunglasses and race hats fill out the look, as does a bag full of souvenirs from one of the trailers outside. Some trucks and vans drop off people on the way into the infield to get the shopping started before the tents are even up.

Atop a little gray 5x6-foot platform in the back of a pickup, his feet propped on 2x4 railing and a beer in his hand, basks a guy who identifies himself only as Red. "Red hair, red neck, I'm red all fucking over," he says, and it's true. He's got a wisp of red moustache; red hair going to gray pokes out from beneath the Confederate flag bandanna that covers his head; and apart from his Hawaiian print bathing suit, he's nothing but bright pink skin. No fewer than three of his group of ten guys go by the name "Red," and they all earn it. He's here for one reason, he says: "Drink beer, sit in the sun, hang out until you sober up, then go home. We're just rednecks here for the music, the tunes, the race. We're here for the rebel flags."

Those flags have started to show up in force. Maybe one out of every three encampments has a long flagpole, lashed to a platform brace, to a tent pole, to a pickup. Atop the poles flags are going up: colored flags for the drivers, checkered flags, flags with the NASCAR logo, pirate flags. But above all the Confederate flag. Stand on Red's platform and even now, with the vast infield no more than a third full, you can see dozens of rebel flags snapping in the breeze. "I love it!" Red says, raising his Bud. "This is the first race I been to in three years."

Oh. Busy?

"Prison," he says. Then a girl walking by 50 yards away catches his attention: "Oh, my lord, looky there, looky there," he says. "I love you!" One of his pals—a bearded, bellied guy named Red—stands up to show off his shirt: "Rose Racing" it says, from Big Prairie, Ohio. "In Memory of Mike Rose, 1956–1992." Mike died racing at a dirt track, and everyone in Red's crew has a shirt for him, not that most of them are wearing them. Red sits back down on his platform. "I'm here for the fucking race, man," he says. "Charlotte Motor fucking Speedway."

❖

Charlotte Motor Speedway, all right. Inside the Winston Cup garage, it's a day off, which means though the garage is open, there is no practice time allotted on the track for Winston Cup cars. For the Cup guys, according to Humpy Wheeler and everybody else, this is supposed to be a day off to compensate for qualifying taking Wednesday and Thursday. At any other racetrack, haulers would just be pulling in this morning, and teams would run qualifying laps this afternoon; but this is Charlotte, and the teams have been here for two full days already. So Friday is a day off. A nice relaxing day off.

For some teams, that actually turns out to be true. Look down the row of cars in the Winston Cup garage and you see at least half sitting quietly under their covers, tires or jacks leaning on the covers to hold them tight against the car, duct tape covering the fuel intake and the catch-can spigot to keep moisture from getting in. Engine sounds come from across the asphalt in the Busch garage, but here in the big show things are quiet. Only teams that didn't accomplish what they needed to on Wednesday and Thursday are here, or teams that are facing long odds. Or guys who just won't give up. Guys who talk racing in their sleep.

"I was the first guy through the gate this morning," Frank Good says. He's been getting the car ready since then, waiting for Jeremy to arrive with the race engine.

The qualifying engine is set up to run a few laps at high revs real fast. The race engine is set up to run 500 laps under more control. So Frank is waiting for the race engine.

To race teams, an engine is just another part, just another piece of the car that they can replace in an hour, that they can adjust and tweak to tune the maximum performance to their particular needs. Of course, you do a lot less tweaking when you're renting engines from someone else, especially Robert Yates, who doesn't like to share. Frank laughs when asked for a tour of the Yates engine shop. "He won't even let *me* see it," he says. "I went over there one day to pick something up, and I walked through the shop. He saw me and pulled me over to the side. He said he'd appreciate it if I didn't walk through the shop anymore and see what they've got." He shakes his head. "It's just the same stuff, only more of it," he says.

If seeing the top of the line is out of the question, a tour of the Filmar Racing engine shop being prepared for next season in a space rented from the number 8 car's shop just down the road from the Filmar shop shows how the other half lives.

Engine builder Keith Almond, who's built engines for winning race cars driven by Bobby Allison, Dale Earnhardt, David Pearson, and Terry Labonte, is glad to give a tour. With gray hair and moustache going to white, Keith's lean, smiling face still doesn't look anywhere near his 41 years. As he walks through a rabbit warren of windowless rooms filled with lathes, drill presses, and engine hoists, he explains a race engine.

"It's really just a big air pump that's got fuel mixed in with it," he says. Its job is to take in air, mix it with fuel, spark it to cause the explosion in the cylinder, then blow the exhaust gases out as quickly as possible. "And every part is adjustable, from the carburetor to the tailpipe, just like the race car. Throughout the whole deal what you're shooting for is to move as much air through the engine as fast as you can."

The engine block comes from the Ford factory 70 percent machined. That leaves a lot of leeway for the race teams. For example, the cylinder bore in the engine isn't determined by NASCAR. The total engine displacement—the total volume of the eight cylinders in which the pistons stroke—is limited. "But you can use any combination of cylinder bore and stroke combination to come up with a maximum of 358 cubic inches," he says. Which piston you use is up to you. Whether your cylinder is shorter and fatter or longer and leaner is up to you. What kind of valves you use is up to you.

"One of the keys is getting the valves open and closed as quickly as you can," he explains, setting up a valve, cam, and lifter assembly to demonstrate. The camshaft is the rod that controls when the intake and exhaust valves open and close, and it has 16 little elliptical lobes of steel that control that, pushing on the lifters with the elongated ends. "We get that inside a thousandth of an inch, within two minutes of angle," he says of each lobe. Say it ain't rocket science all you want to, but precise is what it is. (And for the record, the heat-deflecting material used on the race car floor to protect the drivers' heels from the 1,000-degree heat of the exhaust gases was designed by NASA for the Space Shuttle.) The point of engine tuning, he says, "is to control air column movements on the intake and the exhaust sides of the engine." When the fuel and air have been mixed and the spark is being released to cause the explosion that'll drive the piston, both valves have to be closed. Where he wants the piston to be at that moment dictates how he wants his air to be moving for that particular engine, set up for a particular track, and for qualifying or for racing.

More ellipsoid camshafts give you more torque, which you can think of as bottom-end power, good for starting up, for grinding out of corners; think of when you're driving away from a red light, Keith says. More rounded gives you more top-end power, which is good for long stretches at top speed. Where you're going to be racing determines where you want the engine to deliver its power, which in turn dictates how you set up your valvetrain. "We move the torque curve up and down the rpm ladder," Almond says. "You're more or less catering the power curve to the track's rpm rates." At Martinsville, for example, your car runs from about 5,000 to

9,200 rpm each lap, "so you cater to getting torque number as low as you can to keep the car getting off the corners. It's hard to do that and still get a good power number. Charlotte, on the other hand, your rpm range is more like 7,000 to 8,800," since the driver rarely applies the brakes and the car never really slows down. "It's a narrower band, but the speeds at Charlotte are roughly 60 miles an hour higher." So at Charlotte, "We don't care about protecting what happens below 7,000 rpm," whereas at Martinsville what happens between 5,500 and 7,000 rpm may determine who wins the race.

To demonstrate he punches a few numbers into a computer connected to the shop's main engine dyno—a glassed-in room in which engine after engine is hooked up to gauges that can tell you everything from the torque and horsepower at different rpms to the temperature of the exhaust. It measures 62 different things every tenth of a second. The printer spins into action and produces a graph showing the power curve of the two engines: The Charlotte engine has less-oval camshafts, because the engine wants to run smoother at higher speeds. The Martinsville engine has more radically oval ones, so its valves stay shut longer and open faster, thus building up more pressure and more torque. The graph shows that, with the Charlotte engine's best horsepower coming at the top of its rpm range. Back around the 6,500-rpm range, the Martinsville engine delivers about 10 foot-pounds more torque. At the end of its rpm range the Martinsville engine's horsepower starts to fall, but that's not important. By that point—the engine revved that high at the end of those short straightaways just as Kenny gets into the brakes for the hairpin turns—the engine is barely powering the car anyhow. The momentum the car's generated from the first half of the straightaway pushes the car, and the engine is almost an afterthought, Keith says. "It's just making a racket and burning gas."

A qualifying engine will be set up, like the car, to run high and fast for a short burst. For example, it'll have bigger rocker arms, again to put more pressure on the valves. But that banging around on the valve springs can wreck them pretty quickly, and once you lose a spring you lose a valve, and once you lose a valve it dominoes to a cylinder and then your whole engine will shake itself to pieces. A qualifying engine would never last a whole race; it's set for speeds and temperatures that would destroy it. "The piece that goes through the worst environment would be the exhaust valve," Keith says. "At 9,000 rpms, it has to change direction twice during that cycle, on top of being subject to 1,400 degrees. The piston basically goes through the same ordeal, but the piston is a little more bulletproof." The pressure on the piston is about 1,500 pounds per square inch when it's changing direction. And as for that change in direction, Keith says, "Imagine the rope whip a little kid snaps. You know the way that rope frays? That piston goes through the same thing when it changes direction." In fact, the crankshaft, rod, and piston actually expand or contract 35/1,000 of an inch on each change of direction.

Standing in a room filled with computers hooked up to engines, Keith can go on. Two rooms over, his brother, Earle, works on a new block fresh from Ford, and another mechanic walking by comments on what the average race fan knows about engines: "When you push that little pedal down, most times it goes." Engines on little rollers stand like bumper cars along the walls, with their snaking blue electrical cords and their fiber-lined hoses with their cool blue aluminum connectors. Dynos and gauges fill every room, and the walls are lined with gray steel shelves filled with gaskets and carburetors and hoses and belts, with valve springs and camshafts and every piece of an engine you can—or never could—imagine.

Keith wants to go on. He hits a button on a machine called the Cam Doctor and it spits out a sheet of numbers from a test he ran on a cylinder, showing intake cam lift versus crank angle. He points over to other devices he'd like to explain, but he's got things to do and engines to build—for next year. Filmar's new engine program is just getting started, but Daytona is only four months away. He disappears back into his maze of rooms, amid the exhaust fans and the carts full of engine parts.

❖

The amount you can control building an engine is miraculous, and for the Filmar crew at Charlotte on their day off, mostly a rumor. They can control the timing, they can choose their carburetor jets: Bigger means more gas, means a little faster engine but poorer gas mileage, which could mean an extra pit stop over the course of a race. They can even mix up the exhaust pipes to change that air flow Keith was talking about. But beyond that they can pretty much hope Robert Yates is nice to them this week. The car sits waiting, on jacks, wheels off, for whatever he sends.

In the quiet garage, without engine and wheels, the race car loses some of its mystery. You just look under the hood and see clear through to the garage floor. The hubs and spindles and brake rotors hang vertically, connected to the chassis by the upper and lower A-frames, resting directly on the springs and shock absorbers. Tie rods connect the wheels to the steering system, and the sway bar runs across the bottom of the chassis front, stabilizing the car. You can see how the steering works. You can see how the chassis rests on the springs. You can see where the crankshaft will fit into the transmission, and how the drive shaft will power the rear end gear and, in turn, the axles. Back in the rear, you see more springs, more shock absorbers, and the track bar, used to shift weight across the back onto whichever wheel the crew chief wants it on.

It may not be simple, but you can see how it works. It's a pretty straightforward system, really. It looks, suddenly, exactly like what it is: a machine for going fast in a circle. That's all it does, and every piece of the car is designed to do only that. To go fast and to last 500 miles.

Inside the car, painted red—part of the paint scheme—it's simplicity itself. There's the roll cage, with a seat designed especially for Kenny welded in, and the complex, five-strap seat harness that buckles at his waist. The steering wheel is removable so Kenny can more easily climb in and out the window; on it is a button he thumbs to operate his two-way radio when he wants to talk. The doors don't work, of course. They don't exist as more than outlines in sheet metal. Above the passenger door is a Plexiglas window, mandatory on tracks of 1.5 miles or longer (the window was open at Martinsville, to help cool the driver). The driver window is open, but it's protected by netting. The driver can undo the netting himself; he does so after a wreck to signal that he's OK, but he needs a crew member to close the netting after he's climbed into the car. Along the dash are the ignition switch, switches for a fan that will blow air onto the driver and one that will blow air onto the brakes. Gauges for water and oil temperature and electrical output. A tachometer. A switch to flip to the back-up ignition system should the primary system fail. A rearview mirror. In all, a pretty simple place.

Everything starts to ratchet into focus. The maze work of air tubes coiling across the interior on seemingly inexplicable errands begin to resolve themselves. Here one that scoops air from underneath the car and funnels it onto the special radiator for the rear end fluid; there tubes that bring air from the side of the car into the driver's helmet, or onto the brakes, or onto the separate radiator for the oil. Behind the driver is the oil tank, and above that a big plastic container for water with a tube that'll lead to his helmet. Behind all that is the 22-gallon fuel cell, about the size of a big beer cooler and lined with rubber against wreck and explosion.

A clutch pedal. The throttle. The brake. The four-speed stick shift.

And that's it.

Then here comes the engine, and there's a little work to do. Jeremy, the Yates engine baby-sitter, pushes it up on an engine hoist, and he, Frank, Buddy, and Two-Can set about installing it. They hook lines up to it while it hangs on the hoist, checking the valve covers and the headers. They tilt it backward into the car, Two-Can crouching underneath as usual, guiding the drive shaft into the transmission. It's part of the car in less than an hour, and Frank and Buddy are connecting hoses and zip-tying wires and hoses to chassis tubes. They put the plugs in with long socket wrenches, connecting them with long blue wires to the distributor. They spray a little Liquid Wrench into each socket to make sure the plugs don't stick. Two-can applies sealant to the transmission under the car, and it's not long before he leans into the car and flicks the ignition to see how it runs. Frank pushes the throttle from under the hood, and the rev of the engine drowns out thought for a moment.

Then smiles, then big smiles all around. Robert Yates has been nice this week.

"I think we got us a motor today," Jeremy says, and Newt smiles approvingly. "That's a winner! You get the sound of that?"

He can tell just by listening?

Absolutely, Jeremy says. OK, then, what does a good engine sound like?

"Well, it's kind of hard to describe," he says. "You have kind of a real crisp cackle to it, to the exhaust sound."

That's what this one sounds like, rattling around the empty garage like it can't wait to get onto the track. Newt wads up a piece of duct tape and tosses it toward a trash barrel. It goes in, and he allows a smile. "Gonna be a good day," he says.

❖

The engine running for a moment immediately assaults yet another sense. With bright colors, roaring engines, and baking asphalt overwhelming eyes, ears, and skin, you can be forgiven if you haven't taken a moment to do something that sends racing people into a kind of reverie: stop and smell the exhaust.

It sounds ridiculous, but a Winston Cup garage has one of the most beautiful, richest, almost somatic aromas you can encounter. You pick up the harsh, almost smoky odor of tire rubber, which is everywhere; you can get the high, acrid stench of hot rear end gears and fluid, which is so recognizable that the announcers can smell it atop the grandstand during a race: "Someone just lost a rear end—I can smell it," Benny Parsons will say, and a lap later someone will go behind the wall, his rear end gear cooked. You smell the oils emerging from the heating asphalt. You smell brake fluid, SD-20 cleaner, oil, and the ozoney scent of burning metal.

But underneath it all, providing the base scent for the intoxicating perfume, are the gas fumes. Unocal racing gas is leaded, and it's 110 octane, and the burning fuel yields an exhaust that is metallic and rich beyond imagining. Along with it comes the scent of the metal of the motor, as it runs so fast that it literally consumes itself, burning up tiny pieces of metal, which add a sharper metallic flavor to the exhaust. It has a sweetness to it that you can actually taste. You don't so much smell it as absorb it with the back of your palate, and it's overwhelming and dizzying. The relationship between the smell of the exhaust of the car in your driveway and the scent of race exhaust is a lot like the relationship between the stink of manure and the rich, sweet, but cloying smell of silage. Neither is exactly what you would call pleasant, but one has a sweetness and overpowering, almost rotting, richness that seems to cover you, to draw you in.

Walk into the Winston Cup garage once and you might not notice it. But walk in a second time, and it's the first thing you'll say: "Oh, the smell! I forgot about that!" You'll never forget again.

Even though more than half the cars haven't even been uncovered today, that smell fills the air.

❖

In the garage, there's a little more going on than just puttering around on a few cars. Mid-afternoon, a big armored truck rolls into the garage and parks in front of the Winston Cup hauler. A couple of guards come out and stand at the truck's back gate, and Rusty Wallace walks up. So do about two dozen reporters and photographers. A somewhat annoyed-looking NASCAR President Bill France Jr. emerges from the hauler and takes his place with Rusty in front of the guards.

The truck is filled with pennies, big canvas bags full of pennies. Five hundred thousand pennies, to be exact. It's Rusty's $5,000 fine for swearing on the radio after that black flag after his restart cost him the Martinsville race. The pennies weigh about 3,500 pounds, as much as a Winston Cup race car. Rumor is that the truck and delivery cost Rusty as much as the fine itself. He appears to barely enjoy the joke, his jaw set, posing for grimacey pictures handing a big bag of pennies to France, who smiles with equal sincerity.

"What's the point, Rusty?" someone asks.

"I just want to tell all you guys don't never say 'shit,' at least on the radio," Rusty says. Flashes pop, pens scribble. Then Rusty and France climb the stairs into the NASCAR hauler together, and that's that.

The media knot breaks, and most of the writers hurry away. On a day off when not much is happening in the garage, this, at least, is something to file.

❖

In the media center, the activity level is beginning to increase. More writers every day fill the long desk shelves that line the walls and run down the middle of the room. A good 100 to 120 journalists could work on stories at once here without much squeezing, and today, from the briefcases and piles of paper at different desk slots and modem plugs, it looks like at least a third that many have already set up, even though it's an off day.

There are plenty of reasons for them to be here even if many Cup teams are not. Those not covering the Busch teams will still work the Cup garage area, checking on different teams: why Terry Labonte qualified so badly, what Geoff Bodine got just right. Of course, they won't have to work that hard if they're not motivated to. The back walls of the media center are covered with Plexiglas slots just wide enough for a folder of material on a team, a driver, a sponsor, a make of car, or some combination of the above. Chevy, Ford, and Pontiac produce daily sheets of quotes from the drivers running their cars. All the sponsors keep information about their drivers, their teams, and their products constantly updated throughout race weekend, and their representatives are always busy, tidying up their area and making sure their information—and color photographs and pictures of their product—are available. No driver interviewed on television ever drove just a race car. He's always driving the Square D Ford Thunderbird, or the Kellogg's Chevy Monte Carlo or the Interstate Batteries Pontiac. It's part of the deal, and drivers are comfortable playing their role. The reps keep the information coming in the media center. In print, you're much more likely to read about the number 81 car than about the Square D Ford Thunderbird, and every time a sponsor can, through sheer repetition, get a print reporter to mention sponsor or make, that's a victory. They work as hard as the race teams do.

NASCAR pumps out information all weekend long, too. A 49-page statistical summary of every one of the top drivers' seasons is out where everybody can get to it, as is a seven-page file of track data (Charlotte is 1.5 miles; the race is 334 laps, or 501 miles; the corners are banked 24 degrees; the backstretch is 1,360 feet long) and historical data (Darrell Waltrip won 6 races here; Richard Petty won 4; 13 active drivers have won at least one, 33 guys have won at least once in the 75 Cup races held here since the speedway opened in 1960). David Pearson has the most poles at Charlotte (14), and Jeff Gordon has 5, the most of any active driver. Dale Jarrett won the race in 1994 from 22nd position, which is the farthest back anybody has started to win here. It goes on like that for seven pages, and it's always instructive: If you got this and Bob Latford's *Inside Line*, you could write a fair Winston Cup column twice a week. If you got the lists of spoon-fed quotes released after qualifying, during practice, and after the race, you could write an acceptable race-day story without ever leaving the media center. It has a viewing platform on top, but you can stay inside and watch the race on TV if you want to.

Many writers do just that. The speedway staff pumps out information endlessly, too: A printout of each car's fastest times from each practice; qualifying lists; qualifying results; points standings; and money winnings. During the race they produce a race summary every hundred laps, listing not only the top-20 running order every 20 laps but cautions and their causes. No baseball statistician ever produced more information than the people at a Winston Cup race. Charlotte even puts out spiral-bound booklets for each race giving more-detailed statistical data focusing on drivers' histories at Charlotte; NASCAR does the same, only focusing on the drivers' stats so far, producing for most races a statistical volume the size of the phone book of a small city, with charts and graphs and lists and lists and lists.

The media center has coffee and doughnuts in the morning, and it usually offers lunch, sponsored either by the speedway itself or by some company making an announcement. The announcement comes just before lunch, of course. At 11 A.M. the flaks will start preparing the event, piling up Coors Lite cases for one announcement, parking a car against a backdrop of Kingsford Charcoal sacks for another. Then, as the steam trays in the media center are being loaded, corporate higher-ups will stand on the little media center podium and talk about how happy they are to be sponsoring a new team, or to have a new driver, or to be joining "the family of NASCAR racing." Then a team owner will step forward and talk about how very happy he is to have the new sponsor or driver. Then the driver will step forward and say how very happy he (or she—one team announces that Patty Moise will be their Busch Grand National driver for next year, and that Moise is perfect for their audience: "We believe that the mystique of motor racing will sell a lot of home furnishings") is to have such a wonderful sponsor, and then they'll ask if there are any questions and then the writers will break and stand in line for their free chow, usually coming along with a folder about the new sponsor, driver, and team, and a free hat or shirt or cookbook or apron or something like that.

If it's Kenny Wallace you're interested in this morning, you can find a white Square D Racing folder: It has biographies of Kenny and Filbert, a history of Kenny's driving highlights, a short history of Filmar Racing, and information about Square D. Each folder has a business card in it, too. It used to be Steve Post's card, but now it's Danielle's. There's no biography of Newt Moore. He's still too new, and there's never been a formal announcement of his assumption of the role of crew chief. But the biography of the ousted Gil Martin is long gone.

The only other information you can find about Kenny Wallace today is in the Ford Motorsports Notes & Quotes file, where Kenny's comments to the reporter—his "Big Balls Kenny" comments—are repeated word for word.

But what happened yesterday is old news to the people who really count in the media center, and that's speedway public relations director Ron Green and public relations vice president Jerry Gappens.

"The guys shooting that Shell Oil deal are here," says Green, leaning across the desk. "They want to get a shot of their cars on the straightaway." Gappens nods. "Easiest way to do that is wait for a stop in traffic and walk through."

Green makes a note and goes on. "The *National Geographic* guys aren't here until Sunday. Those are the only guys I know of, except the guys following Humpy around. You know about that?"

Gappens nods, and Green, a guy in his 30s who looks like he could be a stockbroker on his way to a golf game, scoots off to solve a problem. Gappens stays behind, hanging on the telephone. A round, florid, constantly smiling guy, Gappens is the main conduit of racing information at Charlotte.

At the moment, Gappens has a fairly immediate problem. He brightens as a voice speaks to him from the phone. "Not too good," he says into the phone. "You guys have shut down our phone lines. Tell John Boy and Billy to tell people to call off that stuff. That's a NASCAR thing, the track has no jurisdiction over that."

John Boy and Billy, a local radio duo whose show is syndicated throughout the country, talk about racing every day. In a kind of quasi-camp High Redneck, John Boy and Billy both play to racing's redneck image and spread the gospel to its growing, newer, higher-brow audience. This morning, bemoaning Darrell Waltrip's fate, they've urged people to call the speedway and demand that he be included in the race. Gappens hangs on the phone and suddenly you can tell he's on the air.

"Another fine mess you've gotten me into," he laughs. He repeats that the speedway has no control over who's in the race. "In the old days I think there was such a thing called the promoter's option," he says. "No more. They also could've put Labonte in on car owner points, and that would have put Ricky Craven [in the 25 car] out, but that's a NASCAR option. So please, please, do not call for Darrell Waltrip."

Outside the media center—it's right next to the garage—another movie crew is at work. An oil-derrick-size floating boom carries a guy with a camera, sighting into that doorway and its sign: "Through these doors pass the world's best drivers." The garage sign-in booth is right there, and the idea of the commercial for race-themed clothing is for some of the world's best drivers to come in through the gates, punching a time clock over which stands a glowering NASCAR President Bill France Jr. Mechanics actually entering the track to do work just make faces at the camera, but a growing knot of fans and hangers-on watches the proceedings. They're rewarded when Jeff Gordon, Dale Earnhardt, Rusty Wallace, Terry Labonte, and Dale Jarrett—with the exception of Mark Martin and Jeff Burton, all the series' best drivers—walk through the gates several times, Chase Authentics shirts slung over their shoulders for easy viewing.

❖

The mechanics coming in that door to work are the mechanics who have something extra to do, like Newt Moore, who's performing a little liposuction on that hippy right front fender on the number 81 car. Kenny pleaded with him to cut the entire front end off and move it 1/2 inch to the left, but Newt did little more than issue a disapproving stare. If the driver needs the right front to catch a little less air, he can do something about that. He takes out a reciprocating saw powered by an air hose and has at it, making angled slices into the fender like it's a pizza.

Busch cars are practicing, roaring around out on the track, but in the garage Newt focuses on that fender like it's the only thing in the world. He makes the cuts, then uses ball-peen hammers to make sure the remaining pieces are set just how he wants them. He clamps them, hooks up the welder from the crash cart, then spot-welds the fender back together a little tighter. Next comes a sander, then some body filler, which causes a moment of joking about how much body filler mechanics run across. "Stirred it, applied it, ate it, snorted it," Newt laughs. "That's why we're here in the first place." The Bondo gets sanded, reapplied, sanded again. It's a little late in the game for painting, so blue duct tape the exact color of the car finish will do the trick. Then comes a layer of wide, clear tape. Then a fresh new Goodyear decal, and then the car has a right front fender that's a little closer to what the driver wants.

It's almost poetic. Watching Newt address that fender, the economy of motion, the volume of intention visible behind his actions, you can feel like you suddenly recognize him. Not him personally, or any of the mechanics personally, but like you suddenly understand who they are.

They're guys who know how to make things work. Guys who took shop in high school and meant it. Guys who built those little electrical buzzers in science class and then took them home and turned them into doorbells. Guys who learned how to weld. Guys who could rebuild lawnmower engines or construct garages. Guys who can make things happen.

And guys who know how to do the same thing in their own lives. Guys like fabricator Jerome Aho, who's at the track today helping Newt with the changes he's making to that fender. He's borrowed a bender-stretcher from the number 24 car guys, and he's making a new valence brace for the front (that's the little brace that runs along the bottom of the nose to support the air dam). The nose has a new shape and it needs a new valence, so Jerome, a guy of 32 wearing a neat Square D hat above his neat, light hair, calmly goes about making one.

Jerome has been in Winston Cup racing for about seven years. He grew up in Stanley, North Dakota: "It's about 50 miles from Canada and 70 miles from Montana." He used to lay on the bed in his room and read racing magazines about "Suitcase Jake" Elder and the race cars he built for David Pearson. Jerome ran dirt cars for about eight years, and then "I figured if I was gonna do it I had to go where the racing was. I packed my bags and told my dad, 'You gotta take a chance while you're young.'"

That was in 1990. He took his life savings of $500, a few clothes, and some tools—"Just a little carry toolbox," he says—and jumped on the bus for Charlotte, like a country singer bound for Nashville with his guitar case and a duffel bag. "I didn't know a person here," he smiles, looking back at the memory as his hands stay busy with the valence. "I went to the Econolodge and said, 'How many days can I get?'" They said for $180 he could stay eight nights and get the ninth night free. "I said, 'That's me, hook me up.'" And he started going through the phone book, looking for race shops. Before his money ran out (he reckons it was about the 50th door he knocked on) he had a job at a Busch shop. That lasted a few months before he got a call from Kenny Schrader, then running cars in every class imagineable. "I got plenty of racing out of that deal," he says. But that was taking up a lot of his time, and like many crew members, he wanted to start his own race team. He took another job in a chassis shop to get more time, but he still didn't have the money to race. From there he ended up at Filmar Racing, where he's happy because he works all week for good pay—in the $30,000- to $40,000-a-year range—and helps young racers at local tracks on the weekends.

Around the Filmar shop, of course, he gets to observe his idol, Suitcase Jake. Jake, for example, doesn't put much stock in writing stuff down; whether he even can is sometimes questioned. When he wanted to set up a car, Jerome says, he would take out four tape measures and stand them on the floor. Studying them, he'd raise the tape of one and then another, setting the heights of the chassis near the four wheels, delicately balancing the weight of the imaginary car in front of him. He'd stand there, thinking, then adjust one of the measures an inch, a half, a quarter, then step back and stare some more. After a while he'd take the four tape measures, put them under the chassis, and get to work.

"He's got a lot of good common sense," Jerome says. And that four-point model of the car that lives in Jake's mind, Jerome says, is exactly the right way to think of a race car and its setup. "It's like a rectangle," he says, putting down the valence and drawing one on a tablet of paper handed to him. With an "x" crossing from corner to corner, it looks a little like a child's drawing of an envelope.

"It's a basic deal, a simple thing," he says. The central point of setting up a race car chassis is balancing weight. The car has to weigh at least 3,400 pounds without the driver, so all the efforts teams undergo to save weight—Duze back at the shop making lighter bushings, teams soaking car hoods in acid to remove metal and make them lighter, teams sanding their chassis tubes to the bare minimum NASCAR demands for safety—are not so much making the car lighter as controlling the weight better. Inside the frame rails of the car are long rectangular lead weights. The more of the weight the team can get out of the immobile components and into the weights they can place exactly where they want, the better they can control the car.

"Think of it like it's cardboard," he says of his rectangle. "If you put your finger under one corner and lift it, the weight is going to shift onto the other three corners, mostly onto the opposite corner." All the shifting, the more- or less-inflated tires, the stiffer or softer shocks, the heavier or lighter springs, the rounds of adjustment in the jackscrews and the track bar are just adjustments to where that race car's weight is going to be. The more weight on the left rear and right front, called "wedge," or "bite," the tighter the car is going to be. A round of wedge, which Newt might tell someone to put into the left rear of the car, will mean putting a single turn of the wrench on that jackscrew. That will tighten the car and raise the left rear up and put more weight on the other three wheels, especially the right front. Kenny runs those hundreds of laps in the car before the race, explaining as best he can how the car feels so that Newt and Vic and Eddie and everybody else can get that weight distributed perfectly.

"It's simple. It's just physics," Jerome says. "That's what I try to tell these Late Model guys I help at the short tracks. But it all has to go together. A car can feel like it's tight, it's pushing, so you put more weight on the front tires," he says, "but then you can have too much weight on the front tires and the contact patch of the tire can't hold the weight that's on it, and it'll heat up and slide. It's like being on ice, then, and it won't steer, so it still feels tight. But it's the opposite problem. The car's going in so tight that he's breaking it loose, and you keep making it worse and worse and worse. So sometimes you just have to back up and start all over again." The ideal, he figures, is to be on the edge of loose. "You can't be loose to where you're scrubbing off speed, but you want to be just about sideways. Yeah, that's the thing; it's *just about* sideways. The tires are grabbing more than they're breaking loose. You have to keep it hooked up all the time."

With his Winston Cup experience and his clear-thinking and good-humored willingness to help any young team that asks him, Jerome has become a favorite at those short tracks. "Last time I was there, someone put a piece of duct tape on my shirt over my name," he says shyly. "It said, 'Suitcase Jerome.' I walk down the pits now at Concord, they go, 'Suitcase!'" He turns back to his valence. "Just to be compared to him means a bit." Jerome is setting up his own race shop in his back yard. "I got the building parts in a pile out there now," he says. "I'm just waiting on someone to pour the concrete."

The setup of the car, of course, is nothing new. This is what guys have been doing since they were filling cars with bootleg liquor and trying to make the monstrously heavy cars look like regular cars, run fast enough to outrun revenue agents, and still handle in turns. A car used for a long run from a still to a warehouse would need to go fast and make a few predictable turns, so it would be set up one way; a car distributing from a warehouse to different bars and homes would need to be more nimble, need to accelerate and decelerate faster, make a lot of turns, would have different gears, different springs. A different setup.

Jerome notices that it's become quiet in the garage. But as soon as he notices, there's a roar as outside on the track 25 Busch Grand National cars rumble into life at once. It's the challenge race for tomorrow's Busch race. At Charlotte the Busch cars qualify like the Cup cars, but for only the first 28 positions. The remaining cars run a race the next day for the final 10 positions. It's called a challenge race, a suicide race, a hooligan race, or a suitcase race. The drivers who come in worse than 10th pack their suitcases and go home.

Newt looks up from his fender. "Is that the hooligan race?" he asks. "The tin can that couldn't make a shitbox red dog race?" That's what it is. And, of course, if yesterday had gone a little differently, it's one more race than his crew would have run all weekend. But that's yesterday.

❖

Back out on the infield, under a high sky with filmy white clouds, the fans barely pause in their own setting up to notice the hooligan race. There's a scant crowd of less than 10,000 in the grandstand, and those in the infield are much too busy to pay much attention to a race that's just to see who gets *into* the sort of AAA-level Busch race. The fans in the slots right next to the track in the turns climb aboard their platforms and raise their beers to the cars and wave at the drivers as they go by, but most fans are paying closer attention to their tents than this little—well, tin cans that couldn't make a shitbox red dog race.

That's not to say that they don't notice the race cars running while they carry around their coolers, while they pull around their wagons, while they set up their tents and lay out their horseshoe pitches.

In fact, that's why they're here. Watching the fans set up with the roar of the cars in the background is almost surreal—it's something beautiful. Red, back near Redneck Hill, doesn't climb his platform to watch the hooligan race. He takes his beer in hand, waves a cigarette, closes his eyes, and starts dancing to the music of the motors.

Stand on Redneck Hill and it's not just Red dancing. The whole infield is a hive, cars and trucks coursing in evenly through the Turn 3 tunnel, slowly cruising the infield looking for their assigned spots. Row TB, or UB, or AA, a little cement block in the grass will say, and then you'll follow down to find 8, 10, or whatever, either spray painted on asphalt, if there's asphalt, or set in a little block of its own if it's lawn. Then the truck opens and out pour women in tank tops and tattoos, men in shorts and long classic rock hairstyles. They stand for a moment as if sniffing the air, but what they're doing is listening.

And there's so much to hear. When the Busch cars are in the near turn, thought is almost drowned out. When they're far off, the hollow sound echoes off the empty grandstands and makes an airplane drone everywhere. Generators putt, and Lynyrd Skynyrd and Hank Jr. sound from different corners. Everybody works on their camping setups, as the cars go around and around.

That's the lovely part. Even after the hooligan race is over, the Busch cars come back out to practice. As the fans set up, their background noise is the sport they've come to see. And it's not in front of them, it's not across some fence from them: It *surrounds* them. They're the only sports fans who are quite literally in the middle of the action. Race fans never say they're going to see a race. They say the same thing the teams say: "We're going racing." They're not just watching the sport. From the infield, and from the stands and outside among the souvenir trailers, they're part of the scene. They're part of racing. And when they set up in the sun, surrounded by the sounds of the cars, smoking and drinking their first beers and greeting the neighbors they haven't seen since last year or last race, they know it.

❖

Kenny Wallace stops by the garage during the hooligan race to check in with the team, and he watches Newt finish his fender. "They're doing what I want, but it's just a cobble," he says. "I want the whole body moved over to take air off that right front, but this'll do for now."

The driver always has an opinion. If you want to get those opinions in detail, you have several options. You can head into the back of the hauler and sit on the leather seats of the office, and you can chat while you watch whatever's on ESPN or MTV. You can head out to the infield and visit with him in his motor home, before his wife or friends and family show up. He'll give you a little tour: The motor home has beveled mirror cabinets, a separate bedroom filled by a queen-size bed, a full bathroom and kitchen, air conditioning. If motor home driver Eddie Jarvis is there cooking up some spaghetti, he'll probably invite you to stay and have a plate.

But your best bet is to go out to his suburban Charlotte home. There, for once, he won't have crew members, fans, his team owner, his public relations rep, journalists, or anybody else fighting for his attention. So you can pull up to his big but modest brick split-level (until a couple of years ago, it was just a double-wide on that lot, and he and Kim and the kids were comfortable) and knock on the door. Kim will come to the door in a comfortable slacks suit and a brown sweater and lead you back to the immaculately clean kitchen, where Kenny is performing race driver job one: He's signing autographs.

"It gets to feel like it's all I ever do," he says, smiling from behind a stack of several hundred 8x11 postcards. Kim says, "We got him down to he's gonna give us four hours every month," she says of the fan club she runs for him from a building out back of the house. "They'll send him ball cards, but we only do two per mailing," she goes on. Of course, they're all free. Like most Winston Cup drivers, the next autograph Kenny Wallace gets paid for will be the first he gets paid for.

Even when he's not signing autographs at his kitchen table (or watching old race tapes from the same table—"I like to see the in-car cameras," he says. "I learn stuff that way"), his life follows a pretty predictable routine. Late Sunday night, back from the race, wherever it is. Sometimes his three girls will be waiting up for him, but more often not. It's a school night, after all.

Monday morning he wakes up around 10:30 and spaces out a little to MTV or VH-1, but not for long. "Usually when I get up my conscience bothers me. After a race when you don't do so good, you get to the shop right away, because you can't let the stew brew. Guys in the shop get to analyzing the race by themselves."

You don't want that. "I'm the quarterback, so it's up to me to debrief them," he says. The races haven't been going so good lately, so he's out at the shop most days after the race—like he was this week—in the afternoon, sometimes with the girls. Then it's home for more time with the girls. "I have three beautiful girls," he says. "They need my attention."

Tuesdays and Wednesdays he's usually gone, either testing with the team—each team gets seven two- or three-day testing periods per season—or making a personal appearance for Square D or one of his 25 or so different endorsement or licensing contracts. Square D gets 56 appearances per year, "but it's not as bad as it sounds," he says. Thirty-three of those are morning hospitality appearances before the races, and then about 20 times a year he flies anywhere in the United States they want him.

Once a month he does a TV show called *Tailgate Talk* on the Speedvision cable network.

If Thursday's free he tries to spend more time with the girls and Kim, "and she'll try to pin me down and sign autographs," he sighs. Then Friday it's a plane ride to a race track, and it's race week until Sunday night. "It gets monotonous. It seems like right after Daytona, it's just nonstop."

The spring and fall Charlotte races, of course, are the hardest weeks: "Charlotte is the biggest circus, because not everyone can get to Daytona." This week he and Kim will have family members staying both in their home and at the racetrack in their motor home. That makes his job harder: "You've got family members coming up to you, friends coming up to you. Sometimes it's hard for people to understand that you're coming into my office" when you approach him at a racetrack. "You've just climbed out of your car, you're holding a shock, you're talking to your crew chief, and they see you and think that you have time."

Of course, that access to the drivers, to the garage, to the pits, is part of what makes NASCAR different from any other sport, and it won't change soon. "Bill France has said many times that we're in show business and that access is what made the sport so big," he says. More, "A hundred out of a hundred times, it's better to stop and sign the autograph." Those fans make the sport, and he hasn't lost sight of that.

"But I can't believe nobody has got run over."

Has the extreme growth of the sport, the maddening crowds in the garage, taken the fun out of Winston Cup racing?

Kenny doesn't hesitate. "Yes. Racing ain't fun anymore. Racing used to be fun because there weren't no rules. There were racing rules, but no etiquette rules. Now, you say the wrong thing, people get on you. You used to could show up at the race track with a T-shirt. Nowadays if you aren't wearing a shirt with the logo on it, somebody's yelling at you."

One thing Square D has been pretty good about, he says, is letting the team conduct its own business. "The number one thing that a sponsor wants is performance," he says. "When you go through a dry spell, the pressure is immense." But what saves them is "the numbers. They say, 'Hey, we're running 25th every week, but look at these numbers!' " Numbers, provided by market research firms, of people who now recognize their name who had never heard of it before; of people who say they buy their products now that they're in racing; of people who do business with Square D because they can go to a race, can go in the garage, can meet race car driver Kenny Wallace in a hospitality tent Sunday morning.

Square D Marketing Vice President and Racing Program Director Jack Carlson "told me in their plane that the racing program has united their company," Kenny says. "In the factory, there's a forklift that's painted up like my race car." That's part of what Square D pays its $3.5 million for every year, and even if the team isn't winning races, so far it looks to them like money well spent. The sponsor wants a competitive race car, but just as important is a driver who can communicate with sponsors and their clients. Kenny knows that he's getting paid a lot more for the latter than the former, and he accepts that as part of the deal. "I'm Kenny Wallace," he says, "because of the way I give interviews. I won't play the game as far as lying."

Then again, he says, the other thing that's saved the team is those couple of poles they won this year, which yielded ecstatic phone calls—and even visits—from Square D bigwigs.

He waxes for a while on how complex racing is now. He says there are three races each weekend: qualifying; practice (which he calls "monitor racing" because of the way team members check the computer monitors to see how their practice times stack up); and the race. How money buys speed, but you need speed to buy money. If they don't finish in the top 30, they'll have to go ask their sponsor for more money next year, which the sponsor, being a business, would like to see the other way around. They'd rather reward the team for doing well, when they wouldn't need the money so much.

He's a little frustrated running such a small team against such large enterprises as Roush, running three cars, or Hendrick, running three more. He knows Rusty's team gets close to $8 million a year, and Filmar Racing is struggling along on maybe half that. "You're not given the same equipment as the guy that's winning, but you're expected to outrun him," he says.

But he thinks his little team has heart. "You've got Frankie," Kenny says. "He reminds me of myself when I was his age." When Kenny won his first pole, he says of Frank, "he purchased a duplicate of the pole trophy and he's got it in his house. The kid's a true racer."

Kenny runs down his own history as a member of those racin' Wallaces of St. Louis, Missouri, the youngest of three brothers, all racers and sons of local short-track legend Russell Wallace. "I spent so much time helping them that I didn't get to drive a race car until I was 22," he says. He won the race, but didn't race again for two years. "I felt like my brothers needed me more. In the St. Louis area I was known as a good mechanic, not a racer." Then in 1986 he started running the American Speed Association series, where he was rookie of the year. He stayed there until 1989, when Rusty started a Busch Grand National team and gave Kenny his first ride. Kenny was rookie of the year in Busch, and by 1991 he was winning races. "I won eight races, eight poles," he says. "I was twice voted most popular driver.

"And here I am, 115 Winston Cup races, and I have never done anything as hard as this in my whole life."

Cup is just the top of the world. Every Cup driver is better than the best Busch drivers. If the Busch drivers can make a race car dart between two other cars, a Winston Cup driver can almost make it hop, like a tailback juking a defender. If a Busch driver can take the high line and then slide down around a slower car that won't move, a Cup driver can skate from side to side like a skiier on a slalom. "If you run in the top five of the Busch series, to run in the top five in Winston Cup, it's ten times as hard. Mind you, I could have said two times as hard, so I mean ten times as hard." Busch cars have 200 less horsepower, they weigh less, and they're smaller. They're race cars, but not Cup cars.

"It's the most competitive sport in the whole world." And, of course, you spend most of your time signing autographs and making personal appearances. "You don't get to practice much, you have so many people to deal with it's phenomenal."

Then he sighs. "But then again, I love getting in the race car and driving it. I'd love it a hell of a lot more if I didn't have to put up with all the crap. If you could ever get through all the smoke and mirrors and just go racing . . . Through all the peaks and valleys, if you still get to get in the car and go racing, it's worth it."

He ain't driving no race car now. He's got about 1,000 more autographs to sign, and he gets back to it.

Kim offers a tour of the fan club office. First she walks through a big room filled with mementos, not of Kenny's career but of careers it's brought him into contact with: He's got signed St. Louis Blues and Cardinals jerseys hung up, and souvenirs from his favorite band, Aerosmith. On her way she talks about being an outsider racing wife. "We have a few friends who are associated with racing," she says, "but I've got some really good friends we meet through the girls." She doesn't do what she calls "the walk," when some racing wives, usually in high heels, totter along with their husbands on Sunday before a race "and tuck them into their cars," kissing them good-bye like they'll never see them again. As Kim points out, they surely will. In fact, if they keep their eyes open, they'll see their husbands every thirty seconds or so for the next four hours.

"And the RV park," she says, shaking her head. "They move into those things. And they sit out there, waiting for their husbands." She can't do it. She'll read a novel or do crossword puzzles. "And I don't belong to the wives' auxiliary, either," she says.

It's had the reputation of being little more than a gossip meeting, but Kim Wallace wouldn't join whatever it was; she doesn't even belong to the PTA at her kids' schools. "Our lives are so complicated that any spare time I have I want to spend with my family, so I don't have time to meet up with all their functions. Lynn Bodine has tried to get me to join, saying it's not the way it used to be, but I refuse to do that." She's not criticizing the other racing wives, she says, but she's an independent woman, and she keeps her own life, even at the racetrack.

During races she's on a special radio channel with Eddie Jarvis, atop the war wagon, and Kenny, plus she can hear the team channel. So she stays as hooked up as she wants to be. During the summer she rotates and takes one of her girls to the race each weekend—they usually arrive on Saturday—and her parents, who live in a house she and Kenny have had built behind their own, look after the other two.

On the bottom floor of that house is the fan club office, a big carpeted rumpus room filled with mementos, everything from a grandfather clock Kenny won in a Busch race at Martinsville to pole awards and gloves, shoes, and uniforms he wore during memorable races. The fan club database is on a computer. Kenny used to send birthday cards to fans, but now there are too many, so he calls two per month on their birthdays, surprising them. Though 4,000 fans isn't large for a Cup fan club, it's an active membership. Kim estimates she gets 10,000 pieces of mail a month and feels that these are more than just fans. She sees them as a kind of ancillary friends.

"One couple, every place in Virginia that we go, they're there." They'll cook for the team and bring food to the hauler, where they're welcomed. It can get out of hand, of course. Kenny invited some people over one year to run go-carts on a little track he had bulldozed behind the house. It was fun and the party was repeated for a couple of years until thousands of people started showing up and John Boy and Billy started hyping it on the radio. Someone claimed to get hurt on a go-cart, and the party disappeared.

Still, the fax machine is always busy, and Kim sits on the desk for a second. "I cannot pick out one of my fan club members that if they called on the phone we couldn't have a normal conversation." She takes pride in that, being normal. "I tell my girls, not everybody has what they have." She doesn't mean money and fame: "They have parents who love them and take care of them," she says. The best thing about her marriage, she says, is that she and Kenny "are always there for each other and for the girls," that they function as individuals, and especially that they have more than their share of laughs.

Then again, certain things will never be normal. Her job every day is reading letters and fielding calls from people who adore her husband. "I could really sit and listen to that all day," she smiles, "people telling me how great he is."

❖

In the Winston Cup garage at Charlotte, nobody's telling anybody how great Kenny Wallace is, but his crew is doing all it can to let him prove it in Sunday's race.

Around them, fewer and fewer other teams work, until they are almost alone. The Busch cars finish their practice and go silent; the fans disappear from the stands. Nikki Taylor, the woman in the red straw hat who helped Morris Metcalfe with the qualifying lottery, roams the garage with her husband, Bill, pulling a wagon with copies of *Winston Cup Scene* on it, delivering them to each hauler and the media center, itself almost empty. Representatives of the Simpson race equipment company, Nikki and Bill have been part of the Cup garage for years, doing one thing or another, Nikki as sort of den mother of the Winston Cup hauler, Bill performing one job or another, such as checking the decals on the sides of the race cars to make sure each car has what it's supposed to and receives only the race winnings it's entitled to according to which programs it's participating in. They also deliver packets of powdered Gatorade and Gatorade cups to each hauler.

Beyond them, there isn't much going on outside the number 81 car's garage stall. Late in the day, a NASCAR official shows Newt a list on a clipboard, and Newt chooses a pit position. Not much good out of this one. With the 26th pick (it's done by qualifying position) he's well down the straightaway near Turn 4. Still, it's a pit, and it could be worse. The 43 car and the 25 car, the two last provisional qualifiers, have to *share* a pit. They'll have to coordinate when their cars stop at first, and as soon as some other car wrecks out of the race, one of those teams will have to run down pit road pushing war wagon, tires, and tanks to set up in that car's vacated pit.

Pit choice is simple: Most important is having a pit that doesn't have anybody in front of it, so the farthest pit down pit road and the pits directly before entrances to the garage are picked first. When those are gone the pits just past the entrances are taken. Ease of getting out of or into a pit during a race can save 10ths of a second when they're most valuable. The pits farthest along pit road are most valuable because they're beyond the stripes by which NASCAR measures pit road speed, so the cars in those spots can drop and squeal out, revving to gain track speed, without worrying about the pit road speed on the way out.

Anyhow, pit stall 29 will have to do.

Not long after that, Newt gets the guys to cover the car. "We got to get out of here," he says. Enough is enough. This is supposed to be a day off, and there's practice all day tomorrow and a race on Sunday. It's time to go.

He's not the only one who thinks so. Look down the row of race cars in the garage and you see something remarkable: Every single other race car in the garage is covered, quiet. Only the guys from the number 81 car are still working. Newt's trying to hurry them out, and he quickly gets help from the NASCAR officials. It's 5 P.M., and the garage is officially closed. They don't want to be hard-asses, but a few of them filter over toward the car, standing around pointedly watching, arms folded.

The guys cover the car, stop by the hauler, and head for the garage gate. They're the last ones out, and the NASCAR officials lock the gate behind them.

❖

On the infield, the end of the day brings little change. The flow of buses and motor homes and pickups coming in the tunnel has only increased. People are off work now, race weekend has started for true, and it's just more, more, more. More viewing platforms going up into the dusk; more Allman Brothers and George Thorogood blasting into the night in Turns 3 and 1; more men with puffy eyes and ponytails drinking more beers and smoking more cigarettes, yelling good-natured, not-quite-drunken greetings to each other from their platforms as they're built. Fires from gas grills and charcoal barbecues dot the rows of campers; tendrils of smoke rise from the infield, snaking together into a light haze in the deepening sky, as though the track itself has just exhaled the smoke from its first evening cigarette.

Things are getting started.

Outside the track, things are getting started, too. Along the backstretch campers and motor homes are parked in tidy rows, stretching into the hills as far as you can see, disappearing into the trees a quarter-mile away. Flags—black number 3 Earnhardt flags, rainbow number 24 Jeff Gordon flags, dozens and dozens of confederate flags—flap in the cooling breeze, and more fires flicker and reflect off aluminum motor home sides. Young boys and girls ride the rows on bicycles, and families sit around baby pools and picnic tables as lanterns go on and card games start. Generators power televisions and radios, though out here, among a great many more families, the mood is more State Fair than approaching decadence like it is on the infield.

Pickups and golf carts official and unofficial scurry around the track on its service roads, carrying ice, carrying fans waving open beers around, carrying pieces of television equipment, carrying food and beer. A Dominoes cart scoots around the infield and the outside camping area, selling pizza for $3 a slice, $18 the whole pie. Street sweepers roll by, and garbage trucks ride by every row of campers, every knot of tents in the infield, every inch of the garage. People with plastic bags migrate over the stands, harshly lit by the track lights as the twilight deepens.

In front of the track, events have started for tomorrow's Busch race, the All-Pro Bumper to Bumper 300. Behind Turn 1 is the Hospitality Village. Tomorrow and Sunday mornings, the yellow-and-white-striped tents will hold breakfast events during which team and race sponsors will bring their groups of fans to meet drivers. For now, only one tent is active. Beneath a balloon sculpture of the All-Pro/Bumper to Bumper auto parts stores logo, a cover band plays "That's the Way (Uh-huh, Uh-huh) I Like It" and a lone khaki clad couple gets down on the plywood dance floor. Others wander among racing video games and a tiny high-banked track where radio-controlled NASCAR racers run. Everything is yellow and white, and it looks like this crowd had a fine time before they got tired. They'll go home ready to come back and sit in a suite with the sponsor to watch tomorrow's Busch race.

❖

Across the street, the rows of souvenir trailers are mostly closed; open trailers line Route 29, but the biggest ones, the haulers painted with team colors and stocked with the newest merchandise, have closed for the night. The remaining trailers, specializing in year-old or older stuff, in discounted shirts and hats, in die-cast race cars painted like the cars used to look three years and two drivers ago, have a flea-market feel to them. Knots of fans in NASCAR T-shirts wander the rows, eating hot dogs and drinking icy, watery Cokes.

They're not buying too much—the checkered-flag seat cushions, can cozies, die-cast cars, key chains, hats, knives and board games, and shirts, flags, banners, radios, and everything else can probably wait until tomorrow. Tonight, it seems, is just a good time to get a look at everything, to take a nice deep breath and smell racing.

That's what a guy named Lloyd, who runs one of the trailers, says, anyway. He's taking a break and having a fried bologna sandwich at a little food stand, sitting in the lights watching the people walk by. He sells mostly clothes, "but whatever sells," he says. He figures this is one of his best weekends of the year, and he pays about $2,000 for his spot to set up this weekend (a spot actually on speedway ground goes for more like $6,000). "The charisma here is much better than the charisma at Daytona," he says. Places like Martinsville and Rockingham he calls "hokey shows," because the tracks are smaller and more rural and draw a much less wealthy clientele. "That's what I call hillbilly races. People, what money they've got to spend, they spend it just coming to the race." Here, though, "you can just smell their money. A lot of Yankees come down for this race."

He's talking to a woman with bright white hair and a pink shirt. She runs the food stand where he's eating. "We sold out today," she says. "Hot dogs and homemade chili and good smoked chicken go real fast." Hustlers on scooters troll the crowds for tickets as they talk, and the crowd washes by in waves. People wearing straw hats, racing hats, racetrack visors, and Dale Earnhardt-shirts wave at Lloyd, say hey to his companion. "I have people that see me every weekend, and I have people that see me once a year," he says. "It's that transient neighborhood. It's like they're nomad racers and they're all meeting at the event and getting to know each other. That's what it's all about."

Well, that and selling die-cast cars and clothes. "It's all apparel now," Lloyd says. He sold die cast, but bigger companies are taking over that market, he says, and so he's moving to shirts and hats, where he can still make a living.

The light posts give a harsh, high-contrast feeling to his meal. Under the lamps you can forget to look up at the sky.

Then a woman walks by in a Terry Labonte T-shirt, leading by the hand a girl of about four with mustard on her face and a glassy stare. It's pretty late, and it's probably been a big day for her.

But there's one more thing she has to see, and her mom leads her off between the souvenir trailers, onto a gravel access road where it's a little darker. She points to the sky.

"You see the moon?" she asks. "You see that little fingernail of a moon?"

The girl raises her eyes and looks, and she smiles.

And it's true. Where Venus and Mars have been dancing in the sky all week, they're joined by an impossibly fragile sliver of crescent moon, angling down toward the trees to the southwest. Out here that's above a sea of campers and tents. Inside the track it looks like it would be just over Turns 1 and 2. The moon, low in the sky and nearly at the horizon, almost disappears into the barbecue haze above the souvenir trailers, into the milky whiteness of smoke illuminated by floodlights. The stars, above it, still burn brightly.

Tomorrow nobody will be looking at the stars.

CHAPTER 7

HAPPY HOUR

Saturday, October 4

Friday was quiet. Friday was a day off. Friday was the last moment of setting up; the Cup garage was closed, the Busch cars practiced, a few thousand people came to watch the practice and the hooligan race, buy a few souvenirs. People arriving early set up their infield compounds. Friday was the final inhalation, the final getting ready.

Saturday the explosion starts.

Driving in to the speedway before dawn Saturday, you see not just the haze nestled in the little farm hollows along the rural roads leading to the speedway—you see troopers, and you see them every half-mile or so. Their lights aren't on yet, but they're watching. The Busch race starts today at 1 P.M., and close to 80,000 people will be around to watch it. That's going to be a lot of traffic, if only around half as much as tomorrow will bring. So they're watching, getting ready.

The Cup garage opens at 7, and around 50 mechanics wait at the steel gate when the NASCAR official unlocks it and lets them in. The sun isn't up yet.

❖

The day starts at a run. Dave goes about his business as usual. The coolers take their morning leak out front of his hauler like always, and he gets ice to restock them with bottled water and soda pop, but the mechanics grab the race car, whip off the cover, and push it onto their scales. Newt puts a couple more decals on the race car where he fixed the fender, and the job is finally done. It looks like what Kenny said it was: a cobble, but a first-rate cobble. Then again, if a car started a race without duct tape on it somewhere, it just wouldn't be racing.

They adjust jackscrews a couple of times, using little funnels beneath the rear window to guide the wrenches down, shaking the car to settle it after every couple of cranks. They pull the lead weights out of the frame rails, hacksaw a slice here and there off the aluminum tubes used as spacers, and soon enough the weight is where Newt wants it. The scales go back in their little padded steamer trunk.

The Square D guys aren't the only ones running. A brilliant orange sun pops up over Turn 3, casting shadows half the length of the garage and burnishing the whole proceeding in an orange-yellow glow; the shadows dance and reel like a marionette show. Guys from every team crisscross the concrete with tire dollies and ice carts, or with five or six shocks dangling from their fingers, two or three springs cradled in their arms. Generators start puttering immediately. Chatting and goofing around has stopped now. Down along the garage row, it's hoods up and elbows in. Practice starts at 9 A.M., and nobody has an extra second.

Kenny's here, regaling someone else with the story of his qualifying lap. Eddie, checking his tires, seems almost cheerful. "Normally, second-round qualifying is the day before the race. Even if you make the race, you don't ask for your race tires until 2 o'clock Saturday afternoon. You don't get 'em made until 3:30, which means you have to do your work the next day, before the race. Here, we qualified on Thursday, so we get a couple extra days; you know what I'm saying? Same thing for the guys changing the motor.

"So we got lucky." It's the first time I've heard anyone from Filmar Racing say that.

Filbert has shown up, and he stands on the hauler steps in a leather jacket, sipping a cup of coffee, watching, nodding, quiet. Engines roar, air wrenches whine, metal wrenches clatter. The rich smell of exhaust fills the air.

It feels like race weekend.

❖

Same thing out on the infield. Overnight the campers and buses kept pouring in. Some people set up in front of car headlights, but many just rolled in, threw a tarp over everything, and slept in their pickups or vans. More are pulling in now, in a steady stream, and the hammering makes the infield sound like a construction site, only with the race cars roaring in the background. Every now and then, after a particularly loud rev, a fan responds with a rebel yell, which usually leads to another, and the hollers echo around the track. Lines of puffy pink people wearing first-cigarette-don't-bother-me expressions and carrying towels and backpacks or overnight cases—or pulling wagons filled with same—stretch from both the men's and women's showers.

A line stretches out of the Pit Stop Restaurant, too, but more people opt for their own food, cooking scrambled eggs in the grease left over from a package of bacon. Beer usually fills in for orange juice, and the smell of breakfast fills the air like the hammering.

Just inside Turn 1, in the golden morning light, a group of guys puts up a series of platforms and blue tarp shelters right along the fence. A hefty man in overalls, sunglasses, no shirt, and a long braided ponytail moves around sections of plywood. His pal, in a ponytail, jeans, and goatee, wanders down for a beer. He introduces himself as Ralph and says he's an electrician from Hickory, North Carolina. "All of us been coming here eight years, some of us ten or twelve," he says to explain how they've ended up with such a prime spot. He points slightly up the hill to a huge purple-and-yellow pyramidal tent with the Camel cigarettes logo on it. "That's the Camel Roadhouse," he says. There'll be entertainment tonight: music, games, and all kinds of racing—and cigarette—themed stuff. Such as the tire challenge: Fans use a real air gun and change a tire on a real hub. "You change one of the fastest, you get handed a prize," he says. "You can get your picture made with some of the Camel gals, something like that." Flags for the number 6, 88, 94, and 3 cars already flap from their compound, and their platforms will be the first ones to see the race cars as they dive into Turn 1.

"Used to be in here you could park anywhere," he says. "But now you have to go where they tell you." He identifies the hill between the turns as Redneck Hill, and says "down in 3 and 4, I know they call it Hell Alley." He points back to Redneck Hill. "Out there on that hill, on like a road course, they have wagon races. On like Saturday night. Ain't no prizes, just bragging rights, you might say. Your wagon against the world." Their compound, like all the others, has improved over the years, but the most important thing he's determined is the Port-a-Jons. "We rent two, one for the men and one for the women. You pay a couple extra dollars to have a nice seat to sit on. Don't have to worry about a bug jumping on you."

A guy snooping from a couple of compounds over agrees that improvements come every year. "You get different ideas from different people," says Dewayne Moffat, from Denver, North Carolina. "That guy over there showed me how to rope down his tent." He shows off a large, white truck that, along with the Astroturf on the top, he's tricked out with a complete sound and mixing system. "I got over 400 CDs here," he says. "This is one of the highlights of my year. Coming down here and going racing, having quality times with friends, drinking, picking, having fun."

❖

Lots of people are showing up to have fun, and not just on the infield.

For one thing, Big Steve Baker is here. He "rolled in last night" on his motorcycle, he says. It's parked out by the front garage gate, on a little triangle of asphalt that holds about 50 bikes of drivers and crew members. With his scraggly beard, wraparound mirrored sunglasses, ponytail, and comfortable bulk pressing against his Square D shirt, Steve brings a kind of good-natured just-pleased-to-be-here to the garage that cuts some of the building intensity.

"That's what I'm here for," he smiles, adjusting air pressure on tires according to Eddie's specifications. He spends more time helping Eddie than anything else, but he sees his job as a weekend warrior as being the guy to fill whatever hole needs filling.

"Anything to take it off these guys," he says, gesturing to the blue-shirted teammates scrambling around him as he helps Eddie stack tires. "That's all I'm for. If I can go get a bag of rags or drag a grease bucket, it's one less thing they have to do." When the races are far away, he rides to Charlotte and gets on the Race Day Express, a charter that the race teams share to get all their weekend crew members to wherever the race is. "Everybody's pretty bleary at 4 A.M." when it takes off, he says, "but it's like a party after the race." But when the team's racing in the Southeast, he rides his motorcycle. He's been with Filmar for about six years. "I've always enjoyed racing," he says, but he was friends with a crew member long ago, was invited to come by and help out, and he's been part of the gang since then. He looks around the garage, filled not only with crew members but with fans and guests on Busch race-day pit passes. "Every one of these fans wishes they could do this," he says. "I'm just one of the lucky ones." He puts a blob of spit on each tire valve he checks, to make sure it isn't leaking.

Kevand Cross, whose place I took waving the pit sign when he had to go home to his real job during the Martinsville race, is here too. He's a friend of Frank Good's, and he pays his own way from New Jersey to help out at every race. He wipes down cars, cleans the grille, helps scrape goo off tires between practices, and works especially hard Sunday morning setting up the pit. Until then, like Steve, he does what he can.

The garage feels fuller because of the weekend warriors' arrival; each team has a couple of extra guys in uniform now, helping get the car ready for the final two practices.

But it's a lot more than that. Suddenly there are people walking around wearing passes that haven't been seen all week. Team members have what are called hard cards—little ID badges that the team pays for annually, granting access to every race. But the access that NASCAR makes so available to its sponsors and fans is starting to show, as different colored cardboard passes, usually worn in a long plastic cover either around the neck or on a belt loop, flop in earnest now.

The garage is NASCAR's territory, and it issues the passes for that, on 8x4-inch sheets of cardboard, different colors for each event, and with letter codes that identify them for NASCAR officials who genuinely check them before you enter. They say "1997 Garage Pass" and have the Winston Cup Series logo in some kind of spangly, hard-to-forge ink. The track issues passes for the grandstand, the infield, and the pit area, and the passes usually say something about the character of the track. The Martinsville Speedway pass, for instance, was a little red square of construction paper with the date of the event and a serial number; its lone foray into decoration was the speedway and event logos in gold foil ink. The Charlotte pass—the Pit Infield pass issued to journalists, anyway—is bright orange cardboard, the same size as the garage pass, with the event and speedway logos printed in sparkly pink ink, and the date reversed into a holographic cube pattern. The credential itself is an event at Charlotte.

There are different colored passes for each day, from Friday to Sunday; there are different colored passes for just the pit area on Sunday morning; there are passes that last all weekend; there are passes that give you access to the grandstand, too. Charlotte issues more than 2,000 passes of one color or another for this event, and you can often find posted near entrances a sort of Rosetta Stone helping security guards make sure they know what color passes are valid when.

Getting those passes is an adventure. Outside the speedway is a little building where credential seekers line up and are allowed in one at a time, by a guard, and allowed to present a picture ID and hope that the credentials they requested are filed where they're supposed to be—by town of origin, for some reason. Then you have to sign three different waivers that say, basically, that if you get hit in the head by a loose tire or run over by a speeding race car it's just too bad and you should have expected as much. You sign the forms, you sign the passes, and you usually buy a plastic credential holder ($4 at Charlotte; a buck at Martinsville) and you go on your way.

One more way you can get access to the garage and pits for a race is by buying what is called a single-event license for $100. That's issued by NASCAR, and each team is allowed to sign up 14 people per event who get to go through a special NASCAR trailer outside the track and sign their lives away just the same. (Drivers and crew members sign the same stuff, by the way, and at each race the NASCAR hauler in the garage has a thick sheaf of forms that drivers have to sign before they go on the track.)

The strict control doesn't stop people from trying to get in otherwise, of course. It never works at the credential office, but the NASCAR trailer sees its share of wheedlers every week—people who promise the team meant to leave their names and if you let me in I'll make sure they explain it to you, people who left something in there yesterday and I just want to run right in and get it, people who forgot their names until they peer over the list of names at the trailer. "They come in here and you tell 'em they're not on the list," says Amy Treadway, a young woman of about 25 who works the trailer. "They come back five or six more times. Women are the worst." She says she gets about a dozen such hardy efforts a week. "I give 'em the eyebrow." She raises an eyebrow and issues a deadly stare. "They aggravate me and they get the eyebrow." They also get the message.

"The craziest one?" asks Marlin Wright, chief registrar of the trailer. "I had a man come in carrying an alternator. They was on the warm-up lap on the track, and he said he needed to go in and put it on the car. I told him the cars go through inspection two hours before the race. Needless to say, he did not get in." On the other hand, a driver—or someone else known to NASCAR—can come in hours before a race and effortlessly add a name. Everybody wants to cooperate. By the way, no shorts in the garage area. It's a rule, and when the people at the Gateway International Raceway outside St. Louis ran their first Busch series race earlier in the year, they forgot about that and issued garage passes without mentioning it. They ended up handing out hospital-style paper pants at the gates to shorts-clad fans with passes.

In the garage at Charlotte Saturday morning, those passes have started to show up in quantity. This morning, they're green. Suddenly the people who aren't wearing uniforms vastly outnumber those who are, and conditions are getting hazardous. Cameras dangle from wrists, bags of souvenirs swing in the way of guys pushing dollies or pulling carts. They're used to it and pretty much ignore it. Still, officials line up trash barrels and run pennant tape along the yellow lines nearest the haulers to keep the crowds mostly out of the way. Practice will start soon, and cars will be zipping along the concrete in the garage, and there's no way most of these people will know to stay out of the way.

They're a different-looking lot, these inside outsiders, in khakis and golf shirts or jeans and Jeff Gordon T-shirts and hats. They wander in slack-jawed pairs, gathering in knots at the haulers of the most popular drivers, especially Gordon's number 24 and Dale Earnhardt's number 3, hoping to sight the drivers. A man and woman wearing identical Wells Sports white shirts and sunglasses look more like a matched tea set than a race team. Another little group of three women, all in black, totter around on Louis XVI-style flared high heels, clutching tiny black purses. "We're from M&Ms," explains one.

Salespeople wander the garage all weekend, discussing wheels or electrical systems or uniforms or cleaning fluids or hoses with crew chiefs and owners. Race weekends are when they do their business, and they've got to hustle, or so says Ed Cluka, sales manager for Aero Race Wheels, which he's pushing on Newt and other crew chiefs. "He's switching next year to Aero wheels," Ed says of his conversation with Newt. Coming to Charlotte—he lives in Wisconsin—is just part of the deal, he says. "It's like selling anything else. I want a market, I have to come down here to the track and dig it out." Of course, it's not quite like selling anything else. "You only have 60 or 70 customers," he admits. In fact, if he sold his wheels to every single race team on every circuit that could use them, "I'd have 400 customers," he says. A Winston Cup team goes through 110 to 120 of the 25-pound wheels a season. The teams he serves will destroy 40 wheels at a track, between practice, qualifying, and the race, he says. He goes to seven or eight races a year, but the two Charlotte races are where he does most of his business.

The crowd continues to thicken. Sometimes groups come by, identifying stickers on their shirts, on guided garage tours, led by politely bored sponsor representatives holding little paddles with the sponsor logo—Caterpillar, Valvoline, John Deere—like European tour guides dragging gaggles of impressed but slightly overwhelmed Americans.

Welcome to Charlotte.

❖

It's not much different in the media center. Piles of notebooks, briefcases, newspapers, laptop computers stake out virtually every chair. Writers sip coffee from the speedway urns and get going on their daily piles of free smokes.

And of course, it's far more than just writers. TV cameras are piled in a corner, near a reclining chair, next to the press-conference dais, that usually holds a snoozing reporter. Some attempt is made to keep PR types, people working on racing fashion shoots, people working on catalog sales, and other not-quite-press types from the deadline press area, but not much. Pretty much everybody just mixes, country DJs and people from the Cartoon Network mix with people from the *Charlotte Observer* and the *Baltimore Sun*.

One new face belongs to Randy Anthony, a compact guy with light hair who's a producer for NASCAR Country, a two-hour weekly radio program that combines country music and NASCAR racing. "Because NASCAR and country music have a 50-year history," he says. "It's natural." It brings to mind what Bob Latford said about NASCAR racing on Monday in the Martinsville press box: "It's like country music: Nobody likes it except the public." John Boy and Billy, the radio hosts who got Jerry Gappens in trouble yesterday, run on classic rock stations. But the only station broadcasting from the speedway this weekend is a local country station, WSOC, which is one of NASCAR Country's home stations.

"My job is to get the interviews with the NASCAR people," Randy says. Other producers interview country stars, and the two are woven into a weekly show. "Stars talking about cars, and car guys talking about stars," Randy says. "It goes back to Marty Robbins in the 1960s. He was a big local racer in Nashville, Saturday-night racer, and a country star. Race fans and country music are the same demographic. But up until 1990 nobody had ever put NASCAR and country music in a promotional-powered vehicle." It does now: The show runs on 325 stations nationwide, usually from 10 to 12 Sunday morning, directly before the Motor Racing

Network or Performance Racing Network broadcast of the day's race. MRN is almost always carried by a country station, and NASCAR Country just fits.

Randy hands around a few CDs of this week's show, and then he's off to be one more new face wandering the garage, filling the concrete and jostling with team members.

❖

Not that they really notice. Not now. With 9 A.M. closing in, the number 81 car—like every other car in the garage—is pushed up the incline from the garage to pit road, where the cars await the signal to start practice. The stands are filling for the Busch race that starts at 1:10 P.M., but plenty of fans come out early enough to watch the big boys' morning practice. The final Cup practice—Happy Hour—that follows the race keeps fans in their seats after the Busch race, too. It's the most important hour of practice of the weekend. The cars have been pretty well set up, and the teams are fine-tuning the cars as drivers see how their cars handle in traffic. They pass, run two and three wide, and even engage in a little light racing, and fans love it. This morning's practice, the last time the teams are likely to try something radical just to see what happens, is more like batting practice, and about the same kind of race fan shows up for the morning practice laps as shows up for batting practice before a baseball game.

Headsets come on as soon as the car gets pushed up the slope. With Kenny in the car, Newt, Eddie, Filbert, and Vic on the hauler, and the rest of the crew in the garage, it's the only way they can stay in easy contact. There's still a little conversation about Thursday's qualifying miracle: "I was out with my friends last night, I said, 'How'd we do?'" Eddie says. "They said, 'You did great.' This goddamn track needs a lotta right front spring to go fast in a lap. That's the consensus. I guess a lot of people know about what we did."

But then talk turns to how that affects the job at hand. "Kenny," Newt says, "I just want you to know that's the motor that won Darlington earlier in the year." Jeremy has learned that the motor in Kenny's car was in Dale Jarrett's car when he won the Cup race at Darlington in the spring. "Well, that's awesome," Kenny says. "Hey, I need someone down here to pull my screen back up, one of the TV guys here pulled it down."

Then it's 9 A.M., and engines roar. "Daddy's rolling," Kenny says, and practice has begun.

Same as usual, Kenny's in and out, same as usual complaining about both pushing *and* breaking loose in the corners. "I'm still sliding the nose up the track, especially from the middle out," he says. "I feel like I can go if I get the nose to turn."

Despite the importance of the practice, plenty of cheer is still leftover from Thursday. "Looks good there, buddy," Newt says after one lap. "I know it looks good," Kenny says. "Is it *fast*?" After another adjustment Kenny says, "It doesn't feel like I'm as pinched over in 3 and 4 like I was, but I'm still a little tight." Newt responds, "Them shocks I got for you are supposed to take care of those two problems right there."

A moment of silence, and then Kenny's back on the radio. "Damn!" he says. "Those must be some cool-ass shocks."

Adjustments to sway bar, track bar, tire pressure, springs, shocks, don't seem to help much. "We're 42nd on speed right now," Newt says about halfway through the hour. "We need to get at least to 25th so everyone concerned can say, 'Heeeey!' " Kenny clicks on long enough to mutter, "Monitor racing." Then a lap or so later he's back on the radio.

"Hey, I just realized," he says. "They're starting 43 cars in this race. Who are we faster than?"

Up on the hauler, Newt looks at his monitor. "Uh . . . nobody, now."

Eddie makes a comment about camber, and then goes on to point out that they're running on old tires to save money, saving their new sets for the race. He calls the sticker tires some cars run in practice "ego stickers," but Newt breaks in. "We're just trying to get the car feeling good, K. W., on those tires. Then when we get some new ones on there you ought to be able to haul the mail."

Kenny fairly chirps. "I heard you, Newt. This is Kenny Wallace from St. Louis, Missouri, and I heard you." A few more laps, a few more trips in and out, and then the 81 car glides for good into garage stall 33, managing not to run anybody over on the way.

❖

Not that that's easy.

The crowd is increasing exponentially, and one of the clogging factors is the Busch cars lining up for the beginning of their race. Their race starts at 1:10, and it turns out that the best place for them to line up—with their own little generators, just like the Cup cars—is on the east side of the Cup garage. So while the Cup teams are picking apart their engines one last time, changing shocks and springs, having final discussions about what they can try during Happy Hour, every few minutes a little knot of Busch guys comes running through the garage, pushing their car into line, making a long U around the Cup garage. prerace festivities have started out on the track, with little Bandolero cars running a collegiate competition buzzing around a tiny oval right in front of the start-finish line. Half-scale mockups of race cars barely big enough for an adult to fit in, the little cars are a kind of toy race car. It's like watching the little kids play hockey during the period break of an NHL game. They sound like mosquitoes.

The Busch teams push their cars into line, check their generators, put a thick heat shield over the windshield of the car to keep it from getting heated up by the sun, then trot back to their own garage area.

That word—area—is descriptive. The Cup racers have a big concrete garage, with fluorescent lights and fabric sound baffles hanging from the ceiling and even a yellow stripe painted down the middle to give onlookers the idea of where to stay to be out of the way. The Busch drivers have nothing of the sort. The Busch drivers, in fact, have nothing at all.

The Busch compound is defined by the haulers parked, basically, in a big circle, with the same kinds of tents the Winston Cup cars used last week at Martinsville in the rain set up for makeshift shelter. The Cup tech inspection is a bay in the garage, with hooks for the long metal templates and a scale set into the ground; the Busch tech inspection is two tents pushed together, the templates laying on catering tables.

The garage area itself looks completely different, too. The haulers are a couple of years older. A lot of them are old haulers sold off by Cup teams. Tires, rims, toolboxes, war wagons all seem to end up just sort of around, in piles, rather than in organized regiments like the Cup equipment. The Busch cars are 100 pounds lighter, about 10 inches shorter, and, most important, have about 200 less horsepower. "It's just a completely different car," Kenny Wallace of St. Louis, Missouri, has said. "Completely different."

And the series is completely different. Though virtually all Cup dates have some kind of second-tier race scheduled the day before, it's not always a Busch race. It could be a Craftsman Truck Series race, like last week at Martinsville, or a NASCAR Modified Tour race, or a race from one of a few other touring series. But the Busch series tends to travel with the Cup series, and Busch is often looked at as sort of the last step on the way to Cup competition. Several Cup drivers—Mark Martin, Dale Jarrett, Jimmy Spencer, Michael Waltrip—drive Busch cars too, on the weekends where the races coordinate. Cup drivers often use the Busch series to dip their toes into the business of owning a race team, too. Dale Earnhardt owns a Busch team; Dale Jarrett owns a Busch team; Michael Waltrip owns one, though not the one he drives for.

But there's one big difference between Cup and Busch. The money isn't even comparable. The winner of a Busch race takes home in the neighborhood of $50,000; a Cup winner usually takes home from two to five times that much. Teams are smaller. A Busch team will have five or six guys, compared to a Cup team's 20 to 50. With less money comes smaller sponsorship dollars, and above all, less pressure.

"They'd just rather have Sunday off," is how Bob Sutton, one of the owners of the number 38 Busch car, sponsored by Barbasol, puts it. He looks around the loosely organized garage. "Billy, off of the 74 car, he's been up in Cup. But he's happy down in Busch. Lots of 'em like that. It's not that these people didn't have what it takes for Cup. But in Busch you can be home by Saturday night and spend one entire day sleeping."

He goes on. "It's not the same star quality down here, not the same public recognition. I've had people get introduced to Jeff Fuller and told he drives the number 45 car, and they flat-out say, 'Nuh-unh!' Busch drivers, still, some of 'em get a measure of anonymity that the Cup drivers don't have."

He's right. Take a look at any of the dozens of NASCAR-themed commercials that run for car batteries or cars or oil treatment or soft drinks. The drivers who appear are almost never identified. The people the advertisers hope to reach already know those guys. They don't need to be told that that's Jeremy Mayfield, that's Ward Burton, that's Jeff Gordon. They know, and they like knowing. But that's Cup. The Busch guys have still got a ways to go to get to that level.

Gary Cogswell, crew chief of the Royal Oak Charcoal–sponsored number 34 car, agrees. "I've worked at Cup races, and you're exactly right. This is kinda more like being a kid and playing basketball with your best friends. It's a little bit more relaxed over here. You can feel like you're doing it as a hobby." No thousand-pound weights on the shoulders of this crew chief, and this is a car that's winning races—two this year. The cars use their engines two or three races before tearing them down, he says, and they don't always have different qualifying and race engines. It's just much closer to the Saturday-night, run-what-you-brung racing all these guys grew up with.

Some of the haulers—mostly those for the points leaders like Randy LaJoie or Winston Cup regulars like Jarrett or Martin—are as tricked out as the Cup haulers, but there are plenty of plain white trucks, some barely big enough to hold the race car and a toolbox. And Busch still demonstrates a little of that roots racing spirit too. Maybe the 1979 fight at Daytona was what started the modern era of fan interest in Winston Cup racing, but you don't see much of that kind of stuff on the Cup circuit anymore. In Busch, it's part of the show. In a night race at Richmond a few weeks ago, the number 4 and number 6 cars got into a mix-up early in the race. Joe Bessey, driver of the 6, which hit the wall and ended its race, thought it was the fault of Dale Shaw in the 4, who escaped. As Bessey stood under the lights, hands on hips, by his car stranded at the top of Turn 2, Shaw slowed down on the next caution lap to see if he was OK. Bessey took his helmet off and flung it into Shaw's passenger-side window.

Next lap around Shaw slowed again, and the helmet popped back out onto the track. Shaw roared off. After the race, asked about the incident, Bessey said

Shaw was driving arrogantly. "I think his head's getting a little too big for his helmet," Bessey said. "I thought he might need mine."

That spirit, that unpredictability, can look attractive from the regimented Cup side. Jack man Steve Dluzniewski for Filmar Racing once said he still looks fondly back to the days when Kenny was driving a Busch car. "There was three of us, at the most. Build it, paint it, drive it down the road," he said. Of Cup competition, he allowed, "you do have a little more time to prepare, but it's a grind, more than anything. They want you to work 51 weeks a year. We finish our season and then they want you to turn *up* the wick." He sighed, then talked about the weekly racetracks up in Massachusetts where he grew up. He was clearly more comfortable there. He complains about the egos and politics of Cup racing more than anyone on the team. Then again, he made those comments after a night race at Richmond, while taking the opportunity to devour some leftover sweet corn and baked beans he found in containers atop a big pile of trash left by the hauler next to the number 81 team. Anybody perfectly comfortable eating the neighbors' trash can be expected to appreciate the less-formal attitude of the Busch series.

But it's not just Duze, not by a long shot. Even Newt Moore, struggling under the pressure of trying to head the crew of his struggling team, has cast yearning eyes back to lower levels. Kenny won races at the Busch level; in 1991 he came within 75 points of the series championship. The team won races and poles, the trophies and banners and commemorative checkered flags still decorate the Filmar Racing shop.

In fact, Newt sometimes casts his eyes back even further, back to his days traveling with his Late Model car. "That was my college for this deal," he said one night, hunched over a beer before the next day's race in Dover. "Driving all over, setting up cars, doing it all myself." It was hard, but sometimes, when the pressure is strongest, you know he's thinking about it. Winston Cup is the money; it's the top of the racing world. It's ESPN and a thousand reporters asking questions and it's the by-God real deal. "But sometimes," Newt said that night in Dover, "I wish we could just pull in, unload the car, repack the bearings, take a piss, and go racing."

❖

On the track, at Charlotte, the Busch drivers appear to have repacked their bearings and taken their piss, and they are being carried around for a parade lap in open convertibles after their introductions. As prerace festivities continue, the fans file in, carrying coolers filled with beer, bags of food, and headsets, all virtual necessities. The coolers of beer are a race tradition, though they're now limited to 14 inches on any dimension, since fans had started bringing in bathtub-sized coolers.

Cans are OK, but no bottles. Fans bring in seat cushions—you can find the ones with the checkered flag pattern for $5 at the souvenir trailers—and bags of sandwiches, buckets of fried chicken. They bring in race magazines and buy programs, bring in bags of souvenirs they bought—or were given—outside. Security guards check backpacks and bags, but they're just looking for glass or other dangerous items. You go to a race, you can bring in what you want as long as it's not going to land on somebody's head; and even if it is, if it won't hurt 'em, well all right then. The first three or four rows are called "Chicken Bone Alley," and fans live up to their reputation: If you don't want to sit under an arcing rain of chicken bones, empty beer cans, napkins, and other trash, don't sit in the first few rows at a NASCAR race.

But the most important thing fans bring in may be those headsets. Some are simple AM-FM radio sets that can pick up whatever local station is broadcasting the race; as Randy Anthony said, almost always a country station. Many, though, are much more complex. They're scanners: portable walkie-talkie-sized units that can scan anywhere from 10 to all of the teams racing. Available from trailers outside the track, the scanners allow fans to hear not only the broadcast of the race (Motor Racing Network puts its live feed on a scannable frequency so people at the track with scanners can hear it) but the communications of every single race team on the track, plus the discussions of NASCAR officials, usually the live ESPN feed, and any comments the emergency vehicle drivers might make (usually concerning women in the pit area).

The scanners are another aspect of that vaunted access NASCAR allows its fans. Newt, Eddie, and Kenny talking about what changes to make after a few practice laps? Fans can hear. Discussions between spotters and drivers during the race? Fans can hear. NASCAR black-flags a driver for a penalty? Fans can check in and hear why. It would be, people often say, like leaning over the huddle while a quarterback called plays on the football field, though by hanging around pit road and the garage during races NASCAR fans are already figuratively on the sidelines with the players anyhow.

Outside the track, in one of four TrackScan trailers he runs, Glen Aikenhead, of Mooresville, North Carolina, explains the scanner business. "This is a full-time business," he says. "The only things you really need for a scanner are good batteries and an accurate frequency list. Without either one of those things you won't hear anything. So we update our frequency lists daily, every single weekend. That way when Tim Zock shows up in the number 95 Busch car and makes the race, our customers hear him." Frequencies, of course, are also available on dozens of Internet sites, and they're every bit as accurate as those you can buy for $5 from Aikenhead. For $35 for the weekend he offers a scanner that can pick up 10 teams.

For fans who just want to hear the race broadcast, little AM-FM headsets sell all over for $20, but they don't block out much of the track noise. Fans who go to races more often tend to buy their scanners, whether for close to $200 at the track or for $150 or so at Radio Shack.

"We go through radio technicians in the garage," Aikenhead says, referring to the companies that supply radio communications to NASCAR and the teams. Each team has a few frequencies, which it registers with NASCAR and the FCC at the beginning of each season. Fans would need much more expensive and complex equipment to break into the frequencies and talk, he says, so that happens only very rarely. He knows that MRN is a big part of his business, but he thinks the best moment to use a scanner is during Happy Hour, the final Saturday afternoon practice before race day. "You can jump from car to car, they're all talking then," he says. "If they're pushing going in, you know it; if they can't race if someone's behind 'em, you hear about it." The teams listen in on one another—like Eddie D'Hondt does for Filmar Racing—but Aikenhead downplays that in most cases. "The reality is, there's not a single chassis out there that's the same," he says. "Everybody has to do what works for their own car."

What works for Aikenhead in business is to rent these scanners at the races, and it's not cheap. He says his average fee just to rent a spot for a weekend at a track is $5,000. "There's $100,000 a year just in track fees. Then you have to figure NASCAR has to be compensated in there, too." He's selling something the fans really want, so he can afford it.

Those high fees (they're one of the important ways a track makes its money) are a little harder on people selling something people don't want quite as much, though. At the blue-and-yellow trailer that sells souvenirs of the number 81 Square D car and the number 77 Jasper Engines car, Mike Broyles sings a different tune.

"There's probably three or four trailers out here making money," Broyles says. Those are the trailers for the most popular drivers: the number 24 of Jeff Gordon, who was champion two years ago and is sort of the new model of Cup drivers; the 3 of seven-time champion Dale Earnhardt, who with his gruff, country style represents the old school; the 6, the 88, the 5. For Broyles, "This is a labor of love, mostly." He raced himself for years and then got into business, but later in life he's decided, with his wife, Sherry, to open up this trailer. "It was a way I can stay close to the sport, enjoy it, meet some of the greatest people in it."

"It was my idea, actually," Sherry says. They had some money, and Mike had said he'd help Sherry set up a business for herself. "He thought I might want to go into a flower shop or a deli, something like that. Then we were at a race and I said let's do this. Our two kids are grown. One thinks we're crazy, one thinks we're OK." They both hope that Kenny Wallace has a breakthrough year soon and they start making money. "It takes two or three consecutive weeks of a team doing real good before you see a difference," Mike says. They haven't noticed an upturn after Kenny's strong showing last week.

Overall, the racing souvenir business is worth about a billion dollars a year. But an awful lot of the profits from that billion dollars goes to people running souvenir stores, with less overhead, and to the companies that make the souvenirs themselves, like Action Performance, which has quietly amassed a virtual monopoly on die-cast cars and other toys from most of the cars on the circuit. Kenny Wallace, for example, has his die-cast cars made exclusively by Action Performance. NASCAR-affiliated stores like NASCAR Thunder do a lot of souvenir business too.

But as the Broyles say, the souvenir midway is part of racing, and that's where they want to be. "We were going to races anyway," Sherry says. "Being a fan, that's what I want to do. I want to go sell T-shirts."

❖

Back inside the speedway, the Busch race is starting. Fans fill the seats along the front stretch and Turns 1 and 4. Cheap seats along the backstretch are filled too, though the big bleachers in Turn 2 are closed. Pit road is busy with the Busch teams, with their own war wagons and piles of tires and their own dramas. They have their own throngs of women dressed in tight jeans and race-day credentials clogging up pit road and styling in sunglasses. There are Port-a-Jons on pit road and an ice cream vendor. The speedway plays the Emerson, Lake and Palmer song "See the Show!" over the public address system. As the Busch cars start and take their pace laps, a few Cup teams still working on their cars occasionally gun their engines, giving the throaty rumble that the Busch cars, 200 horsepower smaller, just don't equal. It feels a little like the lions roaring in their cages during the antelope race.

For the Cup guys, this is one of the few moments when they can take a second and watch a race or just relax. They hang around inside and in front of the hauler, either puttering at their jobs or just reading. Vic mutters to himself as he fiddles with shock parts in the hauler. "This is not rocket science," he says for about the 90th time. Then he starts talking about shims of 6/1,000 of an inch that control shock fluid flow, and how different manufacturers' shocks make different pieces.

"And none of 'em fit each other," offers Frank, leaning on the aluminum counter next to the dyno, munching a piece of fried chicken, idly leafing through *Speedway Scene*, a tabloid paper mostly about racing in the Northeast. Out front, Jeremy sleeps in a garden chair and Eddie obsessively checks his tires. Sitting quietly, just enjoying the moment of peace, is Two-Can, who finally has a moment to share a story or two.

"I came here in '68, from Glendale, California," he says. He went to high school with a guy who ended up driving on the Cup circuit—in those days before the big money from R. J. Reynolds and other sponsors, it was still called the Grand National circuit—and Two-Can came along, though he's been a mechanic from the start. "I did everything," he says of those early days. "Brakes, gears, tires, plumbing the engine. There was four of us." He crisscrossed the country with the team; the circuit toured more extensively in the Northeast then, and ran many more races: nearly 50 per year, many on weekday nights, many only 100 laps or so. Engines would last more races, and the circuit stayed a little closer to the shade-tree mechanics who had started it all only two decades before, but he says things haven't changed all that much.

"It's all common sense," he says. "A lot of people make it more complicated than it needs to be. Where you used to do everything with tape measures, now you do it with computers." He shrugs. People squawk about money and politics and NASCAR making rules changes and everything else, but one thing hasn't changed, he says. "Winning is what it's all about."

His favorite win of all time as a team member was when his friend Dick Brooks won Talladega in 1973. "It was a borrowed race car," he says, "but it was a fast race car. We had terrible pit stops and it would go from the back to the front by itself. Now you gotta be as good as the best pit crew to win a race." Frank, hearing Two-Can spinning yarns, leans out of the hauler. "Tell him about the Mexico trip!" Two-Can smiles, leans back in his chair a little.

"We was on our way to Ontario, California, and we crossed the border into Mexico, across from El Paso." (Don't ask why; that's not part of the story.) "We got in a ruckus in a bar," he goes on. "Well, we ended up in jail. We was in there three days." They finally paid their way out of jail and got to California, just in time for qualifying. "We had 15 minutes of practice, qualified second. We won the race." He thinks a minute. "We had to win the race, we didn't have enough money to get home! I think we had 35 cents between all of us." Was driver Benny Parsons worried?

"Naah, he knew we'd gotten in some kinda shit. We were always getting in some kinda shit."

Talk shifts to cheating. "They used to have carburetor rings on the big blocks," he says, to restrict the amount of air that could go into the huge engines cars used to run. "We got to making 'em out of paraffin," so they'd fit the templates NASCAR used to check them, but as soon as the engine started running they'd melt. "Nelson, he had a little fuel cell, behind a false panel up above the shocks." That's Gary Nelson, who's now Winston Cup Series director. In the series' most famous example of if-you-can't-beat-'em, NASCAR hired as top official the crew chief who was the best at cheating. "He went out and tested in '83, the year he won the championship with Allison, at Riverside [California], and he rigged the scales. Somebody'd pull on it and it made the scale weigh more," so his driver could drive an illegally light car. Other chiefs used to fill hollow rails at the front of the car with shot, so weight would shift with the car more effectively. "It got so you couldn't even walk down pit road with a gas can" for all the spilled shot underfoot, he laughs.

Frank lights a cigarette, listening. "At Rockingham, we used to stay at these townhouses at a golf resort. We'd stay up all night playing cards, seven-card no-peek, and he'd tell us all these stories. It was like grandpa telling stories to the grandchildren."

No more all-nighters now, though—"too long days," Two-Can says. He figures to stay in racing a few more years—until he's 62—and then quit. Until then, he hopes to keep coming to the track. He's not a stay-at-the-shop guy.

OK, then, one more story. About that name?

Two-Can pretends to try to weasel out of a story he's told so many times, then gives in. "Well, it was back in 1971," he says. "I drove out to California for two engines made by Keith Black. You had to run 305-cubic-inch engines in a Dodge or Plymouth wing car, which was what we was running.

"Back then, all you heard about was Coors beer, everyone said it was the best beer to drink. You couldn't get it back here, so everybody in the shop gave me some money and said, well, bring back some Coors beer. I got 13 cases.

"When I got back, I had two full cans," he says, with a delighted smile. "That's all there was in the pickup. I drank up all their money!"

Then Two-Can stands up and climbs atop the hauler to have a look at the Busch race. "Yep," he says, climbing the ladder. "Them were real race cars, in them days."

❖

Over in the garage, as the Busch race goes on, the number 81 car is getting attention. Not by the team members now, though. Now it's the in-car camera guys' turn. TNN is broadcasting this week's race, and subcontracting for them is Boykin and Associates, which provides the in-car cameras for the race, and the number 81 car gets one, or, actually, three: one in the rear bumper, to show cars behind it, one inside the car to show the driver's view ahead, and another mounted beside the driver by the outside window, which can show Kenny or can pan to show cars passing on the right. Trent Dyer, of Boykin, works on the cameras, setting up a tiny TV screen and transmitter in a backpack that shoots an image up to the helicopter hovering over the track and back down to the screen so he can check the views; the signal also goes over to the TNN control truck set up outside the track. "That's unlike the radio-frequency pit cameras, which go directly to a receiver on the roof."

He connects the cameras, running little wires through the car, attaching them to the bars of the roll cage with zip ties. The whole system weighs about 12 pounds, he says. The team will adjust for the weight after it's all installed. "Of course the bulk of the weight is in the control box and the battery," a black box about the size of a citizens' band radio affixed to a roll-cage bar.

The rear-bumper camera is flat and shaped a little like a portable CD player; the driver's view camera looks like a pocket flashlight. The third one, the panning camera for passing and looking at the driver, is shaped like a toss-away box camera. "That one's called the doggy," Trent says. The doggy? Why's that?

Trent stops. "You know, I don't know." He polls the three other members of his crew, getting a "Dunno" from under the car and from behind it. Then a big guy in a TNN Motorsports T-shirt stands up across the car. "Hey, why's the passing camera called the doggy?" Trent asks.

The guy stares back, perfectly deadpan. "Because it's in the window," he says, then slowly disappears behind the car, like a whale sounding. Informed sources dispute whether it's because it likes to have its head out the window of a moving car or because it's like that doggy in the window, but the doggy it remains.

And how much is that doggy in the window?

The whole camera system runs about $18,000, Trent explains, and then mentions something remarkable: The network doesn't pay the team to put cameras in their car. The *team* pays the *network*, and it pays $18,000 for the opportunity. Makes perfect sense, says Steve Post, on hand with his wife, Julie, and a packet of Square D decals. He'll put a Square D sticker on every surface the cameras can show, looking over Trent's shoulder at his tiny screen. He puts them on the dash, on the tubes of the roll cage. On the rear bumper he fans three little Square D logos so that whichever way the camera pans the Square D is visible. When cameras are mounted underneath cars, like they were in Martinsville to show the brakes, teams put decals under there. Food Lion pays for a camera in the number 18 car, and it's not even a sponsor. It just pays for the camera and puts a decal on the dashboard.

"We got into the in-car camera business in a big way after Richmond," Steve says. The sponsor decided to spring for one to see how it worked out. "I think we got one head-shot of Kenny, and that was it." Steve left an enraged voice mail to Neil Goldberg of ESPN, the senior producer in charge of NASCAR races for the network, which broadcast the Richmond race. Goldberg admitted there had been a problem with the cameras in Kenny's car, so he offered a sort of do-over at the spring Martinsville race, which turned out to feature a stirring duel throughout the race between Kenny, who started on the pole, and his brother Rusty. Kenny finished that race sixth, one behind Rusty (his two Martinsville races were his best finishes all year), and the Square D logo was on camera it seemed like for half the race.

"So we bought up every remaining race," Steve says. "And we're not even in the identity business. I don't know why there's any left at all."

❖

ESPN broadcasts more races than anybody else, and it's kind of the master at it. ESPN started running flag-to-flag coverage of races as one of its charter franchises. It's hard to remember now, but when ESPN started out in 1979, college basketball and racing were underexposed, and that's where the network made its impression. Now it broadcasts not only close to half of the Winston Cup schedule but Busch races, truck races, and shows such as "RPM 2night," which runs every day of the week.

Nowadays, Goldberg and his crew are old hands, and they demonstrated that at the Martinsville race. In the air-conditioned trailer parked outside, Goldberg sat at his desk in front of a bank of about 40 screens of different sizes, each labeled with a camera number, the number of a car (for in-car cameras), or just a letter, for replay screens. He has cameras in the turns, along the backstretch, on the home stretch; he has a couple of cameras roaming the pits. He has a couple of cameras on the roof for the bigger picture. ESPN televises qualifying and Happy Hour as well as the race.

As producer, Goldberg runs the show from that desk. "Our goal is to really make their living room rumble," Goldberg says of fans watching at home. Making calls on which views go on the air, Goldberg and the director communicate with camera people and reporters over headsets much like the teams use. Listen to the ESPN live feed on a scanner and you'll hear about 30 commands every minute, as attention moves from the leader to a tight race among the fifth- and sixth-place cars, to a pit reporter explaining what happened during a pit stop or wreck, to an in-car camera showing another battle for position, to graphics and statistics and back to the race: "Watch your leader, watch your leader, ready for the leader—lead! Lead! Lead! . . . Ready I-4; take I-4. Ready 9; take 9. Watch the iris on 9. Ready 3, take 3; second car—car 21—on 1—5 and 21, they're racing—ready 1, take 1 . . . ready 3, take 3. You're next, Pat . . . ready to dissolve 24 . . . dissolve 24! Yeehaw! Fifteen or 10 please . . . 15 or 10. He's crossing the line right . . . now!" It goes on all race long.

Actually, it starts long before the race and goes long after; like the crews, the TV people show up days before the race and leave long after. ESPN broadcasts the race and pays around $1 million to do so but subcontractors handle the in-car cameras and radio-frequency cameras; subcontractors bring in the generators that power the equipment; and subcontractors run the uplink truck that shoots the signal up to the satellite for relay to the network's headquarters and then broadcast.

It's a massive undertaking, just like what the teams, and the fans, do.

At Charlotte, Jennifer Wells of World Sports Enterprises manages the whole TV setup for TNN, with a gang of subcontractors just like ESPN does, in her threadbare trailer outside the track, its walls covered by schedules, lists of names and jobs, and a big sign warning, "Anyone on the crew caught asking for an autograph or asking to have pictures taken will be *fired on the spot!*" She lifts a weary eye. "I've only gone to the bathroom once today, that's how busy I am," she laughs. Though she's production coordinator, she's a freelancer for WSE, like almost everyone in the TV broadcast business. She talks about what her life has been like this week.

"We had to come in Monday, because we had pole night on Wednesday, then Happy Hour and the races Saturday and Sunday. We had to come in Monday and start setting up, laying cable. Some tracks are precabled, but not this one too much." Monday they had their trailers set up, got the phones set up, "and sent runners out to get groceries for the week."

Since then they've been setting up cameras, running cables, producing graphics in a mobile graphics trailer TNN provides, getting head shots of drivers and crew members, shooting interviews, and taking those scenic shots of the surrounding area you always see: downtown Charlotte, say, or the Piedmont hills. Even during untelevised practice sessions someone has to run at least one camera in case there's trouble. "That's called crash watch," she says. "I don't like it to be called death watch." She will have someone in the NASCAR control tower during the race so they can make decisions. NASCAR can tell them how many laps it expects a caution to last. "We know how fast a caution lap is, so we know if we can get a commercial in."

She drifts through a huge white notebook of Charlotte facts, much like the ones the writers get at the media center, or the notebooks Eddie D'Hondt and Newt Moore keep on car information for each track, only this one's full of her own information. They run about 11,000 feet of triaxial cable at Charlotte, another 8,500 of coaxial. They asked for 167 media credentials, 83 garage passes, 128 parking passes. They set up 11 different stationary cameras. The ones in Turn 2 mounted right on the wall to show the cars' speed are called "speedy—come/go." They'll have access to virtually every one of the cameras the crews hang above their pits, plus three in-car cameras each in six different cars, plus a couple of extra in-car cameras mounted here and there for their own purposes. Plus the mobile radiofrequency cameras, plus the camera in the helicopter. If you figure 80 camera options, you'll be just about right. And each camera person has a spotter working alongside. Camera people only look directly through their cameras about 20 percent of the time, they estimate.

Crew and camera people have been flying in bit by bit all week, working 12-hour days and eating out of coolers under a tent in the TV compound. "It can be very brutal," Jennifer says. "And a lot of people from the outside think it's a very glamorous job.

"But we're family," she says. "We've been working together 15 years, even the freelancers." She's worked other sports, but she thinks racing has a tighter sense of community. "Especially the fans. They are so loyal. And you don't hear a lot of scandal about the sport. Everyone protects each other and looks out for each other." They're as protective and close-knit as a circus, many often say.

And back at the number 81 car, Trent agrees. The people working the races have the same experience as the teams, the drivers, the fans: "We're a bunch of high-tech carnies," he says. "That's what we call ourselves."

❖

But TV is TV. Every sport has a massive TV undertaking and a massive audience. What's remarkable about race broadcasting is that racing turns out to be a fabulous, almost perfect radio sport.

At first this seems counterintuitive. The people who laugh at fans watching cars go around in circles at the race track, who guffaw at fans watching cars go in circles on television, completely dissolve at the idea of fans listening to cars go in circles on the radio. And yet if you listen, you learn quickly that a race broadcast is one of the most entrancing radio experiences imaginable. A race broadcast equals a baseball game broadcast for radio satisfaction.

At the Motor Racing Network truck, parked outside the track at Martinsville last week, announcer Mike Bagley sat in the soundproofed engineering booth, checking facts on a laptop. Bagley is one of the turn announcers for Cup races, and he's one of the lead commentators for Craftsman Truck Series races, and he agreed that racing is made for radio. "Racing is a great radio sport in that we can paint a picture," he says. "It's almost like baseball. You think of Vin Scully, the way he describes things, you get goose bumps. It's actually better than TV."

The MRN announcers—and the announcers for Performance Racing Network, which broadcasts many races—do the same thing the great baseball announcers do, Bagley says: "We describe how full the grandstand is, what the weather is like, we describe the colors of the cars." Racing is like baseball in another way, too. It's a sport where for long periods of time the same thing is happening over and over. Whether it's pitcher-catcher or laps upon laps, it's the same thing, and the announcers fill with description, with history, with lore. Then suddenly a whole lot of things happen all at once—a gapper, a hit and run, a double play; green-flag pit stops, a pass for the lead, or a wreck in Turn 3—and the announcers' voices rise in speed and tone as they describe the complex chain of events. Then, likely as not, there's another 10 or 15 minutes of quiet to discuss the ramifications of what's happened, whether it's how an early inning pitching change affects the opportunities for a double-switch late in the game or how a two-tire pit stop under caution will affect the leader's handling, and whether he can finish the race on two rather than three tanks of gas now.

But what makes racing the greatest show on radio is the seamless interplay of the announcers, handing the call of the race from turn to turn seemingly without effort. The secret of that is that every announcer can come on the air as soon as he has something to say. That is, Bagley says, "All the mics are hot." With the click of a hand-held button, you're on the air. Thus, if the guys in the booth are filling a long green-flag run by nattering about a sponsor or what Richard Petty did in 1976 and then there's a wreck, no director or chief engineer has to cue the booth talent to listen to Bagley. "Trouble in Turn 2! Trouble in Turn 2!" Bagley shouts, demonstrating that he clicks with his thumb and he's on the air. Pit reporters signal the guys in the booth that they have something to add by quickly clicking their mics on and off; the engineer will hear it and clue in the announcers, though it won't be loud enough for the audience to hear at home. And lap after lap, the announcers just seamlessly pass the call from one to another.

That, Bagley says, is pure voice inflection, and he demonstrates: "Hornaday in the lead comes across the line, but here comes Sprague on the inside, and the battle for the lead's in Turn 1, . . ." and as he says "Turn 1" his voice takes a dive that completely demonstrates he's done talking. The Turn 1 announcer will pick it up from there. Listening to it is like watching the Harlem Globetrotters warm up. They don't miss.

His comparison of racing to baseball extends further, too. Racing has developed a wonderful vocabulary, a language as beloved to its fans as baseball's is to its own. Cars going too fast into the turns wash up the track; if they get all the way up near the top, where pieces of tire and crumbled asphalt pushed by the cars make for treacherous going, they're up into the marbles. A driver who spins out and manages to avoid the wall and other cars looped it. A mix-up, or wreck—or, more likely, just "trouble"—doesn't make other cars wreck, it *collects* them.

A car that's keeping all four tires on the track and running well is hooked up; a car that's smoothly running the bottom line through the turns without wavering is on a rail. A great car is a rocket ship; and the best a car can be is dialed in, when everything's working together. A little shake or shimmy in the turn is a bobble; if the driver almost loses control he's out of shape; if he regains control he's gathered it back in. A faster car closing in on a car ahead of him reels him in; a car that blows by another car passes him like he was tied to a stump. Cars running close? You could throw a blanket over 'em. Cars running nose-to-tail? That's a train. Someone passes by getting behind a car to upset the airflow over the front car's spoiler, making him unstable on his rear wheels? You took the air off him. If you do that and pass someone and three other cars come with you, you opened the door. Cars trying to keep up with changing track conditions are chasing the track; if you're trying to catch somebody but you just can't do it, you don't have anything for him.

And above all is the deal. No matter what happens in a race, an old-fashioned door-bangin' wreck, a slip in the oil dumped when somebody's engine blew, or a dropped lug nut, it was "just one of them racin' deals." Everything in racing is a deal. Stand around a pit crew for a few minutes, and before long someone will say to someone else, "That guy over there? What's his deal?" By which they mean a little more than just "What's he up to?" They mean what's his *deal*. Drivers have dozens of contracts, deals—with sponsors, with race teams, with products, with NASCAR. Crew members strike deals with their teams, and with each other, for information and help. In a sport where open, unrepentant capitalism is the name of the game, where getting the money is essential to running the show, the deal is the basic model of interaction.

Everything is a deal.

Bagley's got the best deal there is. "This is a dream come true," Bagley says of his job. He started running errands for MRN at Dover Downs when he was 15, but recalls that growing up in Milford, Delaware, "I used to lay at home on my shag rug in my den, moving Matchbox cars to MRN." This is the only job he's ever wanted, and the only one he ever hopes to have.

❖

Back in the Charlotte garage area, the Busch race is winding down, and the activity is cranking up. Every team has their race car ready, stretching in a long U around the garage, covered and hooked up to generators. This is Happy Hour, the last practice. This is genuine race practice, and it's last changes and last chances for these guys.

The garage crowd level is probably at its worst during the moments before Happy Hour. Not only is every member of every team running an errand of some sort, not only is every official and staff member hurrying somewhere—Nikki Taylor delivering Gatorade to haulers from a little cart; her husband Bill, with a clipboard, checking car decals for contingency money (money paid by those companies to finishers carrying their logo); hauler drivers running to get ice; Miss Winstons (there are two) in red-and-white uniform tops carrying bags of cigarettes to different crew members—but every single fan and hanger-on in the eastern United States appears to show up around Happy Hour. The crowds no longer fill only the areas around the haulers of the top racers. Every hauler is under siege, and every crew member has to keep a hand free to guide strange bodies out of the way.

But the most remarkable change before Happy Hour is in the drivers.

Kenny Wallace comes out of the Square D hauler in his fire suit and protective shoes. His gloves and helmet await him in his car. Standing on the hauler steps, he bears scant resemblance to the laughing guy who sat on the counter on Thursday, or the guy who even this morning couldn't tell the story of his miracle lap often enough. Now, his Oakleys wrapped around his head and his hands on his hips, he's Kenny Wallace, Race Car Driver.

It's the same with every driver. Guys who have been climbing into and out of cars all weekend long, guys who have been having heated discussions with their crew chiefs and team owners, guys who have put a foot on someone else's bumper and shot the shit about how to keep the right front from unloading, are suddenly stern and scowling, bold and fierce. Guys in bright gold or deep blue, guys in forest green or the rainbows of the multicolored teams stride through the garage with cock-of-the-walk intention. The fans, even as the drivers are at their most visible, seem to recognize this, giving them space, shrinking back a little from the guys they usually clamor toward. The drivers look busy; they look unapproachable. They look like they have someplace to be. And that they do.

They're going racing.

As he waits for the moment to get in his car, Kenny is thinking about racing. He's talking with other drivers about the Busch race, in which Jimmy Spencer outlasted Mark Martin. They're both Cup drivers who still drive Busch cars on Saturdays, and it was a good race. "He met his match," Kenny says of Martin's loss. "When you challenge Jimmy Spencer, you'd better be prepared to wreck him." Spencer used the simplest racing tactic to hold off Martin: He "made the car wide," in racers' parlance. "He just made it difficult to pass," Kenny said. "That's what racing's all about. There's nothing wrong with mirror-driving a guy when it's for the win." He wouldn't work that hard to keep a faster car behind him in the middle of a race. It's dangerous and foolish: He'd just be wasting tires and fuel against a car that would eventually pass him. But at the end of a race, it's a different story. "Let's log laps, let's play for 290 miles," he says of the 300-mile Busch race. "Then those last 10 laps, do whatever it takes."

Then he's climbing into the car. The Busch teams have scrambled their pit areas, and the track is clear. Last chance, and it's time to go. Headsets on, and the Newt has a final word.

"OK you guys, you did a great job this week; we got a lot done. Let's get out there and do what we need to. We got a lot of changes to try; let's make 'em fast. The more laps on the track will benefit us the most tomorrow."

There's a moment of silence, then Frank Good: "God, that sounded good," he says. "Did anybody record that?"

Kenny asks if the car has on tires set at race-start pressures. Eddie says he put on the best set he had: "They're black and they got 'Goodyear' on 'em." On the hauler, Newt allows a small smile. Spirits are high, and with an hour left of practice, maybe they'll find the spot for this car. Anything is possible.

The cars roar to life and Kenny speaks the words that bring the slump back to Newt's shoulders in a second. "Tighten me up!" Kenny says after his first laps. "I'm loose!"

"Come on in then," Newt says. "Boys, let's put a full rubber in the right front, or no—two half-rubbers in the right front. And check your oil and water temps, buddy."

And the chase is on.

"Just keep checking how you feel, K. W.," Newt says as Kenny goes back out. "Then we'll see if we can't find somebody for you to play with." A little later, Newt's done just that. "Slow up a little bit," he says. "The 7 car is right behind you, let's just run with him a little bit, if we possibly can."

We can. Kenny slows to see how he runs with the car directly behind him, taking the air off him. He lets the car by, then tries running behind to see how his right front holds the air coming off another car.

Practice goes on. Cars play cat-and-mouse, running two- and three-wide on the front and backstretches, chasing each other down in the turns. Most of the fans have stayed in the grandstand after the Busch race to watch Happy Hour, and they're right to do so. The intensity during practice now is higher than it has been all week. When Kenny comes in for a change, sometimes the crew saves a minute by having him stop on pit road instead of coming all the way into the garage. The change has the feeling of a pit stop, so important are the remaining minutes of practice. Other cars do the same, maximizing those precious seconds on the track. One trip through the garage Kenny sees a crowd running toward the number 28 car, which has had an electrical fire. "God, what happened to the 28?" Kenny asks. "Just concentrate on what you're doing, K. W.," Newt says.

More stops, more changes, and the setup they're chasing never quite comes into focus. "The 400 and a half rubber in the right rear, I could go in and finally rotate the front end, roll through the middle of the corner," Kenny says, but then the next lap he's sliding again.

Other cars work on their race tactics. The 6 and the 3 chase each other around, the 18 and the 88 run nose to tail, the 24 runs up behind everybody and picks them off seemingly at ease. The 81 comes in and out, chasing a setup that just won't come. Finally the caution lights come on and, for better or worse, they've done what they can do. Cars slip into the garage like it's the end of a race; TV crews run from driver to driver to ask about the final practice; a disconsolate number 28 crew pushes their burned car into the garage. For them it's going to be a long evening.

Kenny, flushed and sweaty, stands drinking a soda as Eddie, Vic, and Newt debrief him. "I can really see what's going on," Eddie says. "You come in good, but when you just start to turn, whoooop! You go up. I can really see it."

"Yeah, it's big," Kenny says of his trouble in the turns.

They discuss things over and over, but the problem is pretty simple, when all is said and done: The car won't handle. "It's not driving on the left front is what you're saying?" Eddie asks.

Kenny's been saying that for two weeks, and he says so in the simplest terms he can find: "I want it," he says, "to go like this: Neeeeeoooooowwwwwr!" He drops his left shoulder and raises his right one, as though he's preparing to drive toward the hoop in basketball. "But it's going like this: Neeeeeeeeee-neeeeer!" He raises his left shoulder and leans back, like he's stepping into the passenger side of a very small car.

But neeeeeeeeee-neeeeer is going to have to do: Practice is done. The next time that car gets rolling, there's going to be 42 other cars with it and 500 miles to go. The Filmar crew gets going on the final changes to the car, changing oil and fluids, getting it ready for tomorrow morning's final race-day setup and checks. Frank's wife, Melody, is around, and so is Rhonda, Newt's wife. Not that they're getting much attention, but it's nice to be around. Kenny calls the team into a brief meeting in the back of the hauler, thanking them for their faith and hard work all weekend and focusing under the pressure of the personnel changes, the tough season, Charlotte.

Then Newt, finally, takes a minute to sit down on the hauler steps and think out loud. "If we'd have missed this race . . . ," he says, then trails off. "We had to make this race," he says. "We had to. There was no not making it. I'm just learning how to do this better every day. I've got a noose around my neck, because if I fail, I'm done." Filbert has never said this, and nobody at Square D has said so. But Newt feels certain: Every race is make or break for him. "I missed a race when we went to California because the communication wasn't good, and we couldn't miss another one." He doesn't say the team missed the California race; he doesn't say Kenny missed the race, or the car missed the race. He says he missed the race.

But the fact is, this week they made the race, on a lap that was—miraculous? Inspired? Lucky?

"That wasn't a lucky lap," he's sure. "He probably put the car in better that time." Any special actions he's taking for the race tomorrow?

"I pray a whole lot," he says. Then he nods his head. "Nothing easy's ever worth a shit to have," he says. "We're gonna be a good team next year."

Tomorrow is still up in the air.

❖

Showing up in the garage for the last few minutes of practice is Humpy Wheeler, speedway president, making an appearance, hustling from the media center to the NASCAR hauler to one team or another, hurriedly conferring with Ron Green or Jerry Gappens. In a rush like he is now, this is the wrong time to talk to Humpy.

No, the time to get to Humpy was a week and a half ago, on a Tuesday night, when the teams were testing at the speedway. A track usually has a testing date about 10 days before it has a race. Teams are allowed to run up to seven tests per year, so they choose judiciously. Since Charlotte is home for virtually all teams, they almost all choose Charlotte.

Testing is a wonderful thing to see, especially under the lights at Charlotte. With only a few fans who wandered in—for free!—to the open grandstand, no television, no radio, virtually no coverage at all, the teams come to testing in marvelous disarray. If practice has a little of the feeling of dress rehearsal or batting practice to it, testing, with the cars half-painted and trying out different parts, feels like spring training, or like an early rehearsal for an opera, as though an actor might have on a helmet and braids but the bottom half of a ballet costume, or boxer shorts. This was the testing session where Kenny ran so bad that the team kind of melted down; where other drivers told Kenny his car was jerking and twitching so much it looked like a turkey; where Kenny even asked another driver to wheel his car around the track and verify that Kenny wasn't crazy, that the car was actually almost undriveable.

It was.

Watching the Bondo-yellow cars, the half-painted cars, the primer-gray cars drive around the track late in the evening, a solitary figure went from hauler to hauler, visiting with different teams and owners. Atop one, outlined against the lights, the figure pulled something long and narrow out of a billfold, signed it, and handed it to another silhouette atop a hauler. When he climbed down the ladder to the ground, Humpy—that's who it was—pulled another one out and handed it over.

It's a fake million-dollar bill. His own slyly grinning face is on it, and it's a pretty clever forgery, even feeling a little like a bill. On the back is the speedway's schedule for the year and the motto "In God we trust; all others must pay cash."

Humpy, in a sport coat and tie, comes in the hauler, slides the door closed, and jumps into talking. "That's as close as you can get without the Secret Service bothering with you," he says of his fake bills.

The testing going on is the only truly computerized part of Cup racing. Cars go out with all kinds of electrodes that measure shock travel, engine temperature, and dozens of other things, storing the information and hooking up to little computers that consultants—or, for the big teams, their own engineers—use to make charts and graphs and tables of data. If you want to know how high your right front is on the backstretch at what speed and have it printed out in a chart, testing is when you can find that out. But Humpy doesn't see the tech angle of things. From his perch atop the haulers, Humpy says, "I feel like I'm back at Saturday-night racing, at a short track that happens to have long straightaways.

"It's a bunch of guys that like to go fast, and a bunch of fans that like to watch 'em." And at Charlotte, with qualifying on Wednesday, there's a lot more days of going fast and a lot more to watch, huh.

"Hey," Humpy says about racers. "They like being at the race track. I mean, it's show time! I've always thought that to have a great sports event you have to have great preparation. Look at a heavyweight boxing match or the Superbowl. That's why we have more practice here." He echoes Kenny's sentiments about racing being the only sport where you don't get to practice as much as you'd like.

"I figured out a couple years ago, the average Winston Cup driver spends about 250 hours a year in a race car. A lot of boxers spar that much, and spend twice that on roadwork." Humpy was a Golden Gloves boxer, and he thinks about boxing a lot. "So I like to have plenty of practice for the guys."

Humpy's been in racing his whole life. He started out as a driver, "but I was terrible," he admits. "I was a chronic crasher. I was much better at promoting." And promoting is what he's done, better than anyone on the circuit. He's developed little Legends and Bandolero cars, which cost about $12,000 and run all summer on a tiny little oval in the front apron of the speedway and allow anybody who wants to to participate in racing—low-level, just-for-fun racing, to be sure, but racing nonetheless. He's got driving schools to use his track day and night, keeping his track busy—and making money—virtually every day of the year. He introduced Lugnut.

But more than anything else, he's created race-day festivities. Martinsville's rained-out parade of drivers was pretty much par for the course at most tracks: Driver intros, maybe a parade lap with the drivers waving from convertibles, then let's go racing.

Not at Charlotte. At the Memorial Day race Humpy always stages some kind of patriotic display, whether a show invasion with real Army helicopters and explosives, a parachute drop, a jet fly-by, or some combination of all three. Before the October race, Humpy just has a little more fun. "I think the craziest was probably the circus," he smiles. "In 1984 we had a circus; the elephants left stuff all over the front straightaway." A *Charlotte Observer* columnist wondered the next day whether dancing bears wouldn't be next, and Humpy's still thinking it over. As for this fall's race?

Well, since there's no daily press around to give away the surprise, Humpy will say, "We're going to have an alien invasion here, with flying saucers and spaceships. It's gonna be fun." He thinks a minute. "Anyway, if it makes just five people laugh, we've done our job."

Humpy entertains people at racetracks as well as anyone, though almost anyone who's tried to do it recently has succeeded. Why is racing taking off the way it is?

"It has a lot to do with the culture of the period," Humpy says. "There's a return to the heartland, country music, home remedies. I think people have become so urbanized they want to return to the earth. That's why pickups sell so well. People don't need 'em, they just think they do."

There are other factors, of course. "The drivers are nice people, they talk to 'em. And they do what everybody else does: . . . drive." You have to be an athlete to drain a three-pointer or hit the curve. But *everybody* drives. That may be why people in the Northeast are a little slower to get excited about racing than the rest of the country. With all those trains and subways, Humpy figures, "They don't get in their cars and go to work up there no more."

Television coverage is better. Speedways are better and cleaner, no longer the dirt tracks with filthy rest rooms some still imagine: "We're doing right by the fans, now." He knows there's a lot of grumbling on the circuit that it's not as much fun as it used to be, but he shrugs. "You can't have something as terribly successful as this is without losing some of the fun for the people in it." Wall Street's discovery of racing will have far-reaching effects, he says, and he wants to keep that from wrecking the sport. Like everyone he laments the passing of some of the older tracks in smaller markets. (North Wilkesboro, North Carolina, was bought so that its two Winston Cup dates could be shifted to tracks in New Hampshire and Texas, for example.) Yet he accepts that as part of growth. He just hopes the sport doesn't lose the flash, the gruff charm that seems to be drawing fans to it now. He doesn't want to see technology wreck the sport, and he's glad—the computerization of testing notwithstanding—that unlike open-wheel circuits like Indy cars and Formula One, NASCAR works hard to keep new and terribly expensive components out of racing, keeping it simple.

"People come out to the tracks to see a bunch of guys rub nonexistent door handles and run close together. They're not going out to see a bunch of computer-driven high-tech graphite component racing machines that can't run within 20 feet of one another and never pass. They want to see *cars*. The NASCAR stock car is the only race car that's ever been designed with entertainment in mind: the spectator, the TV audience.

"It's a primitive beast, but it's also on top. The public is voting every week. They've basically said, 'This is what we want.'"

❖

Have they ever.

Outside, among the souvenir trailers, the fans walk around in an attitude portraying, simply, "Gimme." Jaws are not slack, exactly, but everywhere you see a slight bow of the head, an expectancy. Eyes are lifted reverentially. "This is what the Lord has given us," fans seem to be thinking. "And it is good."

On the infield, though, it's different—not so passive, not so respectful. Fans have a swagger, a little pride in their stride. They've come here to be part of the show—to go racing—and by God they're part of the show. All weekend long, tossing horseshoes and footballs, drinking beer on platforms, they've been going racing. Now, late Saturday, as the afternoon stretches into evening and the long, slanting rays of the autumn sun burnish the infield in the same orange that glowed on the garage concrete in the morning, it's party time.

What you do on the infield is you walk. As Eric Clapton and Lynyrd Skynyrd pumps out, as the horseshoes clank and the beer spills, you walk in circles, like a race car, making loops around the entire infield, seeing what you can see. The first thing you find this evening, in Turn 4 among the motor homes, is John Caruso, sitting in a lawn chair in the middle of the gravel road wearing shorts and little else, and he's fishing.

"Fishing for suckers," he says. He's got a dollar bill on the end of a long nylon fishing line, and if anybody bends to pick the bill up off the brown dirt road, he yanks. "I get a bite or a nibble every minute or two; I get a strike about every five minutes," he says. He's been doing this all day. "I didn't even watch most of the race. I just sat down here drinking and fishing. I'll watch tomorrow's race, though." This is the point of the infield, for John. "It's entertainment for everybody. This kinda shit makes you laugh."

A walk though Turns 3 and 4 offers a tour of the best school buses the infield has to offer. Buses painted like the number 33 Skoal Bandit car, like the number 3 Goodwrench car, like the number 6 Valvoline car. One bus, painted bright red, has several drivers' nicknames on it: "Awesome Bill" Elliott, "Ironhead" Earnhardt. Inside it has a stove, a refrigerator, four neat bunks, and a pantry.

"No air conditioning," says a roundish fellow named Boyce, its owner. "You make too many friends."

Viewing platforms atop the buses are getting busy now, with the sun sinking and the beer coming out in earnest. Cries of "Show us your tits!" serenade any young woman walking by, and they're successful at least 10 percent of the time. ("Oh, thanks, honey!" a dancing man shouts from beside one bus after a woman riding by in a golf cart obliges him. "I ain't seen one all day!") Over the fender of one bus a guy leans, puking in what passes for a discreet manner.

It's 7:30 P.M.

As the sun drops over the edge of the speedway above Turn 1, the front-stretch lights come on, illuminating the bleachers, where cleanup crews make their slow ways across the bleachers, filling bags with napkins, chicken bones, and flattened cans. As the evening sky dims toward pale green and purple in the west, the crescent moon, Venus, and Mars seem to increase in brightness again, chasing each other down toward Turn 1. About the time it's dark enough that the darkened disk of the moon is visible, the howling begins.

And make no mistake about it, this isn't garden-variety howling. These are genuine rebel yells, and one breeds another like backyard dogs calling one another through suburban streets. The yells emanate from viewing platforms and tents, from tarp enclosures and from guys in T-shirts and flip-flops carrying beers along the gravel, asphalt, or dirt roads that mark the infield. They start as the infield darkens. They ebb and flow after that, never quite stopping, ending sometime after the race ends on Sunday.

Among the motor homes and buses in Turns 1 and 2, a more subdued atmosphere prevails. Here a family sits in lawn furniture under a neat awning, playing Scrabble or spades by the light of a Coleman lantern, behind a picket fence; there a late dinner fills the air with sweet-smelling barbecue smoke as two families, on a rug in a court between their motor homes, watch baseball on television while one member cooks. Candles and citronella lamps flicker on picnic tables; tiki torches cast lurid shadows. Red or white twinkle lights run along awnings and tarps. Sometimes straightforward party lanterns of red, green, and yellow sway in the cooling evening breezes along with the umbrellas and flags. A few fragments of what used to be called Hell Alley remain here, as a banner saying "What race? We're here for the party!" indicates: One bus has a female mannequin strapped to the front with a bikini on; another has a life-size cardboard replica of Dale Earnhardt, on which is scrawled, "I'm gonna kick Gordon's skinny little ass."

In the "some things never change" department, in front of another is a little iron jockey, holding, of course, a confederate flag. And Big Red yells once from his platform farther up toward the center of the track, "You know why we love racing?

Because all the other sports—football, basketball—the *niggers* has took over!" There are no black faces around to take offense, certainly, and even the rightest-thinking whites aren't going to protest such comments in the infield of a NASCAR race.

Sigh.

But there's a whole lot more than that. There's loud music and beer drinking and horseshoes in the dark. Fireworks start going off by 8 or so, with enough Roman candles going off that the launching of a mere bottle rocket is a disappointment. The home stretch lights are still on, throwing the infield into a place of stark whites and deep shadows and lending the place something of the feeling of a Brueghel painting of madly reeling peasants. The continual rockets and flares bring to mind the bridge scene from the movie *Apocalypse Now*.

Walking farther down becomes an almost surreal exercise. The general level of lubrication rises, and the weird lighting enables people to kind of loom up out of shadows, suddenly there, then suddenly gone. As drinkers, NASCAR fans are built for distance rather than for speed—they're drinking on race stomachs, not qualifying stomachs—and so they mostly end up hugging drunk rather than fighting drunk, hollering drunk rather than screaming drunk. One little court in Turn 2 has a karaoke machine, and a man wearing a rubber hat shaped like a giant penis does what he can to sing along with Hank Jr. If you don't hear "Freebird" at least twice every 15 minutes you are just not listening.

Down near Turn 1, the Camel Road House is in full swing, with a cover band playing "Bad to the Bone" and "Born to Be Wild." People compete in the Tire Change Challenge for the chance to win a race-morning pit pass, and, as promised, you can get your picture taken with a Camel gal in a tight halter top. You can also buy Camel gear—lighters, hats, shirts—but it doesn't cost money. It's all available for "Camel Bucks," which come on—surprise—Camel cigarettes. Which are the only things being sold for cash money, though if you smoke a rival brand you can just give them the old pack and get plenty of Camels for free.

But the highlight of the infield is, just like Ralph in Turn 1 said, the wagon races.

Atop Redneck Hill, on the curving asphalt road running over the top, someone has spray-painted a clumsy "Start" line. Along it are several wagons, some painted like race cars, some with special tires, some with long, steerable handles, some just plain wagons. Inside each wagon is a person either drunk or silly enough to think a full-speed push down an asphalt track in an unstable wagon with no elbow pads or helmet sounds like a whole lot of fun. People line the track for about 100 feet as it descends the hill. There's no finish line, and nobody to see who wins. Then again, most times down nobody finishes, and the whole mess ends in a tangle of arms and legs and wagon wheels about halfway down.

"If I'm behind ya, I'm gonna race ya!" one guy screams, and a friend of his gets ready to push him as three other wagons take similar positions. A drunk guy wearing a bandanna and shorts and holding a Bud jumps in front and yells, "Three! Two! One! Go!" and they're off, flashbulbs popping and suddenly illuminating lines of fans wearing racing hats and T-shirts and holding beers. One wagon falls over almost immediately; two crash into one another after about 40 feet; and the fourth goes careening down the hill into the darkness and is lost. By the time that guy comes pulling his wagon back up, he has to dodge the next race, which has basically similar results. Someone sells hats—"Redneck Hill Wagon Races," with a rudely drawn silhouette of a guy in a wagon—for $10 out of a Bud Ice 12-pack box. "Don't tell anybody," he says. "I ain't got a license." A Piedmont Rescue Association golf cart, dispatched from the motor home headquarters of the fire and rescue teams keeping an eye on the infield, sits by awaiting the inevitable disaster.

They don't wait long. Just as several flashbulbs pop, one woman goes over in her wagon and hits the ground—crack!—with her head so hard people in compounds 50 feet away jerk their heads up at the sound. The golf carts putts over, and before five minutes have passed she's sitting up again, and soon walking off with her friends, the fire and rescue people shaking their heads.

"Sharon!" says a guy named Kenny to a girl next to him in a number 24 hat and shorts, standing on a cooler for a better view. "You see why we don't want you to race?"

Sharon isn't convinced. She's here for fun, she says, "because I just had a baby and I need to release my energy." She comes every year, and it appears that she may have had a beer or six at some point this evening. The wagons keep going, with no significant injuries.

She looks out from the crown of Redneck Hill at the infield, now completely full of tents and campers, buses and motor homes. Little fires flicker here and there; multicolored lanterns glow; music pours from everywhere. Flags and umbrellas flap in the breeze, outlined harshly against the homestretch lights.

"This," she says. "This is the greatest place in the world."

Then the crowd starts booing, because a pickup, making a slow circuit of the infield, is coming up the course. But the driver has the right idea. A nice long loop through the infield is the best way to take it all in. If you sit on the truck's tailgate, dangling your legs and drinking the beer somebody will surely put in your hand, you get a wonderful view of the whole infield. Tiki torches, blue tarps; here someone alone, dancing by himself to music he's conducting with a lit cigarette, waving a beer in the other hand; there two or three guys holding each other up, howling for the sake of it. Bleary-eyed guys sprawl on an upholstered couch on the lawn. Families still up, playing cards while kids fall asleep in front of the TV or slumber in tents. Golf carts, pickups, and cars slowly cruise the loop, and campsites right along main street line the street with lawn chairs, watching the parade. Coolers of every sort lean against every structure, and just reaching in for a beer if you need one is acceptable and even encouraged. Striped tents glow from inside with lanterns, and generator-powered floodlights illuminate Earnhardt flags, NASCAR flags, and rebel flags.

The infield. That's all it is is the infield, and maybe Sharon is right: If racing is what you dig, this is the best place in the world. Or maybe Frank Beatty, one of the volunteers from Concord Fire and Rescue who mans the Speedway Command Post overnight to help people when they have rollerblading accidents or get tire grit in their eye, puts it best. "If you sit up there in the stands, it's just a race," he says. "You come in, sit down, and go home.

"You come to the infield, it's an experience."

The infield experience motors on. The moon, Venus, and Mars have sunk behind the speedway, but even through the smoky haze that's coalesced above the speedway, stars twinkle.

Guys howl and yell at those stars until the sky begins to turn orange in Turn 1.

CHAPTER 8

THE SHOW

Sunday, October 5

PART 1: THE LAST MORNING

The first glimmer of pale light rings the horizon in the fields northeast of Charlotte. Horizontal wisps of high clouds form bands that first are merely dark, blotting out stars, but as the light slowly increases they turn white, thin, feathery. They won't last long. A good day for a race.

Mist fills the low places and hangs in puffs above ponds as you drive toward the track in the half-light. Then you turn onto Morehead Road toward where it meets Highway 29—the corner of Charlotte Motor Speedway. The troopers are out on every street corner along Morehead now, their dome lights on as they read their morning papers and sip coffee in Styrofoam cups, just being present as a low rush of cars speeds to the track. Route 29 is already busy; blue-and-white police lights flash up and down the road as far as you can see.

Crew members. Drivers. Owners. Vendors. Ticket-takers. Cleanup crews. Drivers of the wreckers that line the corners of the speedway. Doctors to work the infield care center. NASCAR officials. Promoters. Public relations people. Sponsors. Hospitality workers. Lots of people need to get to the speedway early.

Lots of them are there already.

❖

A couple of mechanics stand in front of the metal gate at 6:30, as the first orange glow starts to seep above Turn 3, though the stars still shine directly overhead. A few steps away, among the campers on the infield, the weary rebel yells that have kept up all night long are starting to turn into sarcastic—then less-sarcastic—rooster crows. A young woman in a fleece top and a wool hat against the chill of the autumn morning sits in a comfy, stuffed living-room chair, her sleepy eyes taking in the occasional stirrings around her calmly. Friends sleep around her, in tents, in sleeping bags, or just on the grass. Is she the first one up?

A groggy smile: "I'm the last to sleep." But soon it'll be time for bacon and eggs, and coffee, and then beer and sausages. "We'll be cooking all day," she says, taking a little sip of what is either the night's last or the morning's first beer. Generators putt quietly in the half-light; near the top of Redneck Hill a huge television screen stands next to a humming generator. It will improve the views of the fans on the infield and in Turns 1 and 2; other screens are placed around the infield. In the dawn, looming black against the dimming stars, it looks like the monolith from *2001: A Space Odyssey.*

Around it the infield is strewn with beer cans and cigarette butts, though in most places some attempt has been made to keep the trash in piles around the garbage cans. The speedway keeps garbage trucks rolling all day, and the mess never quite gets out of hand. Overall, you've had parties that left your yard looking worse. Lines begin to stretch away from the doors to the showers. You can smell bacon.

❖

By 6:55 the garage gate is thick with mechanics. Frank, Kevand, and Buddy stand, lightly hunched against the chill, among the multicolored crowd, when cries get their attention.

"We're getting married in the winner's circle!" comes a woman's voice. "Get married, and watch the race!"

And sure enough a woman in a bride's dress stands surrounded by fans in T-shirts and hats with car numbers. A guy shrugs and grins; he's the groom. TV reporters swarm the couple, and they're lost in a sea of microphones and lenses. It looks embarrassing, and Frank shakes his head. With a car that hasn't run smooth all weekend, he's thinking about humiliation this morning. "If he's out there getting embarrassed," Frank says, looking down, "just stuff it in the wall. It's destroyed! We can pack it up and get out of here."

But mostly the group just bounces on their heels, nervous. "It's *time*," says Two-Can, who's just walked up, and Frank murmurs, "Come on, let's *go*." Then Newt appears: "Peckerheads!" he says in greeting, and the gate swings open and the mechanics swarm the garage.

It's like the rest of the weekend has been at 33 rpm, and today is at 78. Two-Can fairly runs to garage 33 and opens the door. He and Buddy have the car-cover off, folded and replaced in its bag in a second. Within two minutes the garage is alive with the sound of air guns, jacks, generators, and rattling tools, an instant transition from silence to cacophony. They weigh the car, check its height against those marks Newt made when he set it up, and then get going. The three-page list of race-day checks on equipment and fluids is taped up to the rear quarter panel, and initials start going by items immediately. Guys from every team run their normal morning tire errands, their ice errands, and their parts errands. At one point a mechanic from the number 12 team stops in the middle of the garage concrete and points toward the winners circle, a little asphalt circle surrounded by holly bushes, where at the moment he can catch a glimpse of veils and crinoline. "Hey, look!" he shouts. "Them people over there are getting married!" There's a little cheer from that direction and then the party heads off.

Dave sweeps the trailer and fills his coolers, today protected against the hordes with signs: "DO NOT SIT ON" and "TEAM MEMBER DRINKS!" NASCAR officials check engine compression, pushing around their own little cart of equipment. They reach the number 81 car at the same time someone's climbing inside to check one of the in-car cameras and Rich Vargo hangs out the other window, checking the dials on the dashboard. Two-Can finds his way underneath the car by going between the in-car camera guy's legs. Newt comes to the toolbox and tapes a piece of paper: "Pit #29." In case anybody forgot.

At pit 29, the race-morning operation is underway. Don is assembling the little metal rack that holds the filled gas cans near the pit wall. Kevand tapes down the electrical cords that connect the war wagon to the speedway power outlet, then performs the same operation on the air-wrench hoses as they emerge from the tanks of air in the bottom of the wagon. He makes three perfect coils of the hoses: front, back, and spare. When he's finished he starts setting up the race scoring computer, as Don switches on his gas computer. The television is already hooked up. Country Music Television blares out. "I tried to get him to put on the *Flintstones*, but he kept switching it to that sports station," Don says. This appears to be a compromise. The pit for the number 8 car nearby blasts out rock music, as is its wont. Andy Thurman cleans the Square D banner that hangs over the pit wall. Big Steve Baker comes by with his loads of tires, four at a time, setting them out along the back of the pit area in the order that Eddie has determined. He spreads them out. Soon it will be time to start gluing on the lug nuts. "Not too early, so it has a chance to get brittle," Steve says. "Not too late, so the nuts don't fall off on the way to the car." The sound of drills burnishing the rims echoes along pit road. Kevand assembles the big sign and the brush for scrubbing the grille. Don shares a story that instead of hanging a sign, teams used to have a guy stand out at the end of the pit with a sign. "And that was before pit road speed limits!" he laughs. I'm glad I didn't know that at Martinsville.

Don puts a Square D decal on the metal shade that goes over the scoring monitor: "They're paying the freight," he says. "Make 'em feel good. A lot of bigwigs here today." Out on the grassy apron of the track, a little village has appeared, causing a grin from Don. "Humpy puts on big shows here. They're probably going to blow up the village or something."

At 8 A.M., the gates open, and the fans with race-day pit passes start swarming the pits; others with weekend licenses start choking the garage, and the first fans pop out of the portals into the homestretch grandstand, armed with coolers and headsets. In the morning light, the empty track looks smooth and beautiful.

❖

At the hauler, Steve Post stops by for a moment to talk to Eddie, who wants his help making the presentation to the Square D guys about the Las Vegas race. Eddie has a question for Danielle, so Steve relays it by leaning his head forward and speaking into his chest. Steve, like virtually every public relations person—and every official—in racing, wears an ear-piece speaker and a clip-on mic, enabling him to speak by radio to people on his team. So many ear pieces and little curly cords infest the garage that it sometimes looks like a Secret Service convention, and it's never surprising to see someone get a far-off look on their face, grab their lapel, and start talking into space.

Eddie's scrawled out a list of costs for the Las Vegas excursion. Between airfares, lodging, tires, motors, groceries, and miscellaneous items (ice is included in the budget), he estimates $120,000, and he knows they won't bite. He's asked for Steve's help in coming up with a better budget. Steve huddles with him and stalks to the media center, finds a keyboard connected to the track-supplied printer, and types. Final estimate: $36,000. "No prob," Steve laughs. "This is an easy job. We're trying to help the cause, not hinder it." Then he drops the printed sheet off with Eddie, picks up Danielle at the hauler, and heads to Kenny's motor home in the infield.

The infield itself is in the same kind of uproar the garage is in. People and vehicles travel in every direction on every sort of errand. A Humvee with a "prerace Parade Lap" sticker drives by, heading toward the backstretch, where parade vehicles gather to enter or leave the track. Tractors and golf carts pull little trolleys of fans from parking areas to their garage or pit road tours. Guys with T-shirts and 9 A.M. beers crowd around the garage gates, looking for drivers.

At the motor home, Kenny comes out the door. Even in a bright red golf shirt and those dangerous silver Oakley sunglasses, he looks ready to be done with this. "I will be one happy sumbitch at the end of this day," he says. Kim looks like she feels exactly the same way, only she's too polite to say it. Family friends sit around the side of the coach, which has a recessed television, and watch *Waterworld*. Kenny and Kim slept at home, but they didn't get much more rest. Every spare bedroom is filled with friends and relatives. Kim appears to jump at the chance to walk up to the suite to watch Kenny chat with the guests, and it's hard not to wonder whether she just wants to get away for a few minutes. A quick trip in Steve's van takes the gang to the stairway up to the suites, and Steve has the expected discussion with the guards about who they are and where they're going. But in moments, Kenny's leading an entourage of five down the concrete passageway along the back of the suites, with sun filtering through the chain-link fencing. He walks into the suite, the last one in Turn 2, with a great view of the turns and a long sightline out the side along the backstretch. There are about 15 rows of movie theater–style seats, and a long bar along the back for, at the moment, coffee and Danish. There'll be plenty more food later. Everybody has a Square D plastic bag filled with stuff: a program, a Square D Racing hat, a die-cast number 81 car ("One of 16,488"), a copy of *Inside NASCAR* magazine, earplugs, a catalog of Square D Racing clothing and gear (a mug with the number 81 car on it is $7.50; a gas-powered mini-race car with a 3 1/2-horsepower engine is $1,500), a Square D Racing drink can cozy, and a number 81 car key chain. A tall, sharp-featured man in a Square D golf shirt introduces him, and Kenny walks to the front of the suite to applause.

"First of all, I gotta look out the window," he says, looking up and down the backstretch, out over the infield, filled with campers and tents and flags—and he stops. "My God!" he says. "Look at all those banners!" It's true. A casual sweep of your eyes over the infield picks up 80 or 100 blue-and-yellow Square D Racing banners. Danielle got the idea to distribute a thousand banners the last time she was up in a suite and saw all the other banners fans had appropriated from other teams. Miller, Budweiser, Valvoline, they all put up banners throughout the region of a race, in parking lots like the one used by the ticket hustlers on Thursday night, and the fans swipe them and use them as sidewalls, as roofs, as awnings for their camping compounds. It's the way things work, and now, when guests look out the window of the Square D suite, they can see dozens of those banners. "It was $10 each, so $10,000," Danielle says. Looks like a good deal.

Kenny tells the crowd about the race, explaining that this race—behind Daytona in February, Indianapolis, and the Charlotte race in May—is probably the fourth-biggest race weekend of the year: "As you can tell, this is our premiere racetrack." Then he goes immediately into a description of the week's highs and lows. "It was pretty close this week," he admits, but describes his miracle lap: "It was real cool, the tires were real sticky, and I—Hey, I just realized!" He stops, grinning, and points over to the suites above Turn 1, across the track. "This could be like 'Left field sucks!' 'Right field sucks!' at a baseball game! You guys could get walkie talkies and yell back and forth." Then just as suddenly he's back on track.

"So that kind of gives you an idea of how tense Wednesday night was," he says. "I got up Thursday and told my wife, 'I'll be back, I'm gonna go make the race.' Then I came out here and pretty much stunned the world."

The crowd is delighted by his candidness and his gently poking fun at himself. "We've had an odd year," he says. "Two poles, no top-five finishes. And to be honest with you, we're still not real happy with this car. I ain't gonna win this race." Questions come up, and he answers patiently. He doesn't exactly covet the bigger shops and more expensive equipment of rivals—like his brother—but just the same, "it depresses me. That's why I don't go over there. But we've got a lot of faith on this team, a lot of heart. I've had a lot of offers from other teams, but I've got a good sponsor, a team that likes me, and that doesn't happen much in this sport."

He answers questions about tires, about gears: "One is only to get out of the garage area during the week, two is for pit road, and three is for getting up to speed. I'll stay in fourth the whole race." Behind him, visible through the window, cars and trucks mass on the backstretch for the prerace parade laps. Little Legends cars, tiny Bandolero cars, white trucks, dozens of identical Camaros (since the race is sponsored by GM). Kenny finishes his questions and spends another 10 minutes signing anything anybody brings to him, chatting with people, and filling the suite with his raucous laugh.

Winning races or not, you can see why his sponsor loves Kenny Wallace.

The tall man who introduced Kenny to the crowd turns out to be Jack Carlson, the Square D marketing vice president who's in charge of the racing program, and that's exactly what he says. "If it weren't for Kenny Wallace, I'm not sure we'd be in racing at all," he says. "I'm not sure we could be with another driver. You want everything you do to represent the way you believe and feel. Words like honesty, integrity, fun-loving, competitive, and driven come to mind. He's like a magnet, he wants to be with people." Watching Kenny, up here, around the garage, or at other morning hospitality events, that's always true. Kenny especially seems to have a kind of radar for kids. A kid in a wheelchair was being pushed around the garage at a race at Richmond a few weeks before, and Kenny squatted down to talk to the boy and eventually had to be almost dragged away to a team meeting.

Square D got into racing, Carlson says, a few years ago, almost by accident. Square D sells its electrical equipment through distributors—a Square D junction box might be in your house—and one distributor was working on Kenny's house. He introduced Kenny to the Square D people, and "it just snowballed from a business opportunity to sell some equipment into sponsorship," Carlson says. They dipped their toe in for a couple of races when Kenny was at the Busch level, and as Square D learned about racing, they started to realize what the sport could do for them. "We got bitten by the bug" is how Carlson puts it.

"This is the ultimate team sport," Carlson says. "What I don't think most people appreciate is how much work goes on behind the scenes." They liked the teamwork as a corporate identity; they liked the speed, too. Before they got into racing, they were using a cheetah in their advertising.

Carlson trots out the numbers everybody involved with the sport constantly cites: No other sport is growing as fast as racing as a spectator sport, about 40 percent of NASCAR fans are women (who tend to make family buying decisions), and above all "they take loyalty to a new plateau." Studies regularly show that NASCAR fans polled say they consciously choose products connected with racing and will even switch brands if a product enters or leaves racing. More, race fans seem to know why they're doing it. For them it's a pretty simple proposition: Square D, for example, pays to keep the number 81 car on the track. The fans love seeing those cars on the track, so if they buy Square D products, Square D will see the results and stay in racing and keep the car on the track. Unlike football or basketball, where sponsorship means nothing more than buying advertising time, racing sponsorship actually makes the sport go. Fans know it, and they vote with their wallets to keep it that way. "The number one question we get is, 'Now that you're racing, now that we know what you do, how can we support you?'" Carlson says. "They say, 'Square D, I'm gonna help pay for that car.'"

What's more, Square D is barely in the sport for the fans' support. Much more important to a company like Square D is awareness on the part of its distributors. The Tide car running around the track gets most of its juice by having fans see that Tide logo for four hours every Sunday. The Square D sponsorship pays its greatest return in hospitality events like this one: Distributors and important customers are taken to races, given tours, and treated like royalty, which keeps them loyal and interested. "This is like our golf," Carlson says. "I had a distributor call from Michigan. We've been trying for three years to get their business, and we couldn't get it. But he wanted two tickets to Rockingham. Monday morning we had an order."

Of course, they don't mind that number 81 car being on television all those hours, or they wouldn't buy the in-car cameras. A weekly publication, *The Sponsors Report*, keeps them apprised of what they're getting for their investment. The report watches races and keeps by-the-second totals of in-focus exposure for each sponsor in a race. It also counts sponsor mentions, driver interviews, and everything else you can count in a race. Then it figures out the value of that time based on the cost of a 30-second advertising spot. So at last Monday's Martinsville race, according to *The Sponsors Report*, Square D got $567,890 of advertising value by virtue of the number 81 car's Square D logo being on-screen and in-focus for 17 minutes and 22 seconds. That's more than a half-million dollars on a week when Square D got not a single sponsor mention from the announcers and Kenny Wallace wasn't interviewed once (though he was mentioned 68 times). They discovered this viscerally when they experimented by putting their web site address on the back of the car. "Before the race we were getting 200 hits a week," he says. "Afterwards, 1,100." So they decided to buy the back deck of the car to put the web site on permanently. "That's another $320,000," Carlson says. "What it bought us was an engine builder and some equipment.

"We estimate our TV coverage at $6 to $8 million," Carlson says. With their sponsorship costing "about $3.5 million," he says, you gotta like that return. Of course that's just basic money. They pay a lot for suites like this one, for hospitality tents like the one downstairs today and the one they have at every race, where Kenny speaks to 150 to 1,000 people per race. They pay for coordinated advertising (a fold-out ad in today's race program, for example) and extras nobody can predict, like the trip to Las Vegas Jack doesn't even know he's going to be asked about yet ("You remember the team said they wanted to talk to you?" Danielle gently says to him).

But all in all, Square D is a very happy sponsor. "I'd like to have another $1.5 million," Carlson says, smiling. "I think NASCAR's going to be better off for it the day Kenny Wallace wins a race. A lot of people take a victory lap. Kenny will *run* one."

By this point Kenny has in fact run off. He's gone down to perform the same routine in the hospitality tent, with Steve, who's responsible for getting him there. At some tracks this requires him to check routes days beforehand. If a hospitality is out in a parking lot somewhere, will a car get Kenny there faster or get slammed in by crowds of fans? Can a golf cart negotiate a little hillside to save time? Are there any gates or doors likely to be worked by weekend help who won't recognize Kenny and won't want to let the entourage through?

With Steve, Kenny's in capable hands.

❖

While Kenny's pressing the flesh, his team is finishing getting his car ready. At 10:30 they push it through the final tech inspection of the weekend, dodging a gaggle of people following a willowy man waving a "Ford Credit" sign and saying, "Come on people, stay together!" The Square D Filmar Racing team has no choice. All together, they're pushing their car to its starting position.

Newt, Eddie, Ricky, Jeremy, Two-Can, Buddy, and Kevand lean into the car, pushing it up the incline from the garage onto pit road; Frank follows along, pulling the generator. The parade laps have started, and as the team pushes the car along pit road toward Turn 4, where the cars will line up for the start, they're passed by convertibles carrying, among other luminaries, Lugnut, who waves to the crowd that's already filled close to half the grandstand. Old-style race cars from the 1950s and 1960s follow, as do trucks carrying logos; one for tobacco companies bears the motto, "Freedom of choice: Legal for adults, important to us all." A guy in a golf cart pulling a giant Coke bottle follows a big Coke truck. The Coke bottle shoots T-shirts over the fence into the crowd. All the emergency trucks parked in the corners—wreckers, ambulances, even fire trucks—have their lights flashing.

A NASCAR official stands at the head of the growing line of cars, and he checks the 81 car off his list as they push it by. He points to a spot behind the second pace car, and they slide the car into place. "All right, be back at noon, guys," Eddie says, and everyone breaks to go back to the hauler for lunch. Everyone except Frank. He still has some fussing to do. He checks the taping over the grilles. They're taped to within a couple of inches of the top, but the duct tape is in two long strips, with tabs on the end marked 1 and 2, so that Newt can call for them to be pulled off during the race and there won't be confusion. Frank also turns the little clips that hold the hood down around, so they'll be pulled out to the left rather than the right. "So when the hose comes over during a pit stop, it won't yank 'em off," Frank says. Not much gets by Frank Good.

The walk back to the garage goes through the peak moment of the pit road activity. Only two hours before the green flag, everybody who has anything to do with Winston Cup racing is somewhere in the garage or along pit road. Hank Ausdenmore, the pit crew workout coach, wanders by. "Just keeping the exposure up," he says. "I see the guys a lot, but I don't see the owners that often." Public relations people from every team, from companies that represent big sponsors and small, companies that represent NASCAR itself, walk from garage to garage, pit to pit, slapping backs, shaking hands, squinting behind sunglasses and dropping their heads to hear one another. Salespeople shake hands with crew members, with other salespeople. It's like the world's largest and sunniest convention, only unlike most conventions, in a couple of hours they're actually going to get down to business.

By the Square D pit Steve Baker is replacing lugnuts that the passing crowd has swiped. "I guess they needed one more than they thought we did," he smiles. "Luckily, I have a couple extras right here in my pocket." In every pit along the road, someone is buffing lug holes and stripping down lugnuts. The road itself is a complete color riot. Behind each pit, against the fence to the garage, are piles and piles of shiny black tires. At the front, by the pit wall, is a bright blue or red or green or black war wagon, surrounded by bright orange gas cans and tools painted in team colors. Team members hustle around each pit like a little beehive, setting up and clearing out. The area between the pits and the piles of tires is marked by white and yellow lines, like highway lines: If you're one of the several thousand tourists back there, stay between them and you'll only get peevish looks from team members trying to get around you to do their jobs. Cross the yellow one toward the fence and you're in the crew's warehouse—tires, tools, coolers, jacks—but you'll probably still be out of the way. Cross the white one, into the actual pit, and somebody will probably ask you to leave. Some teams put up pennant tape or plastic chains on standards to keep out the curious or the merely confused.

Sight down along the front of pit road and you see the signs. Arcing above each war wagon, right next to the parallel arc of the camera boom, is a little sign the exact duplicate of the sign the crew member will wave. Each sign has character. The Square D one is, of course, square, with the Square D logo on it, with holes through it to let the wind through. The number 94 team, sponsored by McDonald's, has a sign shaped like golden arches. The number 88 car, piloted by straight-shooter Dale Jarrett, has a simple 88, outlined in red. The number 75 car, sponsored by Remington, has a sign that looks like a target. It's got holes to let the wind through too, of course, but its holes look like the shot pattern from a really good shotgun.

And up and down pit road are men and women in golf shirts, sunglasses, neat haircuts, and jeans or khakis on the men and jet-black trousers on the women. It's almost like a uniform, like someone had called up everyone with a prerace pit pass and told them what to wear. Tour groups still file by, crowding even further. Steve Post brings a group of Square D execs by, explaining the pit strategy, why they make tape marks on the pavement, telling them what he can in the hubbub and the crowd. When he's done, he leads them toward the hauler.

❖

Usually a bastion of quiet, the team's place to disappear, to avoid the crowd, the hauler this morning is buzzing with people. Team wives and family members; team members who work at the shop and rarely come to races; Square D people who have never been seen before, all hang around the hauler. There are baby carriages.

Most of the team members have by now changed into their race-day uniforms, and they sit quietly, finding a spot in the shade, eating sandwiches. Steve Post keeps the conversation moving among the Square D folks. Kenny Wallace is back at his motor home, taking his own quiet time, resting before the race.

Back in the hauler, in the office, is Filbert Martocci, doing what he usually does: Being around without being underfoot. In the office, he can make phone calls, chat with Newt or Kenny or other team members, or just keep to himself. He watches his race team a lot, but rarely does he tell them what to do. He's the owner, and he makes financial decisions, but he works hard to let his team do its own work.

Not that he doesn't try to help. "This week it's been rather extensive," he says of his participation in the team's work. "I negotiated the lease for the Stavola Brothers' engine shop. I interviewed several people to replace several of our departing people. I spoke with the sponsor. They're not happy, they'd like to win, but they just need to talk." The sponsor still asks questions about replacing Gil, he says. "They say, 'Who are you going to hire to replace Gil Martin? Why don't we hire Steve Hmiel?' " Hmiel, longtime crew chief for Mark Martin, is considered one of the best chiefs on the circuit, and he's been pushed upstairs in the Jack Roush organization. Some think he could be lured to another team to be crew chief.

Filbert shrugs. He likes Newt as his chief, but he knows Newt is young and feeling the pressure. "They're gonna have to pony up the dough, if they want that. What I'm trying to do is get some mature assistance for Newt. He's 34. He has limited experience running a race team from the crew chief position. The best example would be Buddy Parrott, at the number 99 car. He's the general manager of that organization and the mentor for everybody."

That's how Filbert tries to help the team. Like any business manager, he tries to find the help his employees need. "We need somebody active," he says. "Who represents a wealth of experience and can be a great father figure, but he won't be hired as crew chief." Eddie D'Hondt appears to be filling some of that role—he has described himself as a sort of auxiliary brain for Newt—but Filbert still wants a little more leadership. "You have to build chemistry," he says. "Like the 24 car; that's a symphony. They come to the track with five people, including the crew chief. Those five people prepare the car, practice the car, qualify the car, and get it ready for race day. That's what you strive for."

He leans over the little table in the hauler office. "You can't do anything in life that doesn't have to be organized. I'm talking about multiple-people activities. It doesn't matter if it's a sport or a business. It has to be organized. It has to have discipline and regimentation. One set of rules to cover everything: from walking into the shop to appearing in victory lane." He figures success is about 80 percent self-discipline and 20 percent leadership.

Filbert says he got into racing in the mid-1970s. Successful in his financial and lighting businesses, he was approached for sponsorship at the Nashville Speedway and got involved. After several years, he ended up sponsoring a team run by Gil Martin and co-owned by racer Bobby Hamilton for $75,000 a year. They wanted to go up to the Busch series in the mid-1980s. "And I said I won't do that unless it's my team. I wasn't going to go from $75,000 a year to $300,000 a year without having total control." So he bought the team from Martin and Hamilton (Martin is actually still part owner of Filmar Racing). They've been through several drivers since then, and now they're on their second crew chief.

Filbert laughs about making money any time soon. "Growing teams like ours spend everything. You would have to get to some of the big teams before you had any money left over." Kenny ran a few Busch races with a car he owned himself this year, and Filbert knew Kenny had learned something when he spun his Busch car out at Richmond, looping it down the front stretch, fortunately not collecting anyone else. Asked about it later, Kenny said, "I just hoped I didn't hit the wall. That car was already sold to Michael Waltrip." Kenny said, during that race, that he was glad he was getting out of team ownership. "This is just a way to lose a lot of money," he said over the radio as he ran his self-financed Busch race. "Filbert, I have all the respect for you now." Filbert at that moment mouthed "Thank you, God," and lifted his hands to the heavens.

So why do it? Many people compare the guys who own Winston Cup teams to old Southern gentlemen raising race horses. It's more an expensive hobby than anything else, and for Filbert, though he works hard as a team owner, that's the case. He makes his money in his other businesses; if he gave up racing, he'd only be richer next year, not poorer. So what's in it?

Filbert plainly loves racing, loves the excitement and the community; he loves being part of an enterprise. But more than anything else, Filbert wants to win. "It's an exhilaration all its own," he says. "You work so hard for it, and it's so long in coming. We went to Busch, and we thought we were the best: Then we missed the first race," he says of his crew's first year in Busch with Hamilton. Then the team worked and worked, and later that year they ran at Richmond, and Filbert was intimately involved. "Three laps into that race the mirror fell off the windshield," he says. "I was Bobby's spotter. We had to run 200 laps with no mirror. I had to *be* his mirror." The car moved to the front late in the race, and to Filbert it's like it was yesterday. "You get so engrossed, you don't notice you might win the race. Or you notice, but you can't think about it. You gotta worry about the guy bumping his ass . . . 'Protect the bottom, he's behind you, keep going. . . .' "

Then came the white flag with a lap to go, and then the checker, and Hamilton had won. "Nobody can give you the words that can give you the feeling of what it's like to live it," he says. "And you're the *only one*. Everyone on your team are the only ones who know that this is the culmination of what you've been working on for years. That day, *you are the best*."

He thinks a minute. "You want to know what it feels like? I don't remember what the steps down from where the spotters stand look like. My eyes were too full of tears."

❖

Outside the hauler, the day is revving its engine. Kenny and Newt have gone into the drivers' and crew chiefs' meeting that precedes every race. A race official stands in front of about a hundred guys, most sitting in folding chairs, some standing around the back, in one of the Goodyear buildings in the back of the garage. He tells them what the pit road speed will be, that the race will be 334 laps, where the restart line is—when they can get into the gas on a restart—and urges them to be careful, cooperate, and race clean. He tells them to observe the pit road speed. He thanks them for their attention.

After that comes chapel, led by Motor Racing Outreach, a Christian group that ministers to the drivers and their families. This is a worship service, but it's tailored to its audience. It's NASCAR to the core. For example, the service usually includes some unusual pop culture reference. One week one of the leaders, a tall brunette women, acted the role of host of "Inside Nazareth," for which she interviewed the minister, playing the role of Nicodemus the Pharisee. "Next week, a guard brings us his own story," she concluded: "It's rumored that Jesus is missing from his tomb!" Another week, another leader urged the crowd to join her in a familiar song. "It's 'Amazing Grace,'" she said, "but we're going to sing it with a twist! I want you to sing it to a tune you all know." And then she broke into the familiar words, but sung to the tune of the famous Coke jingle, "I'd Like to Teach the World to Sing." (Think this in your head: "A- *ma*-zing *grace* how *sweet* the *sound* . . . That *saved* a *wretch* like *meeee*!") Some drivers stay for chapel; Kenny doesn't. He returns with Newt to the hauler to get into his fireproof suit and get ready to race.

The crew hangs around the hauler, eating sandwiches and, at this point, basically waiting. Don is the only animated member of the crew. He's got last week's missing air wrench back from a NASCAR official, considerably the worse for its trip around the Martinsville track in Kenny Schrader's wheel well. The sandpaper coating, making it easy to hold in mechanic's gloves, has been worn off and one corner is abraded completely through. "Don't look too bad," Frank says, looking over his shoulder. "They apologize for trying to keep it?"

Don smiles to himself. "NASCAR don't apologize for nothing. NASCAR don't have to apologize."

Duze reads *Speedway Scene* and squawks at a caption underneath a photo of the number 81 car. "Look at this!" he snorts. " 'A bad pit stop put Kenny Wallace at the back of the pack.' That ain't true!" Two-Can shrugs. "A flat tire, anyway."

❖

The line of cars in tech inspection has dwindled, and now it's empty. Everybody's through, everybody's ready to race, everybody's lined up in Turn 4, from Geoff Bodine on the pole to Terry Labonte in 43rd spot, almost all the way back in Turn 3. Pit road is choked; there's simply no moving. Fortunately the crews have finished most of their work by now and have headed to their haulers. Eddie D'Hondt is the last Square D guy at the pit. Sure, he says, the people underfoot are annoying.

"But we realize everything has its place in this sport," he says. "At one time we all been one of these people." The garage, though, has begun emptying as fans and guests head for their seats. The garage enclosure itself seems empty now, a couple of tool chests left waiting to be loaded up later, but otherwise nothing but a long room with 25 garage doors open on each side and neat piles of floor sweepings and torn or cut belts and cables near every door.

The grandstand is nearly full. The announced crowd is 143,021, which everyone connected with the track points out doesn't include people working the race and no matter who it includes would be the fourth-largest city in the Carolinas. These fans have been entertained by the Legends race and the parades of fire trucks and old race cars, but it's time for some real action, and the crowd along pit road thickens as a helicopter flies low overhead and out parasails . . . Lugnut.

The alien invasion begins—an ambulance with the words "Alien Eliminator" stenciled on the sides roars through the towers of the little village Humpy has set up. As it goes by, the towers explode, revealing old wrecked cars inside. The eliminator crashes halfway through, and a rescue crew saves the driver. This happens twice more; it's hard to tell whether the stunts were supposed to end in wrecks. "Was that supposed to happen?" one fan asks. Another nearby says, "This is Charlotte. If it happened, Humpy *wanted* it to happen." (A couple of months later this stunt ends up on the "Spanning the World" highlight reel on the *Today Show*, right after a clip of a bull charging around, a pair of underpants on his horns, after a bullfight spectator ran into a bull ring.)

Flatbed semi trucks clear away the debris, and the drivers come down a roped walkway from the garage, climbing a riser for their introductions, starting with Terry Labonte in 43rd and working their way up to Geoff Bodine on the pole. Kenny is given his $500 award and a Busch Beer cap for winning the second-day qualifying. He goes up alone, but not everybody does. Jeff Gordon walks with his wife, a former Miss Winston. Ernie Irvan has his daughter; Chad Little brings his 5 1/2-month-old. Jeff Green, who drives the Cartoon Network car, comes up with Tom (that's the cat, remember).

After the introductions, each driver takes a convertible ride around the track. Points leader Jeff Gordon and seven-time champion Dale Earnhardt, the guy he's supplanted as the sport's biggest star, get the biggest cheers, which follow them around the track—mixed, of course, with an almost equal volume of boos.

PART 2: A LITTLE BIT SIDEWAYS

At the Square D hauler, Newt has called and held his meeting. "He told us to focus," one crew member says with a sly smile.

Filbert is heading for the spotters' booth. "All set?" Newt asks. "Water? Headset? Hat?" Filbert has no hat, but he doesn't want one. Off he goes.

Gloria runs off to the scorer's booth. Eddie heads over to the car to make a final air-pressure adjustment. "I gotta do it while I still can," he says. He'll decrease the pressure a pound or so to accommodate for the growing heat of the sun, but as he walks he's thinking about other stuff, too. He got a chance to make his presentation to the Square D guys about Las Vegas, and he's hopeful. When he gets to the car, Two-Can and Frank are there already. "Now you look like one of us," Two-Can says to Eddie, who's changed from dress-for-success clothes into his race uniform. "You looked like a diplomat a while ago."

The double row of cars and generators in Turn 4 is nearly as busy as pit road, but bit by bit, as the clock nears 12:30, the people drift off. Each car is surrounded by a few team members, a couple of spouses (Frank Good's wife, Melody, is here), and a few hangers-on or unidentifiables. Trent Dyer stops by again, checking those in-car cameras once more. Melody asks Frank why the car has cameras today, since the car runs so poorly here. Frank just shrugs. Then Kenny walks up.

For the first time all week Kenny is silent. He leans on the car with his team, but he's distant, arms crossed, keeping to himself. Other drivers do the same. Some arrive with wives and family members, others alone. One car over, Kenny's brother Rusty goes over notebooks with his team before climbing in. Then starting from the back, a Motor Racing Outreach preacher has been working his way up through the cars. He comes to each driver, puts an arm around him and murmurs words into his ears, then heads over to the knot at the next car.

Kenny lets out a sigh and slides feet-first into the window of his race car. Frank leans in and tapes his water jug tube to a seat strap, tapes his radio earphones onto his ears with duct tape. Frank puts a little piece of white tape around the steering wheel at the top—so that Kenny will know where straight is again without resorting to trial and error, and so he can keep the wheels straight during pitstops—and then pulls the Square D insulating blanket off the windshield of the car. The interior fills with light, and there's Kenny Wallace in there, ready to drive a race car. He puts his helmet on but leaves the visor up. He takes another deep breath, then expels it.

From the car next door, Russell Wallace, Kenny's dad, comes over. Kenny looks up with a smile that appears almost grateful. "Hi, Daddy," he says meekly. He hesitates, then goes on. "Say, Daddy—did you ever have to race like this? Just holding on 'cause you was rolling over so much?" Russell leans over and has a few words for his son. Then he's gone. Frank leans in with a comforting pat on his shoulder, then he cinches up the protective screen. He unplugs the generator, and he and Two-Can head back to the pit as a little girl sings the "Star Spangled Banner" over the public address system. The track is clear. Kenny Wallace is alone in his race car.

Then track owner Bruton Smith gives the signal, and Kenny's on the radio: "Motor's running, baby!"

"Ours too, baby!" Newt says. "Have a good run!" Then Filbert, from the roof: "We all got running motors, baby."

Eddie walks around the pit, slapping shoulders and high-fiving. Newt, in his streak-of-lightning Square D hat and his oval sunglasses, has taken his position on the war wagon, hands on hips. He looks like a little general. Vic, the shocks guy, and Eddie Jarvis, Kenny's motor home driver, sit alongside him, checking the lap computer and the gas computer. Air wrenches whir in a kind of call and response up and down pit road, and then, with a NASCAR official holding out three fingers to indicate three laps, the field starts moving behind the pace cars. Red, yellow, and blue balloons are released, and the crowd gets onto its feet.

"OK Filbert," Kenny says the first time through pit road. "Second gear, 4,500." Filbert repeats it. The crew walks to the edge of the pit, standing on the wall, cheering him the second time he comes through. "Just keep it smooth and steady," Newt says. "Got a long race today. Filbert will do your green flag for you, he can see it better than me."

"Ten-four, baby," Kenny says. "Five hundred miles." They come around once more, and the pace car darts onto pit road ahead of the field, and Filbert yells. "Green flag!" he shouts. "Green flag!"

❖

The start.

That's why you're here. It's all been leading up to this. For this you came.

From the moment you drove up to the speedway and heard the whine of a single car testing on the track, from the first moment a race car reached out to you with that noise, you were mad to get inside. What was that noise? That was *loud*, for Pete's sake. What *was* that? You wanted to know, and you wanted to know *right now*. The rest of the week was a rush of images and sensations—the heat of the sun, radiating back from those four banked asphalt turns. The endless hours of practice, the cars droning around the track singly or in bunches. The sickly sweet exhaust smell of the garage. The qualifying and requalifying. The sound of rebel yells reverberating all night long. The pain of a stinging sunburn. The grogginess of dehydration mixed with the beer and fatty food constantly on offer from friendly infielders.

And then finally, on race day, you reach a state of torpid open-spiritedness created by immersion into something that only gets better with every hour. And that's when three guys named Randy, Lindsay, and Mike invite you into their green-pick-up-and-blue-tarp shanty on the hill between Turns 1 and 2. Lindsay, a guy of about 30 with a ponytail and a tan so deep it almost obliterates the artwork covering most of his torso, demonstrates the basic infield ethic while slicing tomatoes in the shade under the tarp before the race starts. For one thing, you always have a beer, he says, handing you one. When someone comes in your camp, you always give a beer. If you can, let someone else use your Port-a-Jon. Yell a lot and listen to music. "Other than that," he says, "fuck it." Randy, with tousled hair, sleepy eyes, and a three-day growth of blond beard, demonstrates the behavior of a car by extending his hand like he's warming his palm in front of a fire, only sideways. He explains tight and loose better than anyone else: "Loose is when the car goes into the corner and goes like this," his right wrist, demonstrating the car's rear wheels, angling up and away from him. "When it does this"—his wrist comes back down, his fingertips instead angling up and away like the right-leaning steering of a car with a push—"it's tight." Simple as that.

Mike, in denim shorts and nothing else other than a mat of chest hair, has sat all weekend almost silently, on a barstool screwed to the plywood viewing platform, rotating and following one practicing car after another with binoculars as he listened in on his headset. Sometimes he trains those binoculars on the rich folks up in the Turn 1 condos. These guys have watched practice intently; they have reeled madly in 2 A.M. drunks. They have smoked joints and ate breakfast steaks and bought a bottle of tequila and drank it.

And then race time. They climb into the sun on their platform, pulling you up alongside them, and the racers start around, following the pace cars. They explain how the two pace cars each pulling a group of 20 or so Cup cars make it easier for the race cars to set their pit road speeds. They demonstrate that you need to cheer when the second pace car disappears, and the group of cars so bright they vibrate closes into a snarling, roaring mass for the second or third pace lap. They explain how the drivers wiggling back and forth are warming their tires to set the rubber and clean off any goo that has been picked up.

Then the cars come rumbling by again, bunching together, seeming almost to hunch their shoulders, to crouch in readiness for the start the next time around. The guys stand on their platform and cheer, and you cheer too. You can't know what is coming, but you feel it. You know it. Some part of you, after all this, is ready.

Then, just barely visible all the way across the infield, all the way across that sun-drenched miracle of flapping flags, of sunburned bodies, of tents and trailers and buses and lawn chairs and baseball hats and circling arms and raised beer cans, the tiny-looking pace car shoots down out of Turn 4 onto pit road. The cars bunch up like fans ready to storm the field after a ball game. From the corner of your eye you see the flag stand, and a sudden figure-eight of green as the flagman, on the signal from the NASCAR control tower, gives the go. The cars jump in speed, almost hopping forward, their noses barely rising as the cars rear back under acceleration.

And then the noise.

You've heard the cars practicing all weekend long. You've heard 43 Cup cars on the track all at once. You thought you understood. But now, when the green flag drops and, half a mile away, in Turn 4, those drivers get in the throttle, you hear a noise that starts a fear, an awe, a surrender in your chest.

And then just as the full force of that Turn 4 sound has reached you in Turn 1, the cars are upon you. Screaming into the turn, bunched like a swarm of angry bees and seeming to fly, sideways, directly at your height on the steeply banked track, the cars dive into the gray turn, literally going down, and the sound you have been hearing all week turns physical, beating into your tender skin so hard it makes you gasp, makes you cover your throat in shock.

And then, echoing back on itself from the high-banked asphalt turns, it gets *louder*. It rises so loud that it leaves sound behind and becomes a new kind of perception, a sort of air-pressure plasma; your ears give up. The screaming roar breaks up into staticky fragments, a noise so buffeting and profound that it surpasses the very concept of hearing. Not a white noise—a *dark* noise.

So you stop listening, and you do by instinct what the others do by tradition: you scream. You scream, you howl, you tilt your head back and let 35 years of civilization out in a long, roaring, bellow. So do the others, and as you catch your breath, as you wipe tears from your cheeks and try to regain some sense of where you are, you see the most unusual thing. Randy is holding his forearm loosely, but intentionally, along Lindsay's. The cars have sped into Turn 3 a quarter-mile away, and for God's sake they're coming back, but you still have to scream to be heard. "What are you doing?" you bellow in Randy's ear. So he puts his arm along yours and offers a beaming, gapped smile.

"You too!" he says. "You too!" And yes, when you look, most assuredly, you too.

Goose bumps. Goose bumps from your wrist, up along your arm to your elbow, and from there all the way up your neck to the base of your hair. Goose bumps.

There's nothing like it. You try to tell people: Loud sound is one of the most profound and terrifying phenomena, whether it's cars or a bomb explosion or nearby thunder or the sound of hoof beats during a horse race. Something about overwhelming noise reaches some part of your brain stem that is programmed to cower, to perceive the thought, "MUCH MUCH BIGGER THAN ME" and crouch in amazement and terror.

You try to explain, in long terms about sound, culture, unity, and participation, about sports, marketing, television, and the great American need to just do something, but it's hard. Then you come to the short version: You saw God.

And that's it. *You saw God.* You know where he *lives.* You've been to his *house.* It's between Turns 1 and 2 in the Charlotte Motor Speedway *and all are welcome!*

That's the start of a Cup race. That's the point. That's why you're here. And every time there's a caution, the cars collect into a bunch and when the green flag drops they repeat the same thing again. And again, and again, and the cycles just never end. That's racing. That's the point.

❖

Or that's the point on the infield, and in the stands, and to a lesser extent on TV and on the radio.

For the drivers and the crews, the start is simply the beginning of a long day's work, with almost none of the excitement, none of the explosive sense of power, speed, madness, and color, especially down in the pits. They concentrate, and they take deep breaths, but they've seen it before. The cars wheel by a few times slow, then the green drops and they flash by louder and faster. The crew is there to work, and the start of the race is just like clocking in.

At Charlotte, today, it's even less thrilling, because there's a wreck before the race even gets started. Up the line, with every crew chief or spotter yelling "Green! Green! Green!" into every driver's ear, someone has trouble making the instantaneous run up through the gears, and down the line guys just getting started have to quickly get out of the throttle or even hit the brakes—get on the binders, they say. The hesitation hiccups its way through the pack; Kenny manages well, avoiding the accordion crush to come, but the cars behind him don't, and before the race is a lap old—hell, before the wrecking cars have even crossed the start-finish line—there's smoke, there's the sick, shopping-center parking lot sound of crunching cars.

It looks like Bill Elliott's 94 car has to stop hard, and Ernie Irvan in the 28 taps into him. Hut Stricklin in the 8 behind Irvan hits a little harder, and Jeremy Mayfield in the 37 plows underneath Stricklin's rear hard. Both Irvan and Stricklin spin onto the apron, and the rest of the pack spreads back out, trying to keep position as they race one lap around back to the start-finish line under caution. Irvan and Stricklin roar down pit road, getting quick duct-tape bodywork, but already bidding farewell to their chances in the race.

On lap four, the field starts again, and this time they get through OK.

❖

For the Square D guys, that early restart is about as good as it gets today. The car is tight going into the corners from the first laps, and it moves back through the pack as though it's late for an appointment with 43rd place. Filbert's comments as spotter could be put on a tape loop: "Looking under . . . underneath . . . clear behind him." The car holds up OK in Turns 1 and 2, but in 3 and 4 it pushes, climbing up the track and forcing Kenny to turn left hard to come out of the turn. He gets almost completely sideways, washing further to almost the top of the track before he can gather it in at the end of the turn and jet down the straightaway. Pushing going in, loose coming out. Pushy loose. Which is to say, everything that can be wrong with a car that has four tires and eight cylinders is wrong.

Jeff Green passes him in that Cartoon Network car. That is, on the first green-flag lap of the race, he's passed by Tom and Jerry. By lap 9 he's running 30th, by lap 19 he's 39th, and by lap 23 he's in last place. He moves backward through the field so fast that he has to keep asking Filbert: "Am I clear? Am I clear?" He doesn't even have a moment to tell Newt what's wrong, though Newt knows. Eddie hands him a little piece of paper with some tire suggestions on it, and Newt shrugs. He makes a left-turn steering motion with his hands, then uses his hand as a car, skating it up an imaginary track. Once Kenny's at the back of the pack and out of danger, Newt says, "Keep cool, buddy. Tell me what it's doing."

Kenny doesn't have much to say. "It's tight," he says. "It's pushing in *and* loose." By lap 30—the race is barely 15 minutes old—Filbert gets on the radio: "That's the leader in your mirror . . . you're clear . . . he's gone."

Lapped. Thirty laps into the race. "I'm fixing to fix it," Newt says. Filbert says, "Newt, I don't know if you can see it, but about a third of the way through, he gets loose." Newt, disgusted, says, "Ten-four." Can he see it? The car has gone from 26th to a lap down in 30 laps; nobody at the track *can't* see it. The astronauts can probably see how loose this car is from space.

❖

Maybe that right front spring should have stayed a little stronger. Maybe the body was just a quarter inch too far to the right like Kenny said, and there was nothing for it at all. But Kenny goes through 1 and 2 all right, then going into 3 you can see him, like Vic and Eddie said all week long, just climb the turn sliding his rear, catching the car about halfway in, and then going into a more controlled slide the rest of the way up, until suddenly, at the outside top of Turn 4, that balky right rear that has just never seemed to have enough weight on it finally catches hold and seems to sling the car up the straightaway like a jai alai player, like a pitcher with a wide sidearm delivery.

And then *zing,* Kenny flies up the straight. You can tell that this is the engine that won Darlington. The car is a rocket down the stretches. Kenny spends lap after lap hunkering down and roaring by people on the front stretch, holding his own in Turns 1 and 2, then getting a little more distance on the backstretch, and then having them eat his lunch in Turns 3 and 4 while he tries to gather his sliding car back in. Two or three laps of that cat-and-mouse and then, once again, it's Filbert saying "Clear low. . . clear behind him," and another car has passed the number 81 Filmar Racing Square D Ford Thunderbird.

On lap 57 Kenny roars into the pits, and the team tries to deal with the car's tightness entering the turns first, raising the track bar on the right. "OK boys, here we go, four tires good and smooth," Newt calls, and the pit stop goes just so: Frank Good makes the track bar adjustment as the right rear tire is being tightened, and the car, which came in running 41st, leaves the pits in 36th. "Good job boys," Newt says. "And that ought to help you out there, brother." Then someone runs to refill the gas cans, everybody prepares the next set of tires Eddie's chosen, and then while Eddie makes tire sheets it's time for smokes and Gatorade.

The rest of the race, at the beginning, is almost as dreary. Bobby Labonte in the 18 car—he started second and everybody has been saying he's fast all weekend—is dusting the field, opening a lead of more than five seconds. He puts a lot more than Kenny Wallace a lap down. "Do all you can in 1 and 2, because I know 3 and 4 are terrible," Filbert says. "That 18 car is putting a lot of cars on the same lap we are." Labonte picks cars off one by one, effortlessly, like he's swinging around to pass a bicyclist. By the 100th lap of the race—by which time he's lapped Kenny again—he's lapped 34 of the cars in the field, and only 9 remain on the lead lap. Kenny can run only the high line, and even that barely; Mark Martin can concentrate on that low line. Bobby Labonte? He can run the high line, the low line, the in-between line; he could run on the apron, on the retaining walls. He could probably run on the catch fence, that's how controlled and just flat-out fast his green-and-black number 18 Interstate Batteries Pontiac looks.

Then, of course, disaster.

❖

During a wreck in a Winston Cup race, time does for everyone watching, especially the people in the pits and on the infield, what it does for the pit crews during a pit stop: It takes a mind-shattering deceleration, going from blindingly fast to sudden slow-motion without the tiniest signal. Time just changes. Cars going at close to 200 miles an hour are suddenly doing what they don't normally do: slowing down. The change accentuates the thickening slowness, as do the graceful, almost stately loops the wrecked cars start making. A car hurtling around the track at speed looks fast, and it's moving in a straight line: None of the parts are moving relative to one another. When it starts spinning, though, your eye catches the spin, focusing on the slow, gentle counterclockwise loop the car will make over the length of, say, a straightaway, instead of on the fact that it's covering that straightaway, out of control, at 140 or 150 miles per hour.

Perception changes, too. From the flaring brightness of shiny reds and yellows and greens, the track shifts entirely to shades of gray. Light gray smoke from tires; dark gray patches of track; cloudy gray smudges against the retaining walls, where cars are skidding; tiny black tire fragments filling the air along with the smoke and the steam from engine parts and fluids spilling onto a 1,400-degree exhaust system and engine. And a glance at any in-car camera view of a wreck shows that the drivers see even less. A driver heading into a wreck sees gray smoke, and that's it. Sometimes oil or rear end fluid spatters, and then the driver sees nothing at all. Conventional wisdom says stay high on the track. The turns, banked at 24 degrees, are self-cleaning, people say. The wreck will climb the track with centrifugal force, hit the retaining wall, and then slide lower and lower on the track as it loses energy.

Driver Kenny Schrader has famously recalled seeing a wreck ahead of him and saying, "I'm about to get real busy," but ask Kenny Wallace or most drivers what they do during a wreck and they say, pretty much, just stand on the brakes, jam in the clutch, and hold on. Dale Earnhardt Jr. was once asked to describe a wreck at Daytona that ended with him barrel rolling down the grassy apron of the front stretch. Given the opportunity to expound on his feelings during an accident of such magnitude, Earnhardt shrugged, saying, "All I saw was sky, grass, sky, grass, sky."

The wreck at Charlotte starts on lap 102 when the number 96 car has a gear problem and dumps rear end fluid in Turns 1 and 2, starting a melee that has about a dozen cars sliding and in trouble. The 91 slides up into the 7, and both end up severely crunched into the outside wall; the 10, with nowhere to go and no way to stop on the slick surface, plows into the back of the 8, smashing its rear end and emptying its oil cooler, further slicking the track. Most important, Bobby Labonte, tiptoeing through lapped traffic and just trying to keep his untouchable 18 out of trouble, has to turn a sharp left to avoid the mayhem, locking his brakes and traveling through the turns completely sideways, smoking the whole way as cars pass him. Several lapped cars pass him to get back on the lead lap, including series points leader Jeff Gordon in the 24.

Mark Martin in the 6 takes over the lead as the racers gather behind the pace car. As the wreckers clear the sheet metal and tire fragments out of Turn 2 and an ambulance takes injured driver Hut Stricklin of the number 8 to the infield care center (he's fine), Kenny Wallace gets on his radio, pissed off. "You gotta pay attention!" he shouts, probably at Filbert. "I just lost the opportunity to get a lap back from Mark Martin! When there's a crash and the leaders pit, watch that monitor! I could've got that lap back from Mark Martin, but I didn't know he was the leader!"

"Ten-four, buddy," Newt says, calm. "We got a lot of time left." Kenny comes in a few laps later for new tires and a good scrubbing of his grille. Oil-dry, a sort of kitty litter that soaks up oil and grease and fluids on the track, clogs grilles as the drivers go through it. The pit stop is OK; 19.82 seconds. "Awesome, boys!" Newt says. "That's the way we do it!" Kenny's passed a lot of the cars involved in the wreck, and a couple of other cars have had engine problems, so the number 81 came in 33rd and went out 31st. "I helped you getting in and I helped you coming off," Newt says of changes to the tire pressure he and Eddie made. "So I think you should be better."

Kenny isn't so sure. "I'm killing myself in 3 and 4," he says. "I push, get loose, and then both ends want to come around. Gives 'em a chance to get their nose underneath me, and they get me out of position. Or else I have to slow way down to run that low line."

Newt takes a look at the information Eddie's giving him. "K. W., we got some really good tires for you. We're only gonna get better from here on in."

"I just need to be able to turn that nose down without the ass end swinging around," Kenny says. "I can come in OK, but I want to be able to come in high and turn down."

"Ten-four," Newt says. "We put you a half a round of right rear, so that ought to help you coming off." It doesn't help much.

❖

For the leaders, the lap-102 caution has changed everything. Bobby Labonte's car hit nothing, suffered no body damage. But by locking his brakes, Labonte flat-spotted the tires and had to get them changed during a pit stop. Add to that the time he spent out of control on the racetrack, being passed by not only the cars racing him but cars he'd lapped, and he ends up in 15th place, the last car on a lead lap that is suddenly far more crowded.

The good news is his car, though it doesn't handle the way it did before, is still outstanding. If he can't fly anymore, he can still leap tall buildings in a single bound. Labonte and his team start trying to pick their way back through the crowd.

Other plot lines abound. Jeff Gordon, trying to nail down his second Winston Cup championship, had lost a lap after pit road speeding earned him the black flag for a stop-and-go penalty. With his closest competitor, Mark Martin, keeping the number 6 car at least in a strong race for second with Dale Jarrett, who's also in contention for the championship, Gordon was having a bad day, his competition looking to bite into his points lead by at least 50 or 75 points. Add in that his season collapsed the year before during this very race: Entering the day leading Terry Labonte (brother of the recent race leader) by 111 points, he finished 31st, worth 75 points. Labonte won the race, scoring 185. Labonte then trailed by only a point, and over the next three weeks he swiped the championship from Gordon. So moments ago Gordon, a lap down, was in trouble.

But the wreck has changed that. Gordon snaked through the smoke and wreckage to make his way past the 18 and back onto the lead lap, and now his team has had a caution flag during which they could pit to adjust their car. Gordon and his crew chief Ray Evernham won't waste the opportunity. Says one Winston Cup official about the number 24 car, "Give 'em enough cautions, and they *will* beat you." The Winston Cup series, the official says, is meant to be a driver and crew chief series, not a technology series. The point is guys trying to figure out how to get control of the cars out on the racetrack, not beat you with titanium valve covers. Number 24 crew chief Ray Evernham is the best there is, and given enough chances he'll figure out the setup. So suddenly, running sixth now, Gordon's a factor. Martin and Jarrett are both running strong cars, fighting it out for second place all day so far. Martin's been knocking on the door for years without winning a championship. Jarrett, son of beloved announcer and past champion Ned Jarrett, is one of racing's nicest guys and a sentimental favorite. Sitting third in the points chase he's having his best season ever. After the caution pit stops they still shake out in second and third, behind Jeff Burton, last week's winner. Terry Labonte, the defending champion whose season has gone to hell—it was his crew chief who threw the axle—had to take the previous champion's provisional and start 43rd, but he's raced his way up to 7th. The players are all there, and with the race one-third over, it's finally getting interesting.

But what has the crowd on its feet for the next 100 laps or so is Dale Earnhardt and his black number 3.

Earnhardt, the seven-time champion whose reign as the sport's preeminent driver was ended by Gordon, hasn't won a race in more than a season, the longest drought of his career. The legion of fans of his butt-kicking, fender-rubbing style want him at the front of the pack. The last two weeks he has finished second, and this week, on one of his best tracks, he looks strong, too. He started the race in 19th position, but he's fought his way up to 5th, and he's getting stronger. The track, people say, is coming to his car. As the day gets warmer, the track heats up and oils come out of the asphalt; as more rubber gets put on the track, it gets more tacky, giving the tires better grab. This brew somehow fits the setup of his car perfectly, so he's getting better as the race goes on.

Kenny Wallace, by the way, is in 34th place.

Another caution comes out on lap 152, when the 12 and the 98 get into a fairly small mix-up in Turn 4. On the ensuing yellow-flag pit stops, Earnhardt's crew rips off a 17.1-second pit stop and Earnhardt comes off pit road in second, behind Jarrett in the 88.

Kenny Wallace comes in for that pit in 34th and leaves in 30th after four tires and a crank of wedge in the right rear, but then he comes back in a few minutes later for a spring rubber in the right rear to further loosen up the car, which is still climbing too high in the turns. That pit stop—when nobody else is stopping—is the only pit stop all day in which he doesn't gain track position. Eddie and Newt are still talking up the pit stops—"Thataway to go guys! We can take that all day long"—but the crew's spirit is gone. They won't stop, and nobody's suggesting Kenny run the car into the wall, but racing for 30th place isn't what gets their blood going. The crew is just doing what it can.

But coming in for nothing more than a spring rubber is the kind of thing you do when your race is pretty much over, and Kenny knows that. "I haven't given up," he says suddenly, his staticky, disembodied voice popping into the ears of his crew. "I never will give up. I'm driving as fast as I can; I'm driving my ass off. Ten-fouuuuur, you all are doing a wonderful job."

Frank is talking to his wife, one ear cup of his headset on, the other on top of his head. Don has a cigarette. If Kenny's pep talk has any avid listeners, it's not immediately apparent. Newt stands on the war wagon like a general without an army, his face frozen, eyes invisible behind his sunglasses, hands on hips, turning slow circles as he watches the 81 go round and round, sliding treacherously up the track in 3 and 4. When a few laps later Kenny yells, "My car went to shit!" it gets exactly the same response.

"You keep digging, K. W.," Newt tries. "We're going to get that top-20 before we leave here today."

Kenny says "Ten-four." The crew just waits.

❖

The pit next to Kenny's is the pit for the 99 car, and that team exhibits little excitement when the 99 takes the lead, and less concern when Dale Jarrett in the 88 takes it away from him. The businesslike pit road, finally, is just nowhere to watch a race. Since this race is getting pretty good, it's time for a trip to the media center.

Above the media center is a viewing platform, on which 20 or 30 writers, photographers, and announcers lean against wooden fence rails and watch the race.

From there you can see virtually every inch of the track. And that's the perfect vantage point for what comes next. On lap 165—almost exactly the halfway point of the race—Dale Earnhardt passes Dale Jarrett for the lead. The roar of the crowd is loud enough to be heard over the howl of the engines.

Jarrett hangs with him and gets back underneath for a couple of laps, but Earnhardt takes back over on lap 176, followed by Mark Martin on his tail, and for the next 50 laps, Earnhardt and Martin engage in a duel for the lead that is almost perfect Winston Cup racing. At first Earnhardt threatens to check out on the field the way Labonte had, but Martin doesn't panic, following his own line and making up a 10th of a second a lap or so to patiently reel him in.

When Earnhardt leads, Martin hunches behind his tail like he's the back end of a horse costume, following Earnhardt's line perfectly and waiting to spring, waiting for Earnhardt to drift high in one of the turns or loosen up when Martin takes the air off his spoiler, reducing the down force on his rear tires. Then Martin slingshots down underneath him and takes the lead, in racing's most common move, and its least preventable. Earnhardt mirror-drives him, putting him off, but Martin can find his spot. When Earnhardt is behind Martin, on the other hand, he drives like the Intimidator his name makes him out to be, poking his nose underneath Martin whenever he's got the smallest chance, looking high if Martin's hooked too cleanly on the lower line. He's pushy, poking at Martin constantly, trying to force the chance rather than waiting for it. Meanwhile, Bobby Labonte's 18 has made its way all the way back into third place, sneaking by Jarrett and blowing by Gordon's 24 like, as fans say, it's tied to a stump.

Labonte gets behind Earnhardt, and from there he doesn't have long to wait. Earnhardt spent a lot of his tires on his duels with Jarrett and Martin, and his handling is going away. He'll have to try to hold out for the next pit stop without losing too much territory. Martin, sticking to his own line and never sliding up the racetrack, has been much kinder to his tires and appears able to hold off Labonte.

With the roar of the engines making conversation impossible, each fan, each team member, watches this display alone, in a kind of silence, either because the deafening rattle of engine noise makes sound superfluous or because a headset dampens the noise and allows the people watching to listen in on the radio call or the conversations of their teams. Earnhardt and Martin's teams remain completely silent during their door-to-door racing. The drivers each know where the other is, and everybody just watches.

And that's everybody. In the grandstand, everyone is standing. On the infield, grills are forgotten, footballs unthrown, horseshoes unpitched. This is the meat of the thing, and the concentration is unimaginable, limitless, profound. In the deafening silence, they're watching two men compete at 200 miles per hour. Ernest Hemingway said, "Mountain climbing, auto racing, and bullfighting are the only true sports. . . . all others are games." Though NASCAR's ceaselessly improving safety regulations have made a driver dying in Winston Cup racing rare (the last Cup driver to die on the track was Neil Bonnett, in 1994, and four drivers have been killed on the track since 1980), nobody pretends racing can't be deadly. Concussions and broken bones are still common; drivers on local tracks where safety regulations are less thorough still die. After a bad wreck, there's a long period of held breath until those window screens come down. Car fragments can enter pit road, and the stands, as they did in an Indy car race in 1998, killing spectators. It's not just a game. "When the car's hooked up, it's a blast," Kenny has said. "When it's not, you're cheating death."

Hemingway's histrionic quote carries weight.

❖

There's a kind of primacy, of simplicity, to racing. It's human stories, like all sports: Can the young Turk defeat the crafty veteran? Can the guy who's been close for years take the brass ring? But instead of rooting for a bunch of free agents who will leave town next month, NASCAR fans choose drivers because they represent something to them, because they believe in them. Jeff Gordon's nice-young-guy professionalism; Earnhardt's surly redneck ass-kicking; Jarrett's good-dad earnestness; Martin's sincere pursuit of his goal and grace when he doesn't quite get there. Any of these guys might feel like the one you wanted to support. So, for that matter, might Kenny Wallace, with his delighted, engaging geniality.

Driving styles fit in with personalities: Earnhardt, always perceived as on the edge of the rules, ready to wreck you to pass you; Martin cool and smart, running the most technically beautiful race imaginable. Jarrett, above all, races clean, and beats you with heart and teamwork. Gordon, on the other hand, just flat-out beats you. He can make his car stretch like a skater landing a jump; he can make it cut like a forward taking a back-door pass for a lay-up. He doesn't just drive a car, he dances it, and he has physical ability as a race car driver that fills with awe people who have been in the sport for decades.

These are people fans want to believe in, and with NASCAR's iron enforcement of the sport's family-style image, they're people fans *can* believe in. People say this sport is all about money, and maybe so. But they describe it better when they say it's about marketing. What fans do when they choose these drivers is, more than anything else, a kind of branding.

You root for the baseball team that plays in your town, or the basketball team of the college you went to. But if you root for a race driver, it's because he speaks to you somehow. He's your *brand* of driver. You choose him and you stick with him.

Then again, maybe it's just as simple as it looks: NASCAR fans will tell you the first car race took place the day they built the second car, and that's what they're all here to see. Guys just trying to go faster than each other, risking death, taking 3,500-pound cars, filled with flammable liquids and heated up to 1,400 degrees, and running them inches apart, at 200 miles per hour, for lap after lap after lap after lap. Guys trying to go fast.

❖

To stand on that media center viewing platform is to have any remaining questions answered. On the platform you're at the center, the middle. It's all happening around you. One hundred fifty thousand fans in the stands, all wearing racers' colors and eating chicken and drinking beer, standing for the whole race. Thirty or forty thousand fans in the infield, with tents and viewing platforms and buses and flags, all waving their arms and listening on headsets. Forty-three teams hustling on pit road, surrounded by friends, family, and ice cream vendors. Five million or so watching at home, and another million listening on the radio.

And, the point of it all, 43 cars filling the day with a riot of color, of noise, of movement.

It's the biggest thing going, flat out. There's nothing else like this. All NASCAR's numbers—it's the fastest-growing sport, the best attended sport, and on and on and on—are for real. It's all true.

OK, but *why*?

Everyone has an idea. Neil Goldberg of ESPN thinks it has something to do with the closeness of it. When thousandths of a second separate first from last, on any day truly anybody can win. Ask the fans, and they'll say it's because the drivers are approachable, don't charge for autographs, are still "just people." Drivers say the same thing. Cynics talk about the money. Everybody talks about family, about lack of scandal. Maybe it's the way it smells, maybe it's the way it looks, the way it sounds. After all, racing is pretty simple: loud noise, fast-moving objects, bright colors. A six-month-old baby is attracted to those things. Maybe racing is just the simplest, most attractive sensation available.

But that fails to satisfy. There has to be something more. Why racing? *Why now?*

The answer that comes closest is the one Humpy Wheeler proposed: This is about looking backward, about yearning for the heartland. Which, in a way, goes back to baseball. Baseball became hugely successful—completely grabbed the attention of the nation—in the late 19th century. As every writer who ever picked up a pen has noted, baseball is a pastoral sport, a game without a time clock, a game played out in a field, and it exploded in popularity when the nation was abandoning its pastoral and rural past for an urban, industrial present. The more industrialized the nation became, the more it yearned for its rural past, and the more popular baseball became.

Same thing with racing at the end of this century. If baseball was the essential Industrial Revolution sport, racing is the sport of the digital revolution. Back then we were abandoning rural and agricultural for urban and mechanical. Now we're abandoning mechanical for digital, and suddenly we can't get enough of this mechanical, decidedly nondigital sport. The only computer you'll find in a Winston Cup car is that rev limiter to keep the engine from going too fast. That is, the only computer on a Cup car is the thing that's supposed to make it go *slower*. Your own car probably has enough computers to run a communications satellite; same with your phone, probably, and chances are you have a personal computer that you use every day but have no idea how it works.

Then here comes Winston Cup racing, where if something doesn't work you fix it by turning a screw or whanging on it with a hammer. Where guys spend all day getting their hands dirty. Where the most complicated part—hell, where *every* part—is neither more nor less than a wheel. A gear, a tire, a shaft, a crank. These, at the end of the machine age, are *machines* the way we can still understand them.

The men and women who have been in racing the longest often characterize Winston Cup racing as the bastardized, Disneyfied, Bowdlerized, dumb-show shadow of what racing truly is, or was.

But that doesn't mean anything to racing's new fans, who never saw Junior Johnson wreck somebody rather than get passed; never saw Lee Petty deliver a murderous look before a murderous pass, never saw them drive cars off the dealership lot, tie themselves in with ropes, put duct-tape over the headlights, belt the doors shut, and go start the engines. They don't know that old-style racing, and can't miss it. They don't know what this used to be. They only know that now it's utterly unlike any of the other bloodless exercises in mass hypnosis that pass for organized sports.

Compared to the 3.2 beer being offered by those guys, racing is pure bourbon. It's still stronger than anything else out there, so it still mesmerizes, still grabs your attention. Into a computer-monitor world in a plastic case with a matte-black finish comes a race car, made of sheet metal, steel, and rubber, a big hunk of actual matter that's heavy, loud, smelly, and real.

Racing has innards, has physical presence. It sweats, it pants, it chews its food. It's a living entity, and you can learn what it's like. It rewards scrutiny, repays effort. The deeper you look the more there is to see. Stirring recent events notwithstanding, baseball approaches a parody of itself, expanding so rapidly that records become meaningless, dropping like pages in a 365-days-of calendar. Football, serious as death, creates a Super Bowl so overshadowing that the regular season fades. Baseball runs TV ads with fake old clips meant to look like Ty Cobb, and meanwhile Ken Griffey Jr. needs to be educated about who Jackie Robinson is. Jeff Gordon doesn't need to be told who Richard Petty or Junior Johnson are—*he knows Richard Petty and Junior Johnson themselves*. And guys still come up from every tiny racetrack in the country, move to Charlotte, and make their stab at the big time. Racing hasn't managed to forget its roots yet. No track owner has yet held a town up for money, threatening to move his racetrack. Racing makes its own money and doesn't need municipal support.

Racing starts with its Super Bowl, the Daytona 500 in mid-February. The moment the engines fire and the field takes the green flag at Daytona is arguably the highlight of the season, every single year. But then it follows up with 30 more All-Star games. Every single race brings together the best drivers in the nation. Then the final race in Atlanta, in November, crowns a champion. There's no down time, no meaningless mid-August three-game series with Milwaukee, no road trip to Ottawa and Buffalo, no guarantee of the playoffs unless you collapse. In racing, there's no guarantee you even get to participate in the scheduled events. You have to drive your way into the show, every single week. It's driving for money, and if you're not fast enough, you go home. Root, hog, or die.

What's not to like?

❖

Labonte completes his quest, retaking the lead on lap 222. With only 112 laps to go, the rocket ship is back in front. But he's not checking out the way he was, and Jarrett's 88 seems to be able to stay with him. Martin's losing the smoothness of his line a little bit—his handling's going away, drivers say—and Gordon's 24 passes him up for third on lap 276. A day that looked perfect for Martin is losing a lot of its charm. After the final round of pit stops, under the green flag, Jarrett looks stronger yet, and the announcers on the pit road TV screens explain that on the pit stop before, when Jarrett's crew dropped the jack for the car to clear out of the pits, a spring rubber fell out of the left front spring.

The car has run better ever since that. Sometimes it helps to be lucky. Labonte, Earnhardt, Martin, and Gordon switch around behind him some (finally finishing in that order), but at the end of the race Jarrett just has too much car. He passes Labonte for the lead with 57 laps to go and never really gets a challenge, pulling his blue-white-and-red number 88 into the Winner's Circle about 10 hours after that couple got married there this morning. He gets out of the car into the crush of team members, friends, and media, wearing a hat representing his sponsor, Quality Care Fords. He'll take dozens of pictures wearing dozens of hats now, but the familiar mayhem of guys swiping hats on and off the driver's head during interviews is long missing from NASCAR. A guy named Bill Brodrick, who represents fuel-provider Unocal, is the unofficial but completely recognized boss of the winner's circle. He hands the driver his sponsor hat, then when the interviews are over keeps the hats coming, in a specified order, so that the pictures the sponsors need are taken. Jarrett will take a picture for every company that has a decal on his car. It'll take a while.

And lest that sound like NASCAR has lost its rough-and-tumble roots, be advised: Brodrick is the hat man for a simple reason. "Because I'm the biggest," the bulky, yellow-haired guy says. "And the loudest."

❖

Kenny's race never really changes after the wrecks. While the crews for the 10 and the 98 frantically tried to get their cars back on the track, Kenny just kept running circles. The only place the car looks really good is during that one moment each lap coming out of Turn 4, when it just seems to latch onto the ground and hurl itself down the front stretch. "Come out hard, Kenny, this is the leader behind you," Filbert says on lap 280, when Kenny's about to go four laps down. "He likes the bottom in 3 and 4, so you should be OK."

"Yeah," Kenny clicks on to say. "My car won't do that."

"Ten-four," Filbert says. "You don't have to." Jarrett is by him that fast. When Kenny's ready to come in for his final stop, on lap 283, Newt and Eddie decide to take only two tires. They're running in 28th position, and every couple of points helps. Dick Trickle and Joe Nemechek, the guys just ahead of him in the points standings, are running 14th and 16th today, so the points situation is desperate. "Time to rock, boys, we need the track position," Eddie says as Kenny comes in for his last stop. "Let's go!"

And they make their final stop, going over the wall neat and coordinated as ever, whipping the right side up and down, changing the two tires, giving the car a gulp of gas, and pushing him out fast enough that Newt goes hopping around the pit, slapping backs. Kenny's in 27th when he goes out.

"I'm still tight," he says when he hits full speed again.

Newt, standing on the war wagon, nods his head. "Ten-four," he says. "I'm gonna get you a car one of these days." With 20 laps to go Kenny starts screaming,

"I'm out of tires! I am *out* of *tires*!" But Newt stays calm. "Keep it smooth, buddy," he says. "We ain't got far to go."

Kenny finishes in 28th place.

❖

And after that it's all familiar territory. With 10 laps to go, Steve Baker starts draining the water tank and Kevand begins taking apart signs, stowing air wrenches, disassembling jacks. Don pops the videotape of the pit stops out of the recorder and hands it to Eddie, who puts it in his briefcase with his pyrometer. When Jarrett takes the checkered flag, Newt says, "Good job, Kenny Wallace, good job. We'll do better for you next time. We're gonna test like we never tested before." "I'll tell you what," Eddie adds. "We made some mistakes, but everyone kept digging."

And then in the sudden quiet Newt jumps off the war wagon and hustles to the hauler as every team scrambles, pushing carts and war wagons everywhere in the garage. If you want to get run over by a race car this is your chance, because except for the top three, held for inspection, every car is gliding back to its hauler, and the drivers want to get out of the cars. Kenny slides right up onto the lift gate and climbs out of the race car, exhausted. Steve Post hands him some cool washcloths and a towel, and with the towel around his neck Kenny sits on the asphalt, leaning against the hauler.

"I felt like I was at fucking Eldora," he tells Steve, referring to a famous Ohio dirt track where the cars slide up and down the turns. That little jackrabbit push he got each lap off Turn 4, he says, came when he slid so close to the wall that his right rear actually started to touch the asphalt berm where the track curves up to the concrete wall and finally found purchase. "You know, I think this car had exactly one lap in it," he says. Good thing that lap came in qualifying, when it could do the most good. He shakes his head. "Well," he says, "we raced all day."

That they did. As the crew loads the hauler, Filbert eats an apple. "I think the car was close," he says. "We're fine-tuning now. We had a good car. At this track, with these people, you gotta have a great car."

Kenny, Newt, Eddie, and Vic sit down in the office, discussing the race. Soon Newt comes back out to help load. Danielle has brought some chicken and potato chips down from the suite, and the crew picks at that as they work. NASCAR officials in the garage rip apart the 88, the 18, and the 3, making their final inspection as orange parallelograms of late sunlight angle across the empty garage floor.

At the back of the Square D hauler, Kenny dresses in the office. "I'm excited," he says. "I see organization. We're not running real good, but we're learning every day.

"You gotta realize. Newt is a rookie crew chief. You take guys like Buddy Parrott [of the 88 car] and Ray Evernham [of the 24], they been here 50 times. Larry McReynolds [of the 3] has been here more times than you go home in two weeks.

"We were unrealistic to hope for a 20th, but you never, ever, ever give up. If we gave up, we wouldn't have been in the race. We were 47th Wednesday night. And we made changes all day, and any one of those changes could have been the type of thing that got us right. What's funny about during the race, is shit happens so fast that we sit around and say, 'When did *that* happen?'" Tomorrow he and Newt and Eddie will sit down in Newt's office for an hour, he says: "Close the door, hold all calls, and write it all down.

"Then next time we come back we'll be better." He's checked the points, too—the 29th- and 30th-place cars not running helped. "We were 212 out of 30th—now we're 164. I'm really excited about next week." He laughs. "You see how racing is? Yesterday in the Busch Grand National race, Dale Jarrett barely made top 10 [he finished 7th]. Today he won the damn race."

Within half an hour more haulers than not are closed up, and the Square D hauler is nearly ready to go, though there's no point in rushing. Hauler driver Dave Ensign points at the line of trucks stretching into the garage as they try to exit. "That one hasn't moved for 20 minutes," he says, pointing at the number 29 hauler. "Where does he think he's going?" Kenny stands for a while, and Newt walks up to the knot of guys—Eddie and Two-Can and Dave—and unscrews the beer cooler and pulls himself out a Coors Light.

They talk genially, mulling over the day. The crew can be happy—since they gained more spots than they lost during pit stops, every guy who goes over the wall gets a $100 bonus. Two-Can says Kenny did a great job of holding off the 97 for 33 laps in the middle of the race. Two-Can has figured that if Kenny had got back that lap when he failed to pass Martin during the wreck, he'd have finished 22nd, not far off their unrealistic top-20 hopes. Kenny looks at the crush of fans at the gate. "I wanna go out," he says, "but I don't know if I can get out that gate." Steve Post, who's going to walk him to his motor home, agrees. "If he stops, we're done," he says. "So just keep walking, K. W." Kenny says 10-4, and Steve leads him into the crowd, which collapses onto them like iron filings to a magnet. "OK folks, walk with us, walk with us," Steve says. "If you walk with us, we'll be in good shape." He and Kenny keep walking, as Kenny signs everything thrust at him.

Just beyond the crowd is the tangle of motorcycles, one by one starting up and taking off as crew members get ready to thread their way out through the lanes of immobilized cars. Putting on a simple black half-dome helmet is Steve Baker, smiling behind those shades as always. He looks over and waves, reaches out a big paw to shake, then starts his bike. As he flashes a final giant grin, the sun glints off those reflective sunglasses, and for a moment the rounded shades reflect everything: The tiny point of sun in blue sky, the crush of people, the race car driver, and around them all the banked turns of the speedway. Then he turns to drive off.

❖

Newt, Two-Can, Eddie, and Dave stand around their beers at the hauler in the emptying garage, and Dave sidles over and starts closing the hauler lift gate, a two-man job. Newt sees him and runs over. "C'mon, big D," he says. "You gotta ask for some help, man!"

Then they're back to their beers. Two-Can and Newt wonder why the spring rubber didn't help, wonder whether another two-tire stop would have. Newt wonders aloud about spring weights. A girl in overalls and a bikini top squeals at them long enough, begging for something signed by Kenny, that Eddie finally opens the side door of the hauler, finds a T-shirt, and unearths a Sharpie. "Look what Kenny wrote," he grins to the guys, then trots over and gives the girl the shirt. Newt and Two-Can get to talking about getting the car hooked up better, and Newt smiles. "That was the awesomest thing at Nashville," he says. "You'd come off the turn and feel that left rear kicking you in the ass, you could just haul ass all day."

They wonder whether Filbert was unhappy. "He didn't look unhappy," Two-Can says. Newt says, "Aw, hell. He'll call just like he always does and tell us we did OK." Two-Can likens building a successful team to building a pyramid. "A lot of rocks in that motherfucker," he says. "A lot of cutting and grinding and sanding. Takes a long time."

Newt sighs. "I'm happy," he says. "I'm drinking beer. I'm excited. We're gonna come to the point, man. Charlotte always wigs everyone out." He's wearing, someone notices, a Busch hat instead of his lightning bolt Square D hat. "That's a pole hat," he says, the hat Kenny was given for his second-day pole award during driver introductions. Kenny gave it to Newt. "He's got the time on it and he signed that. When I'm an old man I can say this shit is what this is all about."

Newt starts wondering about the life of a hauler driver; Two-Can starts reminiscing about the time he won the World 600 with Darrell Waltrip, and suddenly it's about time for these guys to be left alone. They stand together in the garage glowing orange with the setting sun. They stand by their hauler and they drink a beer.

❖

Day is done; the race is over. Yet it's not time to become part of the leisured exodus from the race that marks a NASCAR weekend. Many tracks, when the race ends, become monsters of complexity, with traffic utterly clogged, from the infield to miles away, as everyone leaves at once. But others—like Charlotte—follow the initial two-hour crush with a long, relaxed dissipation rather than a continuous flow. A good 5,000 of the infield fans will stay another night, savoring the race and a low-level last night of beers and friends. There will be slowdowns on the interstates near Charlotte caused by race traffic all day tomorrow. While many compounds pack up and load out, many others take the chance to spread out, enjoy the extra space, and watch the procedure from a lawn chair. They've watched cars set up and go out, cars run laps, the infield around them set up; they can watch it disassemble itself too. So much of a Winston Cup weekend is like a parade that fundamental to NASCAR fans is a long attention span and the enjoyment of just watching something happen. The infield starts to regain the feeling of a hilly meadow, the infielders like people out for a cool evening at the park, or out under an umbrella in the side yard.

The sun goes down, and the evening turns cool. Sitting on the slope down Redneck Hill, facing directly into the floodlit, seemingly vertical bank of Turn 2, three fans sit and relax, drinking a beer and smoking an evening joint. They're Kevin, a heating and air-conditioning worker with long blond hair in weary-looking ringlets; Derek, a man of uncertain living who exudes a kind of frat-boy charm; and Lori, who has long blond hair and wire-rimmed glasses but never says much about herself. They live on the North Carolina coast near Topsail Beach, and they'll drive home tomorrow.

"Our story is our truck is broke down," Lori says. It's a faded green 1982 Jeep Wagoneer, and they're going to have to drive real slow six or seven miles to a nearby junkyard and hope they can find water pump parts. For the moment, they're just enjoying their evening. The sun is completely gone, and they stare with satisfaction as the floodlights cast long shadows of the catch fence down onto the asphalt turn. Above Turn 1, Venus, Mars, and the crescent moon do a little encore dance, with the moon a hand width farther up in the sky than it has been. The camping spot Lori, Derek, and Kevin share is good, but not the best. "We lost our spot on the fence because one of my so-called friends failed to maintain it," Kevin says. He's seen races from the seats, but the infield is the way to go, he figures.

"This place is like a melting pot. Like people from my same neighborhood when I was in Ohio, I see them here." He grew up in Warren, in northeastern Ohio. Lori jumps in. "Guys were throwing a football that whistles down by the fence," she says. "It came up here and I threw it back." It came right back to her: "I don't even know who that is down there, and I was just throwing it and someone else was throwing it back."

They talk about the race, and the number 81 car comes up. "Kenny Wallace!" Kevin says. "He was the first one a lap down. I watched him. Square D was out here passing out banners and hats, so I wanted to see how he did." He thinks a moment.

"Square D took a major knee to the groin, today," he concludes. He free-associates for a while. "I had a girl steal my wagon, once. I borrowed it from my buddy, and she wanted to ride it. I said OK, once. That bitch went down the hill and never came back. I've had a lot of experiences here. I about froze my ass off once."

Lori has a comment. "The PA system?" she says. "The PA system sounds like Charlie Brown's teachers. And the girls showers, there were like no mirrors and no shelves."

Kevin joins in. "And we want more trash cans."

Then it's back to just drinking a beer, smoking a little, and watching the track. Kevin says they went to peer through the fence at the garage during the weekend, and with all the tools and machines, it looked like the robot shop in *Star Wars*. Derek thought the crew members leaving the garage looked pretty tired. "Dejected. They worked all day, and they just wanted to get home."

They did, of course. They spent all day—all weekend—on the edge, flat out, just on the edge of sideways. After five days just trying to keep all four tires on the ground, they have a right to be tired.

"Sideways," Lori says, looking at the steeply banked turn. "The *racetrack* is a little bit sideways. Life's a little bit sideways; we're a little bit sideways. It's *all* a little bit sideways."

They light up again.

❖

Driving out through the Turn 3 infield tunnel, a Quonset-shaped tunnel bright with a yellowish fluorescent flicker all night long, you finally leave the racetrack behind. But beyond the track, it's more of the same. Campers still set up, fans silhouetted against leaping fires, still standing drinking quiet, last-evening beers, tidying up so the load out won't be so hard tomorrow. Every now and then an engine starts and a truck or camper pulls away, keeping a gentle but steady stream of taillights blinking away from the speedway.

Morehead Road is, this late in the evening, free of troopers, but not of cars, and not of race fans. As you creep away, the camping areas get less populated but not empty. Still fans stand, still fans talk. The race is over, but race weekend, it looks like, will take its time. Maybe it's never really over.

The speedway lights disappear behind the first big hill on the way toward Route 49, but campfires still dot the hills to either side. The smoke goes up into the cool air and dissipates. Some of it settles in the hollows, above the ponds, like mist.

EPILOGUE

THE WHEELS KEEP TURNIN'

Friday Night, Wake County Speedway

Kenny Wallace's miracle lap Thursday afternoon around Charlotte Motor Speedway turned out to be just about the high water mark of the 1997 season for Filmar Racing and the number 81 Square D Ford Thunderbird. A good finish at Talladega—15th—gave a little hope, but finishing the year, Kenny never did better than 30th at Rockingham, Phoenix, or Atlanta. Square D popped for the Las Vegas trip that Eddie D'Hondt was trying to organize, and Kenny won the pole at the Winston West race and finished fifth, but that's Winston West.

Kenny finished the year 33rd in Winston Cup points, 107 behind Rick Mast in 32nd, and 207 behind Mike Skinner in 30th—and out of the $7,000 per race stake the team wanted so desperately for 1998. As for the guys running up front, Jeff Gordon needed that strong and lucky Charlotte finish. He dropped to 35th at Talladega, bounced back with a 4th at Rockingham, and closed the year finishing 17th twice, just enough to outlast Dale Jarrett, who went out with a win and two 2nds but still ended up a scant 14 points behind at the end of the line in Atlanta. Mark Martin was 15 points behind Jarrett, 29 behind Gordon. Close, close, close, but Jarrett was still a good racer and a good guy and Martin was still a guy everybody hopes wins a championship one of these days. Gordon was two-time Winston Cup champion.

At Filmar Racing, the revolving door, as Jerome Aho said, stayed stuck on high. Jerome found a job with another team that gave him more free time to develop his own race team. Two-Can left. Duze left. Steve Post left to do the public relations for a Craftsman Truck Series team. Filbert was still searching for that elusive chemistry, and it was hard to imagine that Newt Moore didn't still feel that thousand-pound weight every week.

The 1998 season started rough for Kenny and the guys. They failed to make the opening race, the Daytona 500. Bad enough for missing the big race, but that meant that when Dale Earnhardt, after 20 years of trying, finally won the one race that had eluded him, they watched it on TV. In a moment racing will never forget, the crews of every car in the race that day lined pit road and greeted Earnhardt as he rolled his car toward victory lane, slapping hands with everyone on the circuit. And the guys from Filmar

Racing weren't there. You never want to miss a race, but that was a pretty rough one to miss.

The rest of the season still didn't go a lot better. Wrecks caught them in a couple of early races, and missed setups continued to dog the car. Top-10 finishes at Talladega, Darlington, and Atlanta were scattered among five finishes of 34th or worse in the first 10 races. At Charlotte during Memorial Day weekend, Kenny Wallace got the final provisional starting spot for the Coca-Cola 600. Those Square D Racing banners kept showing up on the infield at races, but maybe the fans were right: Maybe the team's poor performances started to feel like knees to the groin to Square D. In any case, in late July, before the second Pocono race, Square D announced that the 1998 season would be its last with Filmar Racing. Not long thereafter Kenny Wallace announced that he too would leave Filmar Racing, and along with Square D would join Andy Petree Racing, owner of the number 33 car driven by Kenny Wallace's friend Ken Schrader. Driving a brand-new number 55, with Square D as sponsor, Kenny Wallace would finally be part of a multicar team. Newt Moore left Filmar and signed on with the number 77 car.

At season's end, without a driver or a sponsor, Filmar Racing had made no announcements about whether there was more racing in its future.

❖

The only antidote for racing troubles, though, is more racing. So if you didn't get enough at Martinsville and Charlotte, and odds are you didn't, the thing to do is go back.

But every weekend doesn't have to be a Winston Cup race. Chances are there's a nice little dirt or asphalt short track—a half-mile, a quarter-mile, three-eighths of a mile—nearby where the locals get together and run what they've got. Some of them dream the big dreams; some of them just like to mess with cars and go fast. So you end up one Friday night at the Wake County Speedway, in Raleigh, North Carolina.

It's 10 bucks to walk in, 15 if you want to watch from the infield. It's the same 15 if you want to race. When a young guy wins a race, he walks around the outside of the track near the catch fence, touching fingers with his girlfriend, his family, his friends, and there's plenty of them. Friends of the drivers make up a lot of the crowd at the Wake County Speedway.

It's a bumpy little asphalt quarter-mile, sanctioned by nobody, with lights held up by leaning telephone poles, and a melange of aluminum and wooden bleacher seats that will hold a couple of thousand people. Nobody measures your cooler on the way in. Practice gets started at 6 P.M., racing starts at 8, and it's over by 11 so as not to disturb the neighbors. The cars have to have mufflers, so you don't expect to have the kind of experience you have at Charlotte.

There are hard to figure out divisions like Economy Street and Poorboy Four Cylinder, and more common divisions like Late Model Sportsman. The guys race for prizes in the hundreds, not millions, of dollars, and their sponsors, if they have them, are neighborhood garages and muffler shops with their names painted on fenders, sometimes with house paint. Cars run with "For Sale" signs on them and with numbers made of duct tape. It's a starting track.

But it's a racetrack. And when the cars line up for the start of a race, when the pace car pulls off the track and into the infield, the moment is still there. It's still racing, and it's wonderful. Guys bump and gouge the way they do at Martinsville, and the better racers in the shinier cars, in the 75-lap feature race at the end of the evening, set each other up in the corners, mirror-drive each other, and pass door-to-door the way God intended for a race car.

Once you want to see guys driving cars fast, it turns out, you just want to see guys driving cars fast. So you go, and you eat some chicken and you drink some beer and you buy a fried bologna sandwich. You go racing. You probably wonder what it's all about the way you did the first minute you stumbled into the track at Charlotte, but you'll probably wonder that for good. Then again, maybe it's pretty simple to understand. Watching a race start, you look around at the wild shadows thrown by the light poles, by the bare yellow bulbs strung above the track that light up during a caution. You listen to the roar of the engines—a muffled roar, for certain, but a roar without doubt. And you see beside you a man who's brought his son, not more than five, to the racetrack. They walk up the ramp to the front of the sparsely filled stands, and the boy's eyes widen and he rushes the fence.

"Oooh," he says. "Race cars."

Acknowledgments

❖

By rights names should cover this book the way decals cover a race car. But just as the driver climbing out of a winning car gets his sponsor, his team, his owner, and his manufacturer out before he takes a breath, I'll start at the top. Without the support of David and Leigh Menconi, Michael Singer, and Joe and Kathy Miller, no book. Simple as that.

Everyone in racing was helpful, but foremost is Tom Cotter of Cotter Communications, who topped 5 years of assistance by introducing me to the people at Filmar Racing and at MBI Publishing. Kevin Triplett of NASCAR never stopped answering questions. Several NASCAR officials who, as always, wish to remain anonymous, helped tremendously. Dick Thompson at Martinsville and Ron Green, Jerry Gappens, and Humpy Wheeler at Charlotte gave me access behind every door and never stopped offering more.

I thank everyone at Filmar Racing, but especially Frank Good, Eddie D'Hondt, Gloria Ray, Aaron Brown, Jerome Aho, and Steve Baker, who not only answered questions but figured out questions I was too stupid to ask, and also volunteered information. Likewise, among the helpful people at the Motorsports Decisions Group, Steve Post saved my life dozens of times. Kenny and Kim Wallace are the two kindest people in Winston Cup racing and God bless them.

Lee Klancher at MBI Publishing understood this book from the moment I proposed it. His sponsorship made the book happen, his stewardship kept it happening, and his editing substantially improved it.

Gerald Martin, the poet of pit road, writes about racing for the *News & Observer* in Raleigh the way Jeff Gordon drives a race car for Hendrick Motorsports in Harrisburg. From the moment I showed up at a racetrack he shared insight, information, understanding, and sources, but I learned the most from reading his remarkable stories every week. I wish everybody could do the same. Gerald died weeks before this book went to press; his passing is a great loss to everyone in racing and everyone who knew him. Gerald also read this manuscript to try to protect me from any truly humiliating errors, as did Steve Post, Ron Green, and Bob Latford, but any mistakes in this book are my own.

Joe Miller not only read the whole manuscript but helped with the reporting, roaming the infield on race day at Charlotte, and trying to make sense of Humpy's prerace alien invasion. June Spence also read the manuscript and offered comments that made a real difference, as she makes a real difference in so many ways. Lisa and Chuck, as ever, provided help and support unimaginable. I would only look foolish trying to list all the other friends and family who helped, though I should say hello to my sister-in-law Ann because I got yelled at last time for not doing that.

Catering by Leigh Menconi.